attitudes

by the same author

Rhetoric and Writing

Rhetoric: A Synthesis

The Contemporary Writer

Composition / Rhetoric: A Synthesis

The Rhetoric of the "Other" Literature

The Culture and Politics of Literacy

A Teacher's Introduction to Composition in the Rhetorical Tradition

The English Department: An Institutional and Personal History

Searching for Faith: A Skeptic's Journey

The Uses of Grammar (with Judith Rodby)

Senior Citizens Writing

attitudes

selected prose and poetry

W. Ross Winterowd

Parlor Press
West Lafayette, Indiana
www.parlorpress.com

Parlor Press LLC, West Lafayette, Indiana 47906

© 2010 by Parlor Press
All rights reserved.
Printed in the United States of America
S A N: 2 5 4 - 8 8 7 9

Library of Congress Cataloging-in-Publication Data

Winterowd, W. Ross.
 Attitudes : selected prose and poetry / W. Ross Winterowd.
    p. cm.
 Includes essays, poems, and a novella.
  ISBN 978-1-60235-150-9 (pbk. : alk. paper) -- ISBN 978-1-60235-151-6 (adobe ebook)
 I. Title.
 PS3573.I5386A9 2010
 818'.54--dc22
                                    2010007937
Printed on acid-free paper.
Cover design by David Blakesley
Word cloud courtesy of http://www.wordle.net. Used by
  permission.

Parlor Press, LLC is an independent publisher of scholarly and trade titles in print and multimedia formats. This book is available in paperback and eBook formats from Parlor Press at www.parlorpress.com or at brick-and-mortar and online bookstores everywhere. For submission information or to find out about Parlor Press publications, write to Parlor Press, 816 Robinson St., West Lafayette, Indiana, 47906, or e-mail editor@parlorpress.com.

For Marj--to the end of the journey

contents

Part I. Bricolage 3

"Chicken" and Poetry: The Unspeakable and the Unsayable 5
Insomniac Rhapsody on Vitalism 12
Writing Theorists Writing: Life Studies 16
The Seasons: Four Prose Lyrics 20
Tropical Thoughts 26
The Orgone Experience; or, Renewal Is Possible 27
The Ceremony of Innocence 29

II. Poems 35

Vegetables 37

roots 37
Parsnip 37
Carrot 38
Beet 39
Radish 40
Rutabaga 41
Jicama 42

tubers 43
Potato 43
Sweet Potato 44

legumes 45
Pea 45
Soya 46
Bean I 47
Bean II 48

grain 49
Oats 49
Wheat 50

  Rye 51
  Rice 52
 Leafs 53
  Sotweed 53
  Lettuce 54
  Cabbage 55
 magnoliophyta 56
  Okra 56
 Matters Professional 57
  Deconstructionism 57
  The Jaded Compositionist Meditates on His Calling During an Attack of Influenza 58
  Slither, Bustle, Waddle, and Glide, Members of the Departmental Subcommittee on Allocation of Office Supplies and Faculty Amenities 59
  Meditation at a Scholarly Conference 61
 Erotica 62
  Hiking Wheeler 62
  Eudora (on having read *One Writer's Beginnings*, by another Eudora) 64
  The Deep Structure of Desire 65
 Matters Personal 68
  Lenses 68
  With George and Mary 69
  Code Blue 70
  Les Fleurs Sauvages 71
  Mellow Drama 72
  "But a good cigar is a smoke" 73
  How to Read a Page 74

III. Academy Awards 75

 about the author 285

attitudes

Part I. Bricolage

As an attitude can be the *substitute* for an act, it can likewise be the *first step towards* an act.

—Kenneth Burke, *A Grammar of Motives*

attitudes

"Chicken" and Poetry:
The Unspeakable and the Unsayable

I

I like to play "chicken" with my students, most of whom in our post-positivist age have never really experienced the power of language, though every freshman can repeat the truisms retailed by English teachers from the early grades onward and wholesaled by "communications" specialists in the academy, the media, and the marketplace: through language, you discover truth, convey ideas, gain professional and economic advancement, convince individuals, sway the masses, sell products, preserve freedom, defeat falsehood, gain status. . . . Yes, we agree, language is like atomic energy, a mighty force that can be used for good or ill, to heal or kill, an instrument more delicate than the surgeon's knife and more ominous than any other weapon in the history of humankind's arsenals.

Yet, on a less grandiose scale, in a more immediate sense, in the homely atmosphere of a beige, chalk-dusted classroom, with the whirring continuo of a perpetually ill-adjusted air-conditioning system, I like to play "chicken" with my students.

Here are the rules of the game. I'll start with an innocuous expletive, "Darn!" I'll pause and then utter something a bit more potentially offensive: "Damn!" Now the agon reveals itself. Either my oaths will continue to grow worse until I chicken out, can no longer bring myself to the next, more scabrous term, *or* a student will raise his or her hand, indicating that he or she is unable to tolerate the next move in the game. The student is chicken, though usually it's several members of the class who are unable to let me proceed.

The tensions that the game generates come not from mere etiquette, not from formulaic Puritan propriety, rather from, I know certainly, dark caverns of psychic constraints that I as a teacher of language use can experience, but not adequately explain. If the game works—and it always does—the mood of the room seems concentrated in the electric focus of the ambient, unvarying ray of sound from the air-conditioning duct, inhuman, inexplicable (since Carrier's engineers should have been more proficient), and timeless. The pause before we giggle and relax is a suspended moment.

Needless to say, unspeakability comes not only from sexual and other taboos, but from any of the limits set by a given community—including limits of credibility (not many would pay serious attention to the argument that the earth is flat), of genre (as we all know, if something looks like or is called a poem, we lose much of our audience), of beliefs and values (any statements made by officials of the current administration, whoever they might be, are propaganda).

If you think I'm overdramatizing, try "chicken" the next time you have the chance for a parlor game. You'll experience the mystery of the unspeakable.

2

Both D. H. Lawrence and Henry Miller took to painting, though neither was a Rembrandt, choosing palette, paints, brush, and canvas as a first and primary means of expression.

Years ago in Taos, my wife and I saw a collection of Lawrence's art, gathered by the enigmatic Saki Karavas in his office in the old hotel that he ran. His cluttered desk was in the middle of the room, and two pairs of his shined shoes sat on the floor by the wall. The admission charge, paid to the desk clerk, was two bucks each. We had just come from the mountain ranch, where we visited Lawrence's tomb, and had signed the register just beneath the line on which a Nebraskan had penned flowingly, "Lawrence lives!"

"Red Willows" lives in our memory: naked bathers in a stream with a red willow fringe. In the foreground, a young man, crouching like a frog and viewed from the rear. His torso is an optical illusion, a gestaltist ambiguity, an impossibility such as those which obsessed M. C. Escher. At one moment, the figure is a swimmer, about to launch off into the stream. At another, his torso is a penis, the buttocks a perfectly formed glans. He is both swimmer and phallus.

Any interpreter worth his or her salutation can give a perfectly reasonable explanation of this image: D. H. the repressed homosexual doing bugger imagery in a moment of nasty artistry. In language, with such outrages as *Lady Chatterly,* he had reached the limits of speakability, and hence he changed his medium.

And yet, such a reasonable explanation is far too easy, belies what we sense—when we are playing chicken, when we are being honest with ourselves—about the nature of our knowledge, for we know much more than we can say. Not only is language bound by the manacles of propriety (whatever that might be in our daring game of "chicken"), by the limitations on our gutsiness to utter that which is in principle *speakeable;* it is also shackled by the limits of the *sayable.*

D. H. Lawrence, like all of us, knew a good deal more than he could ever say.

Of course Lawrence could have "spoken" his homoeroticism, did speak it both in the suppressed beginning of *Women in Love* and in the conclusion of that novel. In the last scene, Ursula asks Birkin, "Did you need Gerald?"

"Yes," he said.

"Aren't I enough for you?" she asked.

"No," he said. "You are enough for me, as far as a

woman is concerned. You are all women to me. But I wanted a man friend, as eternal as you and I are eternal."

"Why aren't I enough?" she said. "You are enough for me. I don't want anybody else but you. Why isn't it the same with you?"

"Having you, I can live all my life without anybody else, any other sheer intimacy. But to make it complete, really happy, I wanted eternal union with a man too: another kind of love," he said.

"I don't believe it," she said. "It's an obstinacy, a theory, a perversity."

"Well——" he said.

"You can't have two kinds of love. Why should you!"

"It seems as if I can't," he said. "Yet I wanted it."

"You can't have it, because it's false, impossible," she said.

"I don't believe that," he answered.

You say to me, "But 'Red Willows' is nothing more than a pictorial statement of what Lawrence said explicitly in other places, as in the conclusion to *Women in Love,* an obstinacy, a theory, a perversity."

"I don't believe that," I answer. "In part, yes, the painting strains at the limits of 'speakability,' but goes beyond those bounds into the realm of the *unsayable,* the sort of knowledge that is as certain as the flick of a dry fly toward an eddy in Rock Creek and the sort of knowledge that is not certain at all, that flickers dimly and briefly, like a grouse gliding through the aspens across the creek, or perhaps not a grouse at all, for one can't be certain, knowing only that among the white stripes of aspen trunks a dark blur materialized and vanished."

My choice of Lawrence as an example is in part fortuitous, in part predestined. He fits the case, and I am a Lawrentian.

3

What is poetry, essentially, but the attempt to say the unsayable?

Elsewhere I have written that an economic theory can account for wealth, but only a story can explain what it means to be wealthy. The science of aerodynamics explains the flight of a 747,

attitudes

but only a poem can convey my exhilaration when I feel the first lift of takeoff and hear the shocks thump to their full extension as the wheels leave the ground.

It is useful here to think of a distinction made by Susanne Langer in 1942—that between *discursive* forms and *presentational* forms. She is on the track when she says,

> I do believe that in this physical, space-time world of our experience there are things which do not fit the grammatical scheme of expression. But they are not necessarily blind, inconceivable, mystical affairs; they are simply matters which require to be conceived through some symbolic schema other than discursive language.

And the psychologist Endel Tulving helps, with his distinction between *verbal* and *episodic* knowledge. The verbal is conceptual, depersonalized: "The formula for table salt is NaCl." But episodic knowledge is biographical, personal, contextualized: "I remember learning the formula for table salt, NaCl, from a dog-eared, navy blue chemistry text during my freshman year in high school. In class, I sat next to Anne Holt and. . . ."

Perhaps, for a beginning, we can say that poetry is the residue, the excess, after the discursive, purely verbal element of meaning has been extracted—what remains after "alembification," to use one of Kenneth Burke's favorite terms. Once our students have stated and hence removed the thesis of "Sailing to Byzantium," the leftovers are poetry, a kind of knowledge so puzzling that a whole industry labors away to account for it. (No Fermi Lab for this gigantic enterprise, of course.)

If there is an excess, it was created by someone: the author or the reader. Or both. Since you and I can take anything to be a poem, we can create excess—superabundance—in any text. Or, alternatively, we create the excess and hence take the text to be a poem. Guilt ridden as we are, we will always attribute the fecundity to the author, not to our Spartan selves.

In the game of "chicken," we can force our students to experience the principle of speakability. In the game of poetry can we force our students to experience the principle of sayability.

4

Starting, I presume, with Aristotle, "rhetoric" has through the centuries undergone the pressures and counter- pressures of definition. On the one hand, it is the art of finding the available means of persuasion in regard to any subject whatever and, on the other hand, it is the search for identification, consubstantiality. (As I think of numerous other hands, the image of the many-armed Indian goddess arises, but I shall desist.)

Not that I can resist adding my own definition of rhetoric to the hundreds that we could accumulate with a couple of hours in a modest public library. Tentatively, stipulatively, without signing contracts or taking oaths, asking in advance for tolerance and forgiveness, I shall posit, for now, that *rhetoric is the study of the unspeakable and the unsayable.*

Though I will not, in this essay, limn the anatomy of the newly conceived field, we could begin to think of rhetorical theories of scene (for speakability is always an intense agent-scene dialectic), of rhetorical epistemology (following the leads of Kenneth Burke), of a rhetorical psychology, and, not least, of a rhetorical linguistics. (With what fields of knowledge would the rhetorical stop? What area of inquiry is arhetorical?)

But rhetoric has never been merely a "study of" subject; it has always concerned "how to."

> *English 101, The Unspeakable and the Unsayable.* Introduction to the principles and practices of pushing language to its limits. Students will be encouraged to produce writings that test the very limits of speakability. The class will also write much poetry in the attempt to say the unsayable.

English 101 as the "chicken" game and the poetry game!

attitudes

5

Then what about English 400, Advanced Composition? I can think of three possibilities.

The first and most obvious is that it be a course in painting—beyond the unsayable to the visual image.

> *English 400. Beyond the Sayable.* Students will use paints, brush, palette, and canvas to express their ideas. No assigned writing. No class discussion.

The second, and certainly most practical, move turns out like this:

> *English 400. Business Writing.* Instruction and practice in writing such documents as reports, memos, proposals, and business letters. Assignments will be individualized according to the career goals of the students.

"Business Writing," you see, would result from an act of purposeful forgetfulness, a general strategy so necessary for survival in the academy and of the academy that a study of our institutions of higher learning should concentrate on what faculties and administrations don't think they're doing rather than on what they say they're doing and what they actually think they're doing. (The discrepancy between what they say they're doing and what they actually think they're doing is also an important source of understanding for disinterested observers or partisan investigators.)

When it is proposed, the third possibility is almost certain to encounter trouble with the university's curriculum committee, and yet it follows most logically from our argument and is in many ways the most attractive:

English 400. Silence.

Insomniac Rhapsody on Vitalism[1]

July 9, 1985
2:13 a.m.

Insomnia, my God I'm insomniac!
Can't sleep on my stomach or on my back.
Thoughts race through my muddled brain,
Do U-turns and race back again.

I like the last couplet of the quatrain. Definitely, I have a flair for rhyme. In fact, that might be my only flair.

My flares are all burned out. My gifts are silver ashes and hollow red tubes beside life's freeway. The semis roar past, carrying their cargoes into the night, through Wyoming, Utah, Nevada. "Breaker. Breaker. This is Boilermaker. Smokey's parked behind the Little America billboard. So slow down, you hard drivin' mothers."

If I had any guts, any initiative, I'd call ____[2] right now and arrange to meet you in Las Vegas, where we'd see some shows, play some roulette, drink some whiskey—because, you know, Las Vegas is LIFE! The glittering signs, the whirr of the ivory ball as it races around the wheel, the snap of the cards, the clank of the one-armed bandit, all the cigarette smoke, the prime rib din-

---

1. The romantic theory that truth and beauty are in the individual, just waiting to be evoked by the proper instruction.

2. The reader is invited to supply any name he or she chooses.

attitudes

ner (any hour of the day) for $4.99, and look at that fat lady over there in the pink polyester pantsuit: her hair is blue! She's pumping quarters into the slot. A widow from Southern California. (Her husband was a fireman in Anaheim.) My heart goes out to her—poor lost soul in her K Mart clothes, looking for some kind of lease on life (before she joins her late husband in the family plot at Rose Hills Memorial Park), pumping coins into the slot as if . . . as if . . . as if she had found a hypnotic, mechanical act of love to see her through. Oh, may she achieve the three-bar orgasm that will bring a cascade of quarters, enough to sustain her through the next two days, for she's on a three-day tour and has allowed herself only twenty dollars for gambling. Notice her posterior. As the saying goes, it's as broad as two ax handles and a plug of tobacco. If you'll get a bit nearer to her, you can smell her perfume—so sweet that it reminds me of a childhood visit to a candy factory.

No, I'm not tempted by this little bon-bon, the Tootsie Roll. But why am I now turning cynical, for, you see, my intent was to understand and love her, yet the perfume was so overpowering that it subverted my best intentions. Should we, as an act of kindness, tell her how repulsive her scent is?

"Breaker, Breaker. This is Humpin' Harry. Just pullin' into Vegas. Think I can find me a sweet little widow to haul my ashes? Be talkin' to you later. Over and out."

But, of course, the vitalists are right.[3] Just think of what I'm doing now—not what I'm doing, but what the language is doing to me. Gee whiz! The flow of my creativity—the surprises—the twists and turns—the happy accidents—the vivid images—the unintended metaphors. Oh, the joy of it! Why didn't someone tell me about this before? Alas, I was imprisoned by the tagmemic[4] grid! It was my cell, and fool that I was, I didn't know I wasn't free! Lahd Amighty, free at last! I have overcome!

---

3. The rest of the paragraph is, of course, an explanation of vitalism.

4. An overdetermined method used by some English teachers to squeeze or wrench ideas from their students.

Image: my face staring blankly out from behind the grid, my hands clutching the vertical bars.

Oh, if I had the wings of an angel,
Straight out of this grid I would fly,
And I'd land in the arms of _____⁵,
And there I'd be willing to die.

Oh my God! I just realized: the woman playing the slot machine wasn't a California widow at all. She was _____. I should have recognized her sooner. The way she was pulling the handle—definitively, resolutely. The way she was inserting the quarters—reluctantly but resignedly. That scowl! Those practical walking shoes! And I can explain the perfume: she thinks it will attract some truck driver, lure him into a liaison, for, after all, this is her one and only fling, after which she will go back to her work of correcting freshman themes.

Vell, I vill tell you dis: dee only reason vye peoples gembles is dat dey sublimate dare libido. Yust tink of all dem dirty gemblings vords. Poker! Blackjack! Roulette! Craps! Keno! Slot machine! Dat filthy language make me turn blush.

But, of course, we need an explanation for _____'s obsession with the slot machine, and now we have it. None of our characters will be without plausible motive.

Yawn. Calistoga sparkling mineral water with natural orange flavor. Very refreshing.
Truckdriver Harry was in a casino—
Must have been in Vegas or Reno.
He was sippin' his booze and playin' his game
When his eyes lit on a lonely dame.
He finished his drink and picked up his chips,

---

5. The reader should here supply the name of any English teacher that he or she has suffered under. Unfortunately the teacher supplied must be female—not that only women wreak their havoc in composition classes.

attitudes

And he eyed that gal from her chin to her hips.
She was pumpin' a slot with all her might.
He knew that he could score that night.
He stood behind her and nuzzled her ear
And asked if she would like a beer.
She said that she was not a drinker—
Claimed to be a learned thinker.
She turned and looked him in the eye;
His hand crept slowly up her thigh.
What happened next? Please be specific.
To develop an answer, use a heuristic.

Writing Theorists Writing: Life Studies

I

We encounter the Writer in her study. She is at her Underwood typewriter, bending forward, ready to pounce, much like a leopard about to fall on a fawn, or like the favored Polish pianist, claws poised above the keys, ready to leap into an etude. The study itself is stacked floor to ceiling with typescript, so closely packed that only a narrow path from door to typing table is clear. The air is, of course, somewhat fetid; the miasma of aging paper and decades of dust are colorlessly palpable in the close atmosphere.

Following our most recent insight regarding our subject (which is, of course, writing), we ask not "What are you writing?" but *"What are you doing?"*

The Writer is startled, so preoccupied was she with her prepouncing, and she drums her fingers on the typing table, annoyed at both the interruption and the obtuse question.

"I'm making meaning!" she says testily. "What do you think I'm doing?"

The interruption has, of course, temporarily short- circuited the process of meaning-making, and the Writer uses the lacuna to expatiate on her enterprise: "I've been making meaning for years—even you can see that, can't you? In fact, I've made so much meaning that I'm going to have to enlarge my study to hold the meaning that I intend to make in the future. Let me ask you this, pal, 'How much meaning have you made lately?'"

attitudes

Not receiving an immediate reply, the Writer suspends herself again over her Underwood, claws poised, ready to make more meaning.

Realizing that our presence impedes the meaning-making, we retire from the Writer's study, the smell of dust with us even as we step into the fresh air.

II

We encounter the writer in his study. A Camel dangles from his lips, the smoke curling upward, bringing tears to his eyes. He writes with a fat fountain pen, and his mode of inscribing somehow reminds us of a has-been pug, sparring around the gym, punching at shadows, remembering, perhaps, the big fight that should have, but didn't, happen.

Following our most recent insight regarding our subject (which is, of course, writing), we ask not "What are you writing?" but *"What are you doing?"*

The Writer looks at us, and we notice for the first time that he appears somehow to be embalmed. With a whine that is nonetheless a challenge, velvet sandpaper, he says, "What else? What's writing for? I'm creating myself. I've heard all this theory shit, and I'm gonna tell you right now, get off it!"

Timidly we interject, "But we think. . . . ."

"Come on, whatya mean by that horseshirt 'think'? If ya can't express yourself so people can understand ya, then ya oughta shut up. Listen, I've been through hell and back, and what I'm doing is creating the Multiple Me, and anyone who doesn't want to do what I'm doing is a wimp, a wimp, man, see?"Intimidated, we retire from the gymnasium odor of the Writer's study.

III

We encounter the writer in his study. His head is all inclined to the Right, or the Left; one of his Eyes turned inward, and the other directly up to the Zenith. His outward Garments are adorned with the Figures of Suns, Moons, and Stars, interwoven with those of Fiddles, Flutes, Harps, Trumpets, Harpsichords, and many more Instruments of Musick, unknown to us in Europe.

Our writer is sputtering away with a goose quill, ink flying and blotching over vellum. His hands are black with ink, and the end of his nose is India-ink-ebony.

Following our most recent insight regarding our subject (which is, of course, writing), we ask not "What are you writing?" but *"What are you doing?"*

He looks up at us (we think, though we can't be sure) and says mildly, in a Christ-like voice, "I'm discovering what I mean. My son, thou knowest that the pen leadeth to truth. My pen is my staff and my rod, and it guideth me by the still waters and sustaineth me. Join thou me in this journey and thou willst profit thy soul. Thou must learn that believing is holier than doubting."

Moved, we sniffle a bit, wipe our eyes, and step from the smoky fragrance of incense into the cold, clear air of a long marble corridor.

IV

We encounter the writer in his study. Slouched before his computer, he is sipping a glass of sherry and is obviously not completely sober.

Following our most recent insight regarding our subject (which is, of course, writing), we ask not "What are you writing?" but *"What are you doing?"*

"What am I doing? you ask. I'm trying to find a rhyme for 'okra.' I've gone through two bottles of Dry Sack, but I'm stumped. Maybe I ought to abandon okra and go on with 'cauliflower.' Lots of rhymes for that: 'power,' 'Adenauer,' 'bower,' 'cower,' 'shower.' . . .

attitudes

"How's this, huh? 'Ah, snowy, bumpy cauliflower, / Thy aroma hast the power / To make me think of earlier years / With all their joys and their tears.' Man, I'm hot now. Just one more tetch of Dry Sack, and. . . ."

Declining the Writer's offer of a glass of sherry, we depart his study, the cloyingly sweet odor of the wine our most vivid legacy of this visit.

V

We encounter the writer in her study, sitting in front of the screen of her computer, a generic model assembled by her engineer husband. So engrossed in her own lucubrations is she, that for several minutes she is unaware of our presence. Beside her on a paper plate lies a half-eaten hamburger, sans mustard or ketchup, pickle and onion carefully removed and sagging over the edge of the plate onto the desk.

Following our most recent insight regarding our subject (which is, of course, writing), we ask not "What are you writing?" but *"What are you doing?"*

Receiving no answer, we ask again, more insistently, "What are you doing?"

Startled, the Writer looks up, now aware of our presence.

"I'm composing an explication of and commentary on a text by Paul Ricoeur. Perhaps you're familiar with this: 'In some cases the matter to be recovered is so remote, is in a channel of thinking or feeling so alien to our own, that even a savant's "restoration" of the environmental context is not adequate. This is always true in some degree—'"

"That was not Ricoeur," we interrupt; "it was Burke."

"Oh," says the Writer. "Oh."

We tiptoe out of her study, the aroma of cold hamburger lingering in our memories.

The Seasons: Four Prose Lyrics

I

Under the scrub cedars, crystalline snow rots slowly away, rivulets coursing down the mountain, zigzag. A badger lumbers up the trail, pauses, looks at the boy, hisses, and lumbers on. A hawk circles high, falls from sight behind a peak, then struggles upward, a snake in its talons.

The valley below lazes in the afternoon sun, the sagebrush powdery silver, bright in the keen light against yellow sand and moist black earth. The mountains opposite are bare and dun.

The boy watches covetously as Mr. Armstrong's bronze Packard Clipper glides silently along the ribbon of highway. In the Packard Clipper, more desirable than Mr. Holt's black LaSalle or Mr. Johnson's gray Buick, the boy could drive forever: Reno, San Francisco, Seattle—magic destinations.

He closes his eyes. He is on a highway to somewhere in the Packard Clipper, the girl beside him, smelling of Jergen's lotion, her plaid skirt above her knees, her breasts rising and falling under the white blouse as she breathes. The silvery center line stretches ahead endlessly, the boy drives onward, the girl breathes quietly.

II

Like a pride of lions on the veldt, we laze on the grass in the shade of a locust tree, yawning, rolling over now and then, stretching. The heat of August afternoon ascends in shimmers from the sidewalk. In the Dutchman's yard next door, the chickens are settled down in the shade of a lean-to, their feathers ruffled against the heat.

Don Munding rolls over on his side, props his head on his hand, and says, "Wish we had fifteen cents."

"Yeh," says Sonny Markowski.

"Yeh," I say.

"Think your aunt would give us fifteen cents?" asks Don.

"Maybe," I say.

"Then ask her for it," says Sonny.

"Okay," I say, but I don't move.

Nor can I stir until the three coaches of the electric railway have passed on the tracks behind my aunt's house. I hear the horn far away, as the train approaches the trestle, and then nearer as it crosses Redwood Road. And now the electric crackle of the trolley and the metallic thump of the wheels. A blast of the horn directly behind the house and lot sets the old cocker spaniel to howling madly. I feel the earth tremble slightly. And then the sound grows ever fainter, the horn virtually inaudible, the train gone, leaving behind an electric smell, releasing me.

"Go ask your aunt for fifteen cents," says Sonny.

Leonine, I rise majestically, and, feline, slink around the corner of the house, into the back door, and down the basement, where my aunt is doing the laundry. She wrings the clothes through the white rubber rollers of the Maytag, and they fall into a large basket on the floor. The room smells of White King laundry soap, as does my aunt, always.

"C'n I have fifteen cents?" I ask her, without preliminaries.

"Why fifteen cents?" she asks.

"Cause Sonny and Don are out there, too," I reply.

My aunt, a soft touch, but a thoroughgoing Puritan nonetheless, tells me, "You can have fifteen cents if you'll help me hang the laundry out to dry."

The last pair of Mormon garments through the wringer, my aunt puts on her large straw hat with the pink ribbon around the crown, and we lug the basket, she on one handle and I on the other, to the yard and pin each item to the wires that stretch from pole to pole perhaps forty feet. The laundry hangs sodden in the heat, the sagging mid-section of the wires held up by portable forked poles.

When I return to the shade of the locust tree, Sonny and Don regard me through half-closed eyes, but since I don't flop on the lawn, they know that I have the fifteen cents, and they lazily, in slow motion, get to their feet. We walk across the road to the two-pump service station (regular and ethyl), our Keds scrunching the gravel of the apron. Mr. Maw sits in an old swivel chair in front of the small frame building. Barely moving, he nods assent for us to enter, and we go through the open door. On shelves to our left, cans of Quaker State motor oil. On the back-wall shelves, loaves of Wonder Bread, packages of Fisher doughnuts, and cans: Pierce's pork and beans, Spam, Del Monte salmon. To our right, a glass display case (with jawbreakers, Doughboys, Tootsie Rolls, licorice cigars, marshmallow bananas, bubble gum, small wax bottles filled with punch) and a noisy freezer, chug, chugging. I open one lid of the freezer, take out three Fudgesicles, give one to Don and one to Sonny, and, leaving, place three nickels in Mr. Maw's outstretched hand. No words have been exchanged during the whole transaction.

As we are leaving the station, a shining new black Terraplane skids slightly on the gravel as it pulls up to the pumps.

We cross the road, settle ourselves in the shade under the locust, remove the paper bags from the Fudgesicles, and begin voluptuously to lick at the rapidly melting, watery ice cream.

III

Two odors, aromas, smells. Frying pork chops and burning leaves—one richly oleaginous, the other spicily acrid.

In the almost dark of a mid-October six o'clock, the entry light and the windows of the red-brick apartment house glow through the chilly haze. The poplars between the sidewalk and the curb are bare, their brittle gold and brown leaves filling the gutter and lying in puddles on the lawn. Parked at the curb is a shining new Hudson Hornet, silver and gray, sleek, streamlined. A radio somewhere in the building, turned too high (or at least high enough to be heard on the sidewalk), plays "On the Steppes of Central Asia."

The building is two-story, with a front door of oval plate-glass set in heavy, much-varnished hardwood, with a brass loop handle and thumb-trigger.

The carpeting in the hall is worn maroon, with large, stylized flowers in green and yellow. The chipped paint on the wainscoting is off-white, an almost ashy gray. The doors to the apartments are the same much-varnished hardwood as the front door, and each has a brass number: 1, 3, 5, 7, 2, 4, 6, 8. "On the Steppes of Central Asia" is now virtually a roar, but then sudden silence: the radio has been snapped off. The smell of porkchops frying is almost palpable.

Before the door of apartment 3 lies the evening paper. The door opens, and a woman in a cotton housedress (white, printed with violets) stoops, picks up the paper, and glances momentarily down the hall. She has the classic, almost masculine face of a Venus de Milo; her hair is drawn into a bun at the back of her neck; her breasts are full, and her hips are broad and capable.

The hall is lighted by three meager frosted-glass, one-bulb fixtures spaced down the ceiling, and in the light, almost as if from candles or lanterns, the aura is golden, mellow, with the maroon of the carpet, the rich smell of the porkchops, the dark wood of the doors, and the many-layered paint on the woodwork. A woman's gentle laugh is barely audible. And then a metallic clang, perhaps a pan that had fallen, and a man's voice: "Damn!"

The radio plays again, now softly: "In a Persian Market."

A woman appears beyond the glass of the front door and, holding a large brown paper sack in one arm, opens the door and enters the hall. Her tan plaid skirt stops just above her knees. The coat, with its fur collar, is chocolate brown. Her brown hair tumbles from beneath a brown tam. Her shoes are spike-heel black patent leather. She glances down the hall and then hurries up the stairs, which creak slightly with her every step. Behind her hovers the aroma of cosmetics, face powder, and perfume.

Throughout the city, brick apartment houses: sooty yellow or deep red. At six o'clock of an October evening, they glow at entryways and windows. They smell of frying meat. Their halls are musty and dimly lighted. From behind the doors come muted sounds of voices.

In the chill haze of an October evening, brick apartment houses. Mystery and romance.

IV

A new Rambler American, pure white, is parked beside the heaps of plowed, grimy snow. Deep-sunk footprints lead across the snowfield to the river, a quarter-mile from the blacktop road pied with glazes of milky ice.

The river runs green and swift between the snow and snow, here and there a foamy white where a rock breaks the current into eddies. Three stark and hoary trees stand lacy beyond the far bank.

The river gurgles, sloshes around the rocky point where the fisherman stands. He is insulated, puffed with down and kapok, his boots rubberized, his cap synthetic fur with earflaps pulled all the way down.

In his left, heavily-gloved hand he holds his pole; the right, ungloved, he tucks into his left armpit.

The pole jerks. He sets the hook. Another jerk, another sharp pull upward. A third jerk, another sharp twitch. He almost reluctantly pulls his hand from the warmth of his armpit and reels the catch in. The pole bends almost double and is alive with the struggle of the fish. The first breaks water, and he works it as he hauls the second and the third toward the surface. Now all three are moving with the current, strangely passive as though they've given up and, unlike trout, are ready for the net. But no such dignity as nets for whitefish, and he cranes them up, the rod almost an "O" with the weight of three foot-long fish.

With long-nose pliers, he unhooks each one and throws it back into the snow, where a heap of whitefish is growing, maybe twenty or thirty. From a plastic tube, with his right hand, he extracts a maggot, fat, white, but almost inert in the cold, and puts it on one hook. He puts a second maggot on the next hook, and a third maggot on the final hook. He puts his fingers to his nose and smells the putrid flesh in which the maggots were nurtured, the scent of death.

He casts the rig out and waits for the jerk-jerk-jerk of the struggling fish.

Tropical Thoughts

Depending on one's mood, the tropics are either fetid or fecund. The two images, both pervasively green, are, on the one hand, of mildew, scum on stagnant water, ophidians waiting flickeringly for prey, vines strangling nobler growth, the stridently green cries of extravagant birds with grotesquely large bills, Roquefort striations on the milky pallidness of an orchid, a mossy crocodile lying inertly below the surface, only its unblinking luminously green eyes and its snout visible, impenetrable walls of smothering greenness—or, on the other hand, verdure: growth superabundant and languid plenty, the brilliance of a cockatoo uplifting its emerald comb, ripe fruits hanging golden among the leaves, a monkey chattering as it flashes from branch to branch, the ogle-eyed lemur looking through us into its future.

It occurs to me that some inhabit, slither about in, the fetidly figurative while others dwell, thrive, in fecundity. Or, to put the matter another way, some stagnate in greenness while others flourish in verdure.

But I'm not about to name names, not I, no sir, for I'm not a backbiting, wrongheaded bigot.

The Orgone Experience; or, Renewal Is Possible

AUGUST 10 (White Mountains in Maine)

Rain, from drizzle to downpour to drizzle.

We drove to Rangeley and visited the Wilhelm Reich Museum and Shrine.

Reich erected (or had erected, for he was, of course, the great proponent of erections) a granite, three-story Bauhaus atop a peak in the White Mountains. Perhaps fifty yards from the house is the tomb, overlooking valley and mountains: lakes and dense maple and birch forests. Next to the granite tomb (atop which is a bronze bust of the Master) sits one of Reich's most important inventions, a "Cloudbuster," which is a large metal frame supporting aluminum or steel tubes perhaps twenty feet long and a spaghetti-tangle of high-power electric wires. With his Cloudbusters, Reich called down the orgone power in clouds to create deluges (when needed by local agriculturalists).

In his first-floor laboratory, the Master had, among other scientific paraphernalia, a large, black microscope, through which he could view the orgone wriggling of the seed of life; on the top floor, the Master had a great brass telescope, through which he could view the cosmos, powered in its mighty churning by the selfsame orgone that propels the sperm toward the egg. Microcosm, macrocosm.

Awed and inspirited, my wife and I sat in an orgone chamber, feeling the power of the cosmos flow into our aging, failing selves. Emerging from the chamber after some twenty minutes of absorption, we raced, through the mud and rain, to the Buick Regal that we had rented from Alamo ($148 per week, unlimited mileage) and turned toward our home-away-from-home, the Spillover[6] Motel in Stratton, Maine. Our Navy-blue Buick (we would have preferred white or silver!) churned down the muddy road from the Shrine onto Maine Highway 6 and glided faster, ever faster toward the Spillover.

After careening into the driveway and sliding sloshingly to a halt before Unit No. 6, we leapt from the auto; I fumbled, almost in a panic, to unlock the door. We entered. Our raiment flew hither and yon. We plunged onto the queen-sized bed, hardly aware of its thunking collapse, and, our muddy hiking boots still on our feet, we strove for the great, shuddering, liberatory orgonasm.

Later (liberated, Lahd Amighty, Free at Last!), we sat propped in the broken-down bed, sipping diet Coke and watching, beyond the toes of our muddy hiking boots, the Lawrence Welk Show, taped in Escondido. In a small canoe, Guy and Rona paddled about the artificial lake and sang, "My Cup Runneth over with Love." Suzie and Bobby had fun at the pool, dancing to the lively strains of "Ain't We Got Fun." A basso profundo, contentedly angling as he crooned, climaxed (the Reichian influence is pervasive) "Old Man River" by pulling a rubber trout from the artificial lake.

We had dinner at the Stratton Diner: broiled haddock and *real* mashed potatoes and gravy.

God's on the thorn, the snail's in heaven, and all's Reich with the world.

---

6. No kidding!

The Ceremony of Innocence

In my library is a single-volume collection of works by the Marquis de Sade, a book that I obtained for scholarly purposes long ago and read in a strange way: I skipped the dirty parts and followed the amoral, rationalist philosophy that stitched the episodes of pornography together (and that, undoubtedly, in the fertile, fetid mind of the Marquis, justified the Sadism—philosophy as rationalization). I don't claim that I didn't here and there sample the sodomite extravagance and frigid cruelty, for I am, after all, humanly curious.

* * *

Some years ago, my wife and I, clinging to one another in the security of our bed, protected by our down comforter, watched Al Pacino as "Scarface," lurid curiosity and disclaimers about the horrors of the film overcoming our repugnance at the brutality. We shared a huge bowl of popcorn, and as the machine guns rattled and the chain saws snarled, we abstemiously, delicately, one by one, crunched the kernels. Looking down on us from above the bed were portraits of my wife's parents, righteous and undefiled, innocent, in their Mormon youth: lovely Marcella glancing slightly away from the scene beneath her in the bed and in front of her on the television screen, a rose held delicately in her hand; Maitland smiling enigmatically, his high starched collar unfamiliar to a farm boy and clearly uncomfortable.

***

My elder son is an omnivorous reader. When he was in high school, he grazed prodigiously through my library, sitting under the lamp in the family room until all hours, devouring book after book: Conrad and Mailer, Dickens and Tom Wolfe, *Iliad* and *Odyssey*—and his own *Rolling Stones* and other arcana about which we still don't chat since at the farther reaches of his literacy he explores landscapes as alien to me as the mythical planet Golob, on which, our Mormon legend tells us, God lives.

One night—actually a very early morning—I needed my "sleeping pill," an orange, to provide energy for another period of serious log-sawing. Stumbling through the family room on the way to the kitchen, I discovered my son reading, though it was not really a discovery, but a certainty that he would be there.

"So what's interesting enough to keep you up so late?" I groggily asked.

"De Sade," he replied, and pored on through the volume.

I proceeded to the kitchen, peeled my orange, ate it section by section, and returned to bed.

Under the down comforter, beneath the portraits of Grandma and Grandpa, beside my softly breathing wife, I fell peacefully asleep and awoke at seven, for tea and toast and another orange, completely refreshed.

***

Next June, my grandson will attend the family reunion, his first meeting with that huge, fertile tribe of Grahams that are his heritage. They're a righteous, prayerful, joyful, wonderful bunch who eat Jell-o salad, drink root beer, read the Good Books, send their sons and daughters on missions for the Church, and believe that family is more important than state or nation. In the park, as the kids—the best looking, brightest bunch of offspring that any clan could hope for—play their games, and as the older folk

attitudes

bring one another up to date and pour root beer, slice the ham, shoo the flies from the cake, and do just a bit of boasting about this Graham who's finishing an M.A. at BYU and that one who is completing a mission, I'll be thinking about our little boy, whose father, in the wee hours some years ago, read de Sade.

***

Santa Cruz is the punk capital of the world. When we were there a few months ago, my wife and I saw this: A teenager with pink and purple electric hair was restraining a rat, which crawled on his shoulder, by holding its tail between his teeth. Not a white laboratory rat, but one of those inevitably associated with sewers.

***

Our younger son is a theologian, a Presbyterian pastor. Not a tub-thumping ranter or a Jesus freak, but a young man who believes, as I do, that the problem of knowing involves texts. At dinner he, his mother, and I endlessly debate questions about books and the Book.

He's quite a remarkable guy, caught in the dilemma of enjoying the good life and realizing how antithetical those values are to his commitment. He's too serious about his beliefs to imagine himself as a society clergyman, giving witty prayers at country club breakfasts, too dedicated to envision himself as the star of a crystal cathedral, televising easy salvation.

He has not read de Sade, never will. But he watched *Miami Vice*.

***

My wife and I take prodigious satisfaction in our sons, both of whom are clean cut, wholesome, bright, responsible—yes, cultured and poised. With the disinterested objectivity of parents, we say to one another (particularly when the intimacy of a long flight prompts airplane talk about our past and our increasingly brief future), "The boys are all we could ever have hoped for." And then we pause, a bit misty, I suppose, and I take another sip of my preprandial wine as Norma increases the speed of her knitting. Another sip. The needles clink, epées flashing in the gleam of the reading lamp. "And our blessed little boy, Christopher Ross," says Norma, even more mistily.

In the pause that follows, I know her thoughts, and they're mine. How will our glowing little boy work his way through the Cretan maze of cultures and countercultures; of mayhem and murder; of drugs and mindless revolt. What price must he pay to survive the terror of the bomb and of terrorism? Will purchasing a container of aspirin take daring when he's old enough to patronize drug stores? Is he of the generation that finally will have no civility?

Suppose, fifteen years from now, we took Christopher Ross to the Graham family reunion at Saratoga resort on the shore of Utah Lake—and he wore his hair in a pink and purple Mohawk, his pet rat crawling on his shoulder, its tail in his mouth.

Life is clearly too perilous to be lived.

The flight attendant brings our trays of steamed, soggy chicken and watery vegetables.

"It's not too bad," says Norma, who daringly has made the test run. "And the bread is really quite good."

* * *

In our park, a group of young children play "war." We know that they come from caring families, for their camouflage Ranger outfits are clean and pressed, and their plastic M-16's must cost fifteen or twenty dollars each.

attitudes

* * *

My family and friends always accuse me of having a weird sense of humor. Perhaps they're right. For his first birthday, I wanted to surprise Christopher Ross with a camouflage outfit, combat helmet, and M-16.

My wife, who obviously has no sense of humor, vetoed the idea.

* * *

"*Sade, de* \'sad\ Comte Donatien Alphonse Franois 1740–1814 Marquis *de Sade* Fr. soldier & pervert"

—*Merriam-Webster Collegiate Dictionary*

* * *

When I was nine, my mother took me to San Francisco for the World's Fair, an unbelievable sacrifice for a Depression family. Father stayed at home, working as a roofer.

Concurrent with our visit to San Francisco was the international convention of the CIO, the Congress of Industrial Organizations. My mother introduced me to John L. Lewis, then and now one of the great Winterowd heroes. He shook my hand, patted my head, and gave me a quarter. (If I, now a glamorous senior citizen, could choose between Lewis's thick, silvering hair and his furiously bushing eyebrows, I'd take the eyebrows every time.)

One night, Mother had been invited to a banquet, with John L. She gave me a dollar, and I took the cable car from the Hacienda Hotel on O'Farrell Street, to the Golden Gate Theater on Market, enjoyed the show (the film "Song of the South" and Ted Lewis live on stage), and then returned, via cable car, to the Hacienda, where the desk clerk gave me a Butterfinger bar to take to my room as a treat.

* * *

My younger son and I sat waiting for a table in a Chinese restaurant in San Francisco. Having experienced the elation of a USC Trojan victory in football over Stanford, we were mellow, and hungry. I sipped a beer, and Tony, always abstemious, nursed a Perrier. In the camaraderie of father and son out for a fling, I looped my arm in his. He recoiled. "Not in San Francisco, Pop," he said.

* * *

In Greece, shortly after the birth of our grandson, Norma and I translated each experience into terms of Christopher Ross. We perceived him mainly as Apollo, that beautiful, reasonable god. Yet we realized that dialectically Apollo needed Dionysus: no Dionysus, no Apollo. If any word characterizes Greek thought and religion, it is "balance."

We hope to take Christopher Ross to Greece someday, so that he can sit in the shadow of the Parthenon and stroll the Agora. He will experience the holy island of Delos and the holy city of Delphi. And he will learn that once there were brother gods named Apollo and Dionysus. They live now only among the ruins of their ancient homeland.

Through our land prowls a strange new god who doesn't smile benignly like Apollo or roguishly like Dionysus, a rough deity who grins lewdly, malevolently.

II. Poems

Vegetables

Roots

Parsnip

Ah, parsnip, pallid winter root,
Thou emblem, yes, thou very fruit
Of fallow fields and frozen ways,
I alone will sing thy praise
Before I whack thee quite in two
And add thee to this evening's stew.
Oh, vegetable melancholic,
When people dine and drink and frolic,
Thou liest in the basement bin,
A beetle bumbling blind therein.
Thou suffer'st yet the vilest taunts:
You're never served in restaurants.

Carrot

At one time, they were plump and stubby,
Not esthetic, far too chubby;
Often gnarled, but always sapid,
Carrots then were never vapid.
Those sunny roots were full of savor,
Sweet and juicy, earthy flavor.
Carrots now are well designed,
Slim and tapered, quite refined,
But wooden, dry: they have no taste—
For symmetry, gad, what a waste!
Slice it, dice it, scrub it, pare it:
We mourn the passing of the carrot.

attitudes

Beet

In Moscow:
The blood-red beet, da, khorosho,
We use him for our borshcht, you know.
In other lands, tovarishch beet
Is not considered quite so neat.

In the suburbs:
At cocktail party, barbecue,
I've never seen raw beets, have you?
Turnip, carrot, cabbage slice
Dunked in dip is very nice.
Yet palates can by beets be tickled.
Like me, they're at their best when pickled.

In Cambridge:
From Harvard, graduate *cum laude,*
Served usually with quohog chowder,
The beet has been an honored guest
With Kissinger and all the rest
At solemn rites when Derek Bok
Asks famous grads to give a talk.

Radish

Listen, you can hear the crunch.
I eat a radish with my lunch.
The radish, wisest of the roots,
Is never cooked and only suits
A relish dish, not a platter,
Or plate or tureen, for that matter.
Imagine radish casserole,
Baked radish in a Pyrex bowl,
Or think of radish under glass,
A humble root gone upper class.
The radish knows it's best by far
To love ourselves just as we are.

Rutabaga

Forgotten, lost to our cuisine,
Of noble turnip, first *cousine,*
For rutabaga, royal root,
Strike up the timbrel and the flute.
That she at table proud may reign,
From exile bring her back again.
Ma grandmere served her every week,
With mustard greens and ham and leek.
Rutabagas are, *mon dieu!*
At least as tasty as *les choux.*

Jicama

Like the radish, it has crunch,
But if you eat it with your lunch,
You'll find that it has little flavor,
No zip, no oomph, no snappy savor.
Overweight? The thing to do
Is dine on jicama with tofu.
Because that's such a tasteless mess,
You'll lose weight through eating less.

Tubers

Potato

(To be read with a thick German accent.)

At dinner, he is always gut,
Mit Sauerbraten, hardy root,
A glass of Bier, a glass of Wein,
Kartoffel, ja, you're immer fein.
Vegetable democratisch,
Not a snob or autocratisch,
The rich, the poor, the bourgeoisie
At table gladly welcome thee.
Heil to thee, blithe tuber, spud,
Who comes to us from out the mud.
And now at the Oktoberfest,
Salute the root that we like best.
We raise our mugs in heartfelt toast.
For Kartoffel, shout a "Prost!"

Sweet Potato

The sweet potato, unlike yam,
Is very seldom served with ham.
In fact, it's barely fit to eat;
It's mealy and not really sweet.
When we find it's on the menu,
We try to get a change of venu.
Invited out to dine last night,
We'd have gladly taken flight;
As guests, we had no alibis
And met Pale Tuber in disguise,
Posing as a salad green,
The worst imposture we have seen.

attitudes

Legumes

Pea

On the vine, it rises high,
Its goal the vastness of the sky.
Secure within its cunning pod,
It soars beyond the earthy sod.
In the ether there with Jack,
It never dreamed of coming back.
The pea—who ever would have thought
It longed to be an astronaut.
In a row by one another,
Sister pea and legume brother,
Secure against the force of G's,
In their capsule quite at ease,
Had no inkling that their fate
Was actually a dinner plate.

Soya

Since soy bean is a *bricoleur,*
The handyman without a peer,
When we say "soya" in our house,
We always think of Lévi-Strauss.
Fermented juice of soy's a sauce
That saves our rice from total loss
Though honestly I must confess
I think tofu's a tasteless mess.
My farmer friend, I swear, avows
The soybean nourishes his cows.
This legume, whether cooked or raw,
Preoccupies Jacques Derrida.

attitudes

Bean I

John Kenneth Bean is enigmatic.
With wieners he is democratic,
And yet in Julia's *cassoulet*
He turns elitist, slightly fey.
His pronouncements economic
Seem to me a little comic
When with sombrero and guitar
In chili he becomes a star.
With eloquence he makes us humble.
We listen as our stomachs rumble,
Sitting stiff, in mortal terror
Of that most disgraceful error.

Bean II

Professor Twist's Last Expedition

Ogden Nash's exposition
Chronicled the expedition
To the land of crocodile,
The upper reaches of the Nile.
I give you now Professor Twist,
A conscientious scientist.
Trustees exclaimed, "He never bungles!"
And sent him off to distant jungles.
Camped on a tropic riverside,
One day he missed his loving bride.
She had, the guide informed him later,
Been eaten by an alligator.
Professor Twist could not but smile.
"You mean," he said, "a crocodile."
That was in . . . uh . . . let me see,
The year of nineteen twenty-three.
In thirty-three he set out on
A journey up the Amazon.
After hardship you can't describe,
He came upon a savage tribe,
Healthy, happy, without disease—
Twist barely reached up to their knees.
Eagerly he told their chief,
"Your followers defy belief.
They get their vigor by what means?"
The chief replied, "We eat-um beans."
"Beans? Beans? What kind?" Poor Twist was wild.
"Yooman beans!" The chief just smiled.

Grain

Oats

On a frosty winter morn,
I have my choice: oats, wheat, or corn.
In March when all the ways are slush,
I choose to start my day with mush.
Cracked wheat is hearty and nutritious;
Corn meal is soothing and delicious;
But oatmeal laced with heavy cream
And honey globs has my esteem.
You see, in German my name, "Ross,"
Means "stallion." (You can call me "Hoss.")
When offered oats at break of day,
We prancing kind just can't say, "Neigh!"

Wheat

When as a child I walked from school,
Wading through the pool on pool
Of fallen leaves along the way
On lawn and sidewalk where they lay
And heard their rustle and their crunch,
(Three hours ago I'd downed my lunch),
I sniffed the air, a very hound,
Alert to every smell and sound,
The musty odor of the mums,
The chuffing engine's distant drums,
And saw ripe apples hanging late,
Too high for me to depredate.
A block from home, I pause, I freeze.
The smell of bread is on the breeze.
I clasp my "Dick and Jane" securely,
For I understand most surely
That wheat when ground is more than flour:
It's endowed with mystic power.
Baking bread in Bombay, Rome,
Or Salt Lake City signals "home."

Rye

You can serve it slice by slice.
You can pour it over ice.
It goes well with ham or soda,
Vermouth, corned beef, bitters, gouda.
Loaf or bottle, worth a try.
With rye you'll never go awry.

Rice

"I wouldn't leave Beijing," said Mao,
"For all the rice in Sacramento."
You see, the Chairman clearly knew
A fact that's shared by very few:
More rice grows in California than
In all of China and Japan.
It was brought here, to be specific,
To labor on the Southern Pacific,
And then, forsaken, had to stay
In Hanford and in San Jose.
It now speaks English fluently
And sends its kids to USC.

Leafs

Sotweed

One leaf should now be doing time,
Life sentence for its horrid crime,
Its disregard for humankind,
Cruelties that numb the mind.
Sotweed dulls the keenest brain
And leaves behind on teeth vile stain,
A rancid odor on the breath—
Tobacco is the herb of death.
Yet as I pen this morbid dirge,
Struggling with the awful urge
To suck in nicotine and tar,
I'm puffing on a huge cigar.

Lettuce

When it's sliced, I cannot bear it!
Purists always gently tear it
Delicately with their fingers,
Avoiding acrid taste that lingers
From the touch of any metal
On this tender, light green petal.
But lettuce seldom gets its due.
There are really very few
Who eat the leaf 'neath stuffed tomato
Or salad, tuna or potato.
Left on the plate, wilted, oily,
It's often nothing but a doily.

attitudes

Cabbage

A thoroughgoing democrat,
In blue collar and hard hat,
Cabbage has a union card.
On Saturday, he mows his yard,
Watches football Monday night,
Has never missed a major fight;
Subscribes to *People,* scans the *Times*
(For weather, scores, and heinous crimes).
Mr. Cabbage is *sub dig*—
Some would say, "A swine, a pig!"
But this pungent vegetable,
Leader of the plebeian rabble,
Has potential, without doubt:
He's incipient sauerkraut.

Magnoliophyta

Okra

(at the request of Jim Corder)

Family mallow's diverse stock
Includes both okra and hollyhock,
Althea shrub, and, indeed,
Rose of Sharon, and velvetweed.
When you served your okra gumbo,
You undoubtedly didn't know
That your soup was pleonastic—
Rich and spicy and bombastic.
As the dictionary tells you,
Gumbo's "okra" in Bantu.
Consider, then, this irony:
Okra came across the sea
To pick that field, to cut that cane,
To labor on in woe and pain,
While its cousin sat in state,
King Cotton, mallow's line enate.

Matters Professional

Deconstructionism

In the heat, beneath the trees,
Ungainly wood between her knees,
A cellist idly weaves her notes.
The melody, I think, connotes
The lazy, endless whirl of mind—
A nebula that's ill-defined—
Toward a center, resting place,
Stability in boundless space.

w. ross winterowd

The Jaded Compositionist Meditates on His Calling During an Attack of Influenza

Thank God, I say, for student essays!
They let us while away our days
In what we hope is harmless work,
Hunting for the errors that lurk
Within the Twinky prose.
Those acne essays—we've tried, heaven knows,
To improve their complexion
By noting each and every possible correction,
And feeding their authors, without apology,
Nutritious fare from the Norton anthology.
We may do some good; we hope so.
In any case, this much we do know:
The essays probably won't be terrific, Yet they'll serve as a soporific
To deaden the pain of arthritis or flu.
Ah yes, our themes will see us through
The dismal dregs of sniffling Sundays,
The aching, hacking nights of Mondays,
Weekend, weekday—noses or knees, heads or backs,
Wherever the malady, themes help us relax.
Those narcotic anodynes, those horrendous stacks—We need them. We're nothing but pitiful hacks,
Self-righteously flaunting devotion to duty,
To error-free prose and to truth and to beauty,
When we know for a fact (and this is sublime):
Our mission is really just to kill time.

Slither, Bustle, Waddle, and Glide, Members of the Departmental Subcommittee on Allocation of Office Supplies and Faculty Amenities

He Slithers in and hisses greeting.
"This will be a busy meeting."
She Bustles primly to her chair.
"This will be a great affair."
She Waddles dourly to her seat.
"I'm glad," she grunts, "that we can meet."
He Glides along; he doesn't walk.
"We're alone, so we can talk."
Glide looks thoughtful, wise, profound.
Waddle doesn't make a sound.
Bustle's manner is officious.
Slither's start is . . . well . . . auspicious.
"This is," in hiss, "a vital matter."
"Indeed, indeed!" is Bustle's natter.
"I agree!"—that's Waddle's rumble.
Glide advises, "We can't bumble."
Slither strokes his flowing hair.
Bustle wriggles in her chair.
Waddle wakes, her head upreared.
Glide is playing with his beard.
"We'll talk some more," he firmly states.
Waddle's nod asseverates.
Triumphant Bustle says, "Ahem!"
And Slither names her chair *pro tem*.
Slither says, "A job well done."

Bustle adds, "I have to run."
Waddle mutters her adieux,
And Glide: "I've many things to do."
One now Slithers out the door,
And then out Bustles yet one more.
The third one Waddles down the hall.
The last one Glides, and that is all.

Meditation at a Scholarly Conference

We celebrate our solemn rite.
We genuflect; we mumble prayer.
The priestess, personable and bright,
Legitimates the whole affair.
A sermon launched, we sip our wine,
A blessed, welcome sacrament.
Our ardor, though, will soon decline
For the blessed testament.
We endure the sacred mass,
Holding to the ancient creed,
Knowing in our hearts at last
Learned talk is what we need.
We celebrate the frequent rite,
Renewing our belief.
The "Amen" said, our faith is bright,
And we adjourn with great relief.

w. ross winterowd

Erotica

Hiking Wheeler

With candles, groping down through Lehman Cave,
We chased the shadows of reality
And saw the cavern as John Lehman had.
The flicker led him back and back toward
A treasure. In the greatest Saal he dreamed
A courtly dance, the fiddles tuning up,
Their echoes crinoline and riding boots.

Emerging in the blaring sun, we blinked
And wiped our eyes; newborn, we tottered stunned,
Our bleary gaze toward the misted peak.

An easy climb through pine and aspen glades.
I watched the muscles flexing in her legs,
Her working buttocks tight within her shorts,
And heard her breathing deeply in thin air,
The quartz shards clinking with her every step.

When we reached the bristlecones, we paused
To ponder those tenacious trees, so gnarled,
But not eternal, no, yet nearly so
As anything on earth. The cones were bright
With golden honey, fecund, pregnant, ripe.
We ate our M&M's in pinescent air
And sipped the lukewarm water from canteens.

Above the timber, scrambling through the scree,

attitudes

We reached the cirque, the glistening our goal,
Then crunched through ice upon the glacier's face,
And on the farther side, sat peacefully.

We'll take the hike again, again, perhaps,
But someday we'll just stay there, glacier-bound,
Side by side, thinking of the bristlecones,
The M&M's, the water, and the scree.

Eudora (on having read *One Writer's Beginnings,* by another Eudora)

In the sixth grade, Eudora Britton
Had budding bubs.
She wore rouge and lipstick.
She looked, I think, like Ava Gardner,
Hideous,
So repulsive that we boys stampeded,
Terrified when the teacher led her
Toward us across the gym for pairing,
To practice waltz and foxtrot.
I remember her full-lipped crimson smile
Above the sweater and the sagging bobbysox,
That Wonderland smile, fixed, immobile.
As she neared us, towed by Miss Hayes,
We giggled, milling in the corner.

attitudes

The Deep Structure of Desire

If I say to you, "The log is ashes,"
You aren't puzzled in the least.
You've known logs—known your father to chop them
For the black, wood-burning stove your mother used to cook the chili sauce in fall
(Ah, its redolence through the house!)
and to give the upstairs bedrooms
just a bit of heat,
just enough to keep you and Sister Beulah,
huddling together under the heavy quilts
your mother made, huddling there, the two of you together, in the bitter Mormon cold of January—
just enough heat to keep the two of you
not cold, not warm, but in a middle state
that made the huddling sweet.

And yet you should be puzzled.
For, my love and friend,
if the log is ashes it is no longer log.
Something which *was* the log is now ashes.

Here is another puzzle for you:
You, my wife, were born in Fairview.
But, love, when you were born,
you were not my wife—
though no doubt destined by our Mormon God
through eternity, you for me, me for you,

one couple indivisible, with no liberty and much justice
   for both.

Our language fools us.
Our moods are trout that sulk beneath
a log (which is not ashes) and then jump flashing
at a mayfly or a hackled hook.

Finish cooking the dinner.
But if it is not cooked,
how can it be a dinner?

The truth is hard to get at.
Here is a true-untrue story.
Our *oldest* son got lost in the mountains.
(Just Southern California mountains.
Not Alaska. Not that alarming. He told us
that the smog was bad.)
And so I'll begin my story with
"Our *youngest* son got lost in the mountains."
And you'll say, "That's wrong."
So I'll rephrase: "Our youngest son
didn't get lost in the mountains."
And you'll say, "But that's beside the point."
And I'll say, "Someone who is *not* our youngest
son got lost in the mountains."
"Ah," you'll say, "now we can get on with the tale."

So truth is not the exact opposite of untruth.
The truth is hard to find.
Or is it?
My sentences hide the truth.
That is my whole problem.

attitudes

The truth must lurk,
like a trout beneath a log,
somewhere *below* what I say.
The log was once a tree.
The log is now ashes.
The tree, of course, had branches.
And, in this essay, we are led to a terrible
but inevitable pun: branching tree.
I can do an elegant diagram of *The log is ashes.*
In its geometrical neatness, it would satisfy you, my love,
as much as whatever music you wanted to name.
But no diagram will show my desire.
All I can say is that my desire has about it
its enigmas, its ambiguities.
It has a deep structure I could never catch.

w. ross winterowd

Matters Personal

Lenses

Galileo explored the night,
His lens extending human sight
Back and back toward the place
Where time began its stately pace.

Old Dutchman with his home-made lens,
Leeuwenhoek found teeming fens
In a drop of H^2O,
Beasties darting to and fro.

Trained upon a blade of grass,
Great Grandma's magnifying glass
Gathered sunlight to a spot,
Blinding pinhead, shaft white-hot.

Through our lens, our son's first son,
Our miracle, our glowing one,
Past and future gain their focus,
A bright, melodic, fragrant locus.

attitudes

With George and Mary

Somehow the place so fits our friends:
the quiet flow of the river,
the elegant silver trees,
a honker landing just now
and drifting serenely with the current;
the quiet flow of the music,
the elegant, airy room,
the easy talk resumed just now
and drifting serenely on.
Our friends deserve this lovely place,
A house of understated grace,
For all their Acts, the perfect Scene,
A beauty joyful and serene.

Code Blue

The soothing voice, verbal Muzak,
Announces "Code blue. One east."
Some crisis—stroke or heart attack.
"Code blue," the Valium voice repeats.
The young blonde doctor, so patrician,
Crisply practices her trade
And seems the responsible physician,
Until she giggles at a joke I've made.
"Noninvasive Procedures" says the sign,
And so my territory is safe against attack.
A pacifist, I sigh, obey, resign
Myself to lying quietly upon my back,
Looking up at the doctor's serious face,
Hoping that her giggle will not come,
Apprehensive in this alien place,
Wondering if she chews bubble gum.

attitudes

Les Fleurs Sauvages

The savage flowers of Crete,
Geraniums, redder than Achaean blood;
Roses, blood red,
Clustered in the brilliant sun,
Ready for attack.
Oleander everywhere, scarlet phalanxes,
Infiltrating hillsides,
Guarding highways.

More sun than I have ever known,
And brighter, clearer.
Here, just off the coast,
Two small islands—
The next stop Africa.

They ski at Omolo,
And in winter,
The eternal shepherds
Move their flocks
To the coastal plain.

Mellow Drama

"Dear Aunt and Uncle," wrote Denise,
Our daring, nonconformist niece,
"I had my ears pierced. Mom and Dad
"Didn't know, and were they mad!
"I bought myself a pair of earings,
"Lipstick, ruge, and other things.
"I had a big suprise for mama.
"I'm staring in a mellow drama.
"Send some fashion pictures, please.
"From your loving niece Denise."

Dear Niece:
May you be the morning star,
Glowing in the light of dawn.
May you be the evening star,
Shining when the light is gone.
May you ever be the star
Of mellow drama all life long.
Your loving aunt and uncle.

attitudes

"But a good cigar is a smoke"

This hoary joke
Is worth a smile, perhaps a chuckle,
Medicine for those who knuckle
Under to their pumping glands
(The covert leers, the trembling hands)—
Not females, no: testosterone,
The liquor that unmixed, alone,
Taken straight, not on the rocks,
Deadens brains and rouses libidinous desires.
More avidly I puff my stogy;
I'm lecherous, a raw old fogy.
Ah, whatever might have been,
I'm now a senior citizen,
With glabrous pate and sagging skin.
Too late, alas, to live in sin.
Thank Jove, I say, for senile vice;
It's not exciting, but it's nice.
Cigars and such, as Freud well knew,
Keep one going, see one through.
And when at last my hormones cease,
I'll puff away my life in peace.

w. ross winterowd

How to Read a Page

Like Henry Ford, who mined the Mesabi,
Ore for River Rouge.
The great plant smoked and fumed and clanked.
Ore in one end,
And out the other, Model A's.

Like Evel Knievel, gunning his bike,
Metallic thunder down the track,
Up the ramp, over the abyss.
Kerthump! the hind wheel hits the dirt.
Through a cloud of dust and exhaust,
The rider takes his bow.

Like a hawk circling high,
But tighter, tighter, above the rabbit, crouched and trembling;
Then the plunge, the miss;
Wings pulsing, the struggle upward;
The lazy glide on the thermals;
Then circling high in tighter spirals.
The plunge.

Like Grandpa strolling in the park,
Pausing now and then to feel the breeze,
Waiting for the child totteringly to catch up;
Then, hand in hand, onward,
Both silent in the swish of fallen leaves.
Hot chocolate at a sunny table
In the stand beside the lake.

Like Uncle Jim, whose story was the telling,
On the porch at gloaming.

III. Academy Awards

1. Chicken Cacciatore

Professor J. Melongaster Druse had married badly. In fact, his wife was a bowler. Every Wednesday she donned her crimson polyester shirt (blazoned in gold on the back with "Happy's Hamburger Haven," her team's sponsor), lugged her ball and shoes (in a tooled leather bag) to the ungainly red Buick parked in the driveway of the Druse residence, and made her lumbering way to the lanes.

Druse had watched his neighbor, Cynthia Golden, depart for her sets at the Newport Racquet Club, golden Cynthia in her tennis whites (the decorously provocative short skirt revealing just a callipygian glimpse beneath the lacy line of immaculate panties), skipping to her Mercedes convertible, waving gaily at her neighbors, and gliding off for a morning of sociable recreation, followed, no doubt, by lunch at the club.

Tanned, manicured, and perfumed, fastidious, meticulous, and chic, lithe graceful and girlish, Cynthia was overtaking middle age with purring, dignified equanimity, and when Mel Druse saw her, he warmed, not with lust, but with envy of Dr. Greg Golden, who had not only Cynthia, but also the cachet of being an enormously successful neurosurgeon (tooling about in a silver Porsche with the personalized license plate "Brain 1"). Inevitably, Greg was imperially slim and crowned with a glorious, wavy, carefully tended silver mane. Mel, of course, was short, pudgy, and bald. Greg and Cynthia were, naturally, the social lions of the neighborhood, much sought after as guests; the annual Halloween brunch at the Goldens' was the neighborhood's most festive and eagerly awaited occasion. Whether hosting or guesting, Greg and Cynthia were unfailingly considerate and witty, paying alert attention during conversations, listening patiently to accounts of lawns, pool filter systems, golf games, and children gone awry or aright.

In short, Greg and Cynthia Golden were everything that residents of their very upper-middle-class neighborhood ought to be. Greg even played bassoon in the Orange County Doctor's Symphony, and Cynthia was, as might be expected, an active member of the Museum of Art board.

All of this glowing perfection gnawed persistently at Mel's peace of mind. So much glamour and romance created insuperable odds against a literary scholar married to a bowler. Who, after all, would not snicker if Mel recounted his adventures in putting together his book on the fop in Restoration drama: poking about dusty libraries and pecking out ideas on a Dell laptop hardly compared with the tense hum and beepbeepbeeping of the operating room; being mentioned in the *Times Literary Supplement* hardly ranked, among the laity, with being featured in the "Modern Living" section of the Sunday paper, as the Goldens had been. And then there was the vibrant tennis player versus the bowler.

The neighborhood was eclectically expensive, Elizabethan bungalows elbow to elbow with French chateaux, and ranch styles rambling about oversize yards, with split rail fences and wagon wheel motifs. Palm trees and pines cohabited peacefully, but had not gone quite so far as miscegenation.

It was a residential area in which the few churches resembled medical complexes, the medical complexes looked like groupings of expensive cottages, the lawns were as uniformly pruned and verdant as Astro Turf.

The dogs were standard poodles, Irish wolfhounds, Weimaraners, and Dobermans; the cars were Cadillacs, Mercedes, Jaguars, and Porsches. (One neighbor who drove a Rolls Royce was the object of general scorn. Such conspicuous consumption was vulgar and violated the unspoken norms of the neighborhood. Rolls Royces belonged in Beverly Hills, not Huntington Beach.)

It goes without saying that the Druses had a source of income other than Mel's salary; the neighborhood, with its houses ranging upwards of two million dollars, was for bankers, auto dealers, corporation lawyers, proprietors of chain dentistry enterprises, and neurosurgeons, not college professors. In fact, had they chosen to do so, Mel and Bobby could have lived in a much tonier neighborhood than this one, could, in fact, have afforded the very ritziest, for she was the heiress of a very large fortune inherited from her late husband, Bert Redd, the magnate who had owned a great portion of the casino business and less savory enterprises in Nevada. When he was well into his seventies and had divested himself of his fourth wife, Bert saw Bobby, in ostrich feathers and sequins, on the stage at the Xanadu, Bert's most opulent casino, where she was dancing to support herself while she worked on a master's in computer science at UNLV. It was love at first sight on both sides. After a mad weekend of dining and dancing, and after Bert slipped a ten-carat diamond ring on Bobby's finger and draped her with a diamond and emerald necklace, they were married on Monday in The Little Chapel of Eternal Bliss, serenaded before and after the ceremony by an Elvis impersonator. After one year of rapidly waning marital bliss, Bert went to that Big Casino in the Sky, and Bobby was left with all of the loot.

The tale of how Mel and Bobby got together is the stuff of romance novels or TV soap operas.

Mel, a bachelor, had just been promoted to associate professor with tenure, having cleared the hurdle at which at least three-fourths of assistant professors fall. He was elated, and his whole demeanor changed, from unctuous pliability to smug aloofness. As Professor Pottle Tinker put it, "Hrumph . . . Mel seems to be . . . hrumph . . . practicing to become . . . hrumph . . . a dean."

As a reward for tenure well-won, Mel pointed his Toyota Corolla northward on I-15, toward Las Vegas, where he planned a weekend of madcap diversion, release from the serious business of studying and professing Restoration literature.

On Saturday evening, he was grazing at the all-you-can eat buffet in the Xanadu. Walking toward a table, he slipped and splattered a woman at a table with chicken cacciatore and caesar salad. He grabbed her napkin from her lap and began wiping the front of her white blouse.

"I'm sorry. I slipped on a wet spot on the floor."

"Get your hands off me, pal!" said the woman.

When Mel kept wiping, the woman gave him a solid one to the jaw, and he stumbled backward onto an adjacent table, where a couple had deposited a tray overstocked with dessert delicacies, all topped with globs of soft ice cream.

"Oh my goodness!" gasped the lady. "You asshole," shouted the man.

At which point two security guards appeared, one tall and spectrally thin, the other short with a massive overhang above his belt. Each took one of Mel's arms, securing him, and the tall guard, addressing the woman with the bespattered blouse, asked, "Is this man annoying you, Mrs. Redd?"

"Nah. He tripped in a puddle on the floor. Let 'im go." Then to Mel: "Come on. I'll buy you a drink."

> From: Druse@cdu.edu
> To: JMoss@mit.edu
>
> Nov. 7, 2000. I just voted for George W. Bush. The last debate convinced me. Gore is one of those left-wing big spenders. Bush might have his faults, but at least he won't pick our pockets to pay for half-baked socialist projects.
>
> Memorable day. The department just voted to give tenure to Faustino Ajaia on the basis of a first novel: The Gents in Pink. Of course, I had to read this junk about cross-dressers. In our day, Jesse, you didn't

get tenure on the basis of one novel. Of course, Ajaia is a PC shoo in: Hispanic author, sexually liberated subject. Frankly, I don't think writing of any kind has a place in an English department.

Bobby and I are thinking about coming East over Christmas break. If we do travel, we look forward to seeing you. Those years of grad school at Wisconsin were great, weren't they?

From: JMoss@mit.edu
To: Druse@cdu.edu

I can't believe that you voted for Bush. God, the man can't even express his ideas (if he really has any). "Families is where our nation finds hope, where wings take dream." Wow! If he would say nuclear rather than nucular, there'd be some hope. I've always told my students that muddled language is a sure sign of muddled thought. Well, we'll see what happens. Frankly, I think that Bush is an irresponsible jerk.

I'm sorry to tell you that Martha and I will be in France over the Christmas break. Another time maybe.

2. Peppermint; or Heart of Darkness

Late afternoon. Professor J. Melongaster Druse sat at his desk, killing time before leaving to attend the annual departmental cocktail party, looking forward to a few minutes of inert solitude, but on this Friday surcease from the storm and stress of a professor's duties was not to be.

A knock on the door of his office. His response. Mr. Garth Timmins entered and took a seat, forcing Druse to pull himself together and refocus. Timmins, in his snowy white cheerleader uniform, a large purple C in chenille on his chest, apparently found it as difficult to leave his rah-rah attitude and bearing behind on the playing field as it was for Druse to rally the expected professional courtesy and attention. The clash in moods—Garth's sunlamp cheerfulness and Druse's twilit dourness—created emotional smog that hung between the student and his professor.

"What can I do for you?" asked the professor, anxious to get the meeting over with.

"You going to the game tomorrow, Professor Druse?" In his Speech 101 class, Garth had learned that conversations begin most productively with any point of common interest between the parties involved. This bit of wisdom, filed away in both his memory and his class notes, was perhaps the most useful and exciting learning experience in his three years at the university.

"I must confess, Mr. Timmins, the only thing that interests me less than football is baseball. Once the groundskeepers have mowed the lawn and painted the white stripes, the excitement's over for me."

Timmins laughed his professional cheerleader's laugh and said, "Gee, that's a good one, Professor Druse. I'll remember that one to tell the team," and he glanced at his Rolex wristwatch, his smile—the model specially designed for English profs, those strange birds who were for some inexplicable reason necessary for a well-rounded education, which, of course, Timmins wanted to get since that was what he had been told his father was paying for, and if nothing else, the son believed in value received—his smile was frozen on his tanned visage, and his golden hair was tousled just enough to look completely natural, an effect that was a constant preoccupation for the young man.

Druse assessed Timmins. He was a perfect representative of the university's student body, those golden youths whose destiny was a home in Beverly Hills, a Mexican or black cleaning lady ("almost one of the family"), a Mercedes or Jaguar, a ski trip to Utah or even Switzerland in February—two children attending private school, season tickets for one "culture" series (the symphony, the theater), membership in a tennis club, and the deep-felt security that the proper values and accomplishments confer.

"Say, Professor, you know you told us to talk to you about term papers, and I have this idea I'd like to bounce off you. You know, the fops in Restoration comedy—I mean you've talked a lot about them—and, you know, I was thinking: they're all gay."

"Indeed? And what led you, Mr. Timmins, to that conclusion?"

"Well, you know, they dress in lace and all that stuff—and the way they talk, you know."

"Aren't you, Mr. Timmins, simply projecting modern attitudes and your own repugnance for homosexuality onto works of literature from an age in which norms of behavior were quite different from ours? Aren't you, after all, reading too much into the comedies?"

"Well, I'll tell you, Professor Druse, I don't know about Congreve or any of those dudes, but I know that us gays aren't ashamed of ourselves anymore."

"You say '*we* gays.' What might you mean by that?"

"I mean I'm gay."

"Well, I don't suppose that's anything to be ashamed of," responded Druse, after a significant pause during which he formed a new conception of Garth Timmins, the old image—home in the right neighborhood, two children in private school, the proper kind of wife—having been shattered. Now Garth was dancing with another man in a disco and going to bath houses. Druse was even a bit revolted by the possibility that Garth was already infected with herpes or AIDS.

"I'm not ashamed. I'm proud. Danny McLatchy, the tailback, he's gay too. And several fellows on the team are switch hitters. And let me tell you, I happen to know that two of song girls are lesbians."

"Enough! Quite enough!" Druse was genuinely peeved. "I have no desire to discuss the sexual aberrations of our students. If you feel a need to talk about such matters, you should go to the counseling service or the chaplain."

Timmins' smile vanished. He leaned forward, glaring at Druse. "I guess you don't like queers, do you, Prof? We're either crazy or sinners—or both—so we should go to the school shrink or the chaplain and get ourselves straightened out. I'll bet you think blacks should be kept in their place, too."

Druse chose his well-rehearsed role as the icily aloof scholar-mentor. "Mr. Timmins, I haven't the slightest interest in any of my students' sexual preferences or habits. What you do in your own bedroom is your business. However, I don't allow sex either in my office or in my classrooms."

Timmins leaped at the opportunity. "Oh, I don't want to have sex in your office, let alone in your classroom, Professor. All I want is freedom and equality."

"You're not funny at all, Mr. Timmins. In fact, you're downright impertinent. Perhaps you'd better come back at a later time, after you have thought about your manners, to discuss your term paper."

"Look, Prof, tuition at this place is astronomical. Us students pay your salary."

Druse's tone was lethal, prussic acid. "Leave my office immediately. And don't come back. Drop my course. I never want to see you again. Out! Out! Out!"

Timmins scurried out the door of the office.

"These assholes are barbarians," muttered Druse. "What a bunch of shitheads. Why couldn't I have got a job at Johns Hopkins, where I wouldn't have to put up with these philistines? A homofuckingsexual, probably buggering the goddamn quarterback, or the quarterback buggering him. Christ, what a filthy, rotten mess. And I'm stuck. I can't get out."

Druse took a deep breath. The flash of Timmins' ass in the skintight white polyester flannels, when he flounced out the door of the office, had left the professor with a distressing thought. He had another twenty years before retirement, two decades of the likes of Garth Timmins. Graduate students worked on dissertations under the direction of Alex Hamilton, whose whining voice drove Druse nuts; Potty Tinker had graduate students in spite of the perpetual "hrumph . . . hrumph" that made Tinker's lectures virtually incoherent; Max Schinken had to deny requests to serve on graduate committees. But Druse had no graduate-student following; hence, he was incomplete, not achieving the status that adulation from advanced students brings about. Mel shook his head sadly. Twenty years of Garth Timmins.

Druse took *Mr. Sammler's Planet* from his bookshelf and prepared, this third try, to get through the masterpiece, but he had just opened the book to the first page when the door to his office burst open, and Garth Timmins stood defiantly before him.

"I want to inform you, Professor Homophobe, that I just reported you to Dr. Burden, and Monday I'm going to Dean Amore. There are laws against people like you."

Before Druse, astounded and trembling, could respond, Timmins slammed out of his office—the dirty little queer sonofabitch, the goddamn fruit. He probably goes around smelling bicycle seats.

Now nothing could rescue the remainder of the waning day, and the only immediate prospect before Professor J. Melongaster Druse was a two-hour hiatus prior to his departure for Adam Adam's place, where he would meet Bobby, his wife, to endure the rite of the annual departmental cocktail party and get-together. A bleak two hours those would be.

He listened to the sound of a jet overhead, followed by the whack-whack of a helicopter. From somewhere he heard a shrill, brief laugh. Uninterestedly he glanced at the mail on his desk before him.

As he was about to open the first envelope, his phone rang. " . . . Just catching up on a little work before I go to the party. . . . Nothing important. I'll be right down."

Warren Burden, department chair, had asked to talk with Druse. What a pain in the ass. He knew what the subject of this interview would be, and he tensed his system for the walk down the hall and the ordeal of putting up with Warren's namby-pamby remonstrances regarding the Garth Timmins episode.

The outer office was deserted, and Warren's door was open. As Druse entered, Warren said, "Sitzen Sie sich. I mean, setzt euch. Assiez vous. I've got to run down the hall for a minute."

Why didn't the ostentatious jerk just say, "Have a seat"? Druse plunked into a chair by the coffee table, waiting for Warren Burden to reappear. As if in a trance, a deep preconscious state, he stared at an African fetish on the coffee table, an *ojet d'art* that Burden had brought back from his guest professorship in Nigeria. It was about two feet high, in dark wood, glossy and suave. It was a woman, with hair dressed high, like a melon-shaped dome. At the moment, she seemed like one of his soul's intimates. Her body was long and elegant, her face was crushed tiny like a beetle's, she had rows of round heavy collars, like a column of quoits, on her neck. He stared at her: her astonishing cultured elegance, her diminished, beetle face, the astounding long elegant body, on short, ugly legs, with such protruberant buttocks, so weighty and unexpected below her slim long loins.

So engrossed was Druse that Burden entered and settled at the desk without disturbing the trance.

"Uh, Mel, are you with me . . . or in Africa?"

"Oh, Warren. I was in Africa, I guess. I've seen that hideous figure a thousand times, but it's new, different every time I look at it. Deep down, I must be primitive. I'm attracted to that horrible thing. If it comes up missing, you can look for it in my office."

"You should go to the 'Dark Continent.' It's darker now, I think, than when Conrad was there. The old tribes, the old rites, the old ways—they're dying out slowly, but they still exist. That Dark Goddess there still reigns. The old ways, the savage ways are just a few steps outside of town. Oh yes, Kurtz is still in Africa, but he's no longer at a station far up the river. He's in Lagos—where the lights come on and go off according to the whims of . . . . of . . . well, probably, of that Dark Goddess there. And Kurtz is chauffeured through impossibly filthy streets, thudding into potholes, in his Mercedes. He does a little banking, a bit of smuggling; it's even said that he can sell you a slave if you're in the right place and have the right price."

"Yes, I'd like to go to Africa," said Mel. "We've been to the Greek Islands, but they're so tame, so familiar. I mean our family tree goes right back to the Greeks and the Romans, but there haven't really been any Africans in our cultural woodpile. I mean compare Hitler with Idi Amin: the civilized barbarian and the barbaric barbarian, Hitler worshipping Wotan, Idi praying to our Dark Goddess here. You should bring this goddess to the cocktail party tonight. Maybe she'd elicit a refreshing strain of barbaric savagery from our colleagues."

There was a silent pause.

"So," said Warren, "we have a little problem with Garth Timmins, don't we?"

"No problem that I can see," said Mel, rallying his full reserve of inner strength.

"Between you and me, Mel, Timmins is a problem child. I wish he'd stay in the School of Business Administration where he belongs. But he's ours for his general education requirements in the humanities, and we've got to deal with him. He's pretty upset about his interview with you."

"And I'm pretty upset about his interview with me."

"I don't doubt that in the least. He's an annoying guy. I had to put up with him in my class last semester."

"We ought to kick him out of the university. I mean the way he came on to me was unforgivable. I couldn't care less about his sex life. I told him that. He uses his deviation as an excuse for being a goof-off. And you can't imagine how arrogant he is."

"I've checked his record," said Warren in a conciliatory tone. "He had a B-minus average. You aren't thinking of flunking him or anything like that, are you? This is a delicate matter. First of all, there's Timmins' charge of discrimination, and you know what that means nowadays. It can be dynamite. How'd you like to have all the gays in West Hollywood picketing the English Department? And then there's Timmins senior. I happen to know there's bad blood between father and son—over the gay business, you know—but senior, on the other hand, is very proud of Garth's position as cheerleader, and isn't he president of his frat? Anyway, there's big money involved. Mr. Timmins has hinted to Dean Amore that he's ready to make a substantial contribution toward the new science complex. We wouldn't want to be parties to losing that grub stake, would we?"

"Well, so much for Garth Timmins" said Mel. "I need to talk to you about my schedule. Damn it, Warren, you've got me down for another section of composition. Look, I'm a senior person, not a lousy assistant professor or graduate teaching fellow. I asked to teach the seminar in Restoration drama."

"Mel, as far as I'm concerned, I'd like to give every faculty member the classes that he or she wants. But you know that Dean Amore has been looking us over very carefully. To tell you the truth, the last time you taught the Restoration seminar, you had only three students, and that's just bad economics from the standpoint of manpower invested."

"My god, Warren, you sound like that Donald Trump—or like Jack Welch. We're not a real estate empire. We don't manufacture jet engines. We're humanists. Teachers. Literary scholars. Of course, Amore probably thinks he's the Jack Welch of higher education."

"Lester *is* a tough manager, but maybe that's what this university has needed. Maybe we should stop indulging our hobbies."

"Now that's a shitty thing to say. That's just plain rotten. So Restoration literature is just a little hobby, huh? Not worth the time of serious thinkers. What about your field? Is that just an unnecessary hobby, too? I haven't seen *Beowulf* on 'Masterpiece Theater' yet." Mel was red-faced, and spit bubbles had formed at the corners of his mouth.

"Calm down. Calm down. Here, have a peppermint candy. I'll talk to Dean Amore. Don't get excited until we see what the administration is willing to do."

attitudes

"Fuck the administration. And fuck you, too," shouted Mel. Grasping the African goddess, he shouted grimly, "I hate peppermint."

From: Burden@cdu.edu
To: Rodby@Andrew.cmu.edu

Dec. 9, 2000. Well, the fat's in the fire. The Supreme Court in its infinite wisdom has stopped the hand recounts of the Florida ballots.

I'm about to have a conference with my colleague Mel Druse—who, by the way, is a Bush supporter. The jerk, he just had a big set-to with one of our students, who happens to be the son of a major donor to the university and who happens also to be gay. Mel gets as furious as Donald Duck in the old cartoons, and he has the judgment and subtlety of a pit bull. If I can get through that discussion without Mel having a fit, then I have to tell him that he's scheduled for a section of advanced composition next semester. May the good Lord protect me from the wrath of a literary gent demeaned.

I'll see you at the big meeting in a couple of weeks. The drinks will be on me.

From: Rodby@andrew.cmu.edu
To: Burden@cdu.edu

I've run across Mel Druse here and there at meetings. He always seems very intense, humorless. He can't have a sense of humor, or he'd laugh at Bush rather than support him. About a month ago, Bush stumbled into a characterization of himself. You remember he said, "They misunderestimate me."

From my point of view, anyone who has anything good to say about that guy misunderestimates him.

Poor Mel, being faced with the horror of teaching advanced composition. I remember last year at the convention, he read a paper on Vanbrugh. Is he the only person in the world who's now interested in Vanbrugh? Yeh, I think Mel Druse must be one of your many problems

See you soon.

3. Falafel; or, The Education of Bobby Druse

Hearing her voice in the hall, Professor Alexander ("Alex") Hamilton ("Ham"), said, "Here she comes, i' faith, full sail, with her fan spread and her streamers out, and her husband for a tender; ha, no, I cry for mercy."

Her topgallant billowing, Professor Peggy O'Neil sailed into the room, gave a general "Hi, everyone!" and continued the monologue that had preceded her. "I thought my last book would never get out. I'll never again submit anything to Yale. You can't imagine how klutzy they are. I mean that editor is a *real* nitpicker. But, thank God, I have the first bound copy now. I brought it with me. Here it is. The long-awaited book." And on the coffee table she triumphantly placed *A Pound of Mixed Nuts: Insanity and Modern Poetry.* "What a hassle to get here. Alvin was late getting home from the lab. A student called me, and I just couldn't get rid of him. He talked on and on. I'm starved. Is there anything to eat? Did all of you see the article about Stanley Fish in *Newsweek*? Alvin and I don't subscribe to *Newsweek,* but a student brought it to me. Fish is a real fraud, you know. All this stuff about reader response. I bet he couldn't even pass our doctoral exams. I sometimes wonder if he's read Shakespeare. Speaking of Shakespeare, who's going to teach the undergraduate survey next semester? Is

attitudes

Warren here? I'd like to talk with him about the undergraduate courses. Where's Warren? Alvin, get me a drink. Is there anything to eat? I'm starved."

Mel and Bobby entered the room. Catching sight of them, Professor Peggy O'Neil, from her central position, greeted them: "Oh, you. Hi. Mel, have you been sick? You look terrible."

"I hope Warren comes tonight. We simply must talk to him about the undergraduate program. Those people don't know as much as I did when I got out of high school. The other day I found a senior who hadn't read 'Ash Wednesday.' Now that's a shame. Maybe we ought to raise our admission standards. Don't the high schools give students any preparation? After all, shouldn't we be able to expect that our students would know at least the anthology kind of stuff? I don't mean the hard stuff like *Finnegan's Wake*, but everyone—and I mean everyone—should have read *Portrait of the Artist*. I mean, after all, how can you claim to understand the twenty-first century if you haven't read *Portrait of the Artist*? I'm hungry. Is there anything to eat? Alvin, where's my drink?"

Professor Peggy O'Neil now had a fleet of tenders; besides Alvin, there were Mel and Bobby, Alex Hamilton, Bertha Bankopf, Merrill Woodsman, the utility socialites Herb and Nancy Grupp, and more were expected, for this was the annual end-of-semester department get-together and cocktail party.

" . . . I'm starved. Isn't there anything to eat? . . ."

Kate Reese entered the room, pausing to look about and get her bearings and then moving toward the galaxy clustered about Peggy O'Neil. Alex Hamilton put his arm around her waist, and she pecked him on the cheek. Pottle Tinker patted her on the shoulder and greeted her: "I'm . . . hrumph . . . happy to see you. I think . . . hrumph . . . you've been . . . hrumph . . . avoiding me." Kendall Turing kissed her on her ear when she turned her head.

Kate was now the party's cynosure, and Peggy O'Neil was talking largely to herself.

"... and I simply told him, 'Hillis, you, Geoffrey and Harold live in a dream world. I mean, you don't know....'"

The room was filling rapidly. Guests entered two-by-two, three-by-three, and four-by-four. With each set of arrivals, the decibel level rose perceptibly, a cacophonous cocktail symphony.

"... they deal with the cream of crop. The best students. Is there anything to eat? I'm starved...."

The host, Professor Adam Adam, came to the rescue. To save Professor Peggy O'Neil from the horrors of inanition, he offered her a tray of golden spheres and a bowl of sour cream.

"I just don't understand why—What's that?" asked Peggy O'Neil, pausing long enough to notice the proffered provender.

"It's falafel," said a dour Professor Adam Adam.

"Fa- what?" inquired Peggy O'Neil.

"Fa-lafel," said Adam.

"What's falafel?" asked O'Neil.

"It's a Mideastern dish. Actually, deep-fried camel dung," explained Adam.

"Oh!" said a startled Peggy O'Neil. "Oh, you're kidding." And she giggled. "Seriously, what is it?"

"Try it, and see if you like it. Take one and dip it in the sour cream."

Peggy obeyed. "Hm, not bad." she said. "Not bad at all." She took another, dipped it, shoved it in her mouth, and continued: "But I want to tell you about my new project. I'm very very excited...."

Isolated in a corner with Bobby, grumbling Mel muttered, "What a pain in the ass. I don't know why you insisted that we come to this party."

"You know," said Bobby, "you really look like hell tonight. What's wrong? Your hand's shaking so badly that you've slopped your drink. Have a couple more and you'll settle down. Come on. Why don't you try to enjoy yourself? Let's mingle and talk to people. There are Jerry and Bridget."

attitudes

Across the room from the Druses, Professor Gerald Gelb was talking earnestly with Assistant Professor Bridget Heiman. When Bobby and Mel edged into the territory staked out by this pair, Gelb, alternately stroking his beard and raking his fingers through his long hair, was saying, "You understand I don't believe in confrontations, not at all. I'd rather talk to people in private, as it were. A conversation over lunch can do more than all the open meetings in the world. But I think it's time that someone told Warren the way of the world—the way of our little departmental world, that is. He's out of touch with reality."

"So who'd you want to be chair of the department? Waldo Clemens and his goddamn pipe? Or how about Potty Tinker? All we'd ever get out of him is 'Hrumph, hrumph.'"

"Now, Mel," conciliated Jerry Gelb, "I'm not saying there's anything wrong with Warren. Not a bit of it. I just think we should talk to him about the situation. That's all. I'm on his side, of course. You know that."

" . . . but just wait until you see my article in *Critical Inquiry.* Alvin, my glass is empty. . . ."

The galaxies in Professor Adam Adam's living room were rearranging themselves. The cluster of bodies around pulsar Kate Reese was diminishing, the center of gravity shifting toward the constellation formed by Mel, Bobby, Jerry, and Bridget.

Assistant Professor Merrill Woodsman and his companion, Mrs. Bertha Bankopf, joined the growing circle around Bobby and Mel.

"Mrs. Druse," said Jerry Gelb, "I don't think you know Merry Woodsman."

"I'm happy to meet you, Mary," said Bobby.

"The name is *Merrill,*" corrected Woodsman firmly, and he limp-wristedly shook hands.

" . . . Warren? I want to talk to him. . . . some more falafel. . . ."

"And this is Bertha Bankopf," said Merry, presenting a young woman who looked as though she had carefully planned to be the world's most stylish schoolteacher: gray flannel suit, white blouse accented by a frilly red bow at the neck, sensible, though feminine, oxfords.

"So happy to meet you," gushed Bertha. "Of course, I've known Mel ever since I came to the university, and I've wanted to meet his better half."

"If we could drag you away for a minute, Bertha and I would like to talk to you." Merry took Bobby's arm and led her out of the living room and into the bedroom, Bertha following closely.

"Uh, this is a bit delicate," explained Merry, "but I'm sure you'll understand. "Word has been passed down from the top at the university that no one is supposed to approach you about . . . uh, you know . . . about funding. It's being said that you're President Newburn's private property, his new Ophir."

"And," said Bertha, "we wouldn't want the president or anyone in the department to know that we're talking to you about this. . . ."

"About what?" asked Bobby.

"Bertha and I want to conduct a study, an important piece of work. You see, we believe that literature could be very powerful medicine for a sick society. In a nutshell, we want to give inner city delinquents and addicts intensive courses in literature—everything from Chaucer to Ashbery—to see if it will influence their behavior for the better. We need funds to set the project up, to hire teachers, to assemble and analyze our data."

"For two hundred and fifty thousand, we could get under way," Bertha interjected.

"This isn't just an artsy-fartsy project," said Merry. "We're aiming at social action. We want to prove the power of literature."

"Why don't you talk to Mel about your project?" said Bobby.

Merry looked at Bertha, and Bertha looked at Merry. "Naturally we want him in the project," said Bertha. "That is, if he's interested in working with us."

"But we'd like you to make a commitment. We think that wealthy people have an obligation. We're offering you the chance

attitudes

to make a *real* difference in society. We hope you take this opportunity." The look on Merry Woodsman's face was serious, but not lugubrious; the tone of his voice, modulated and sincere.

"Well, I'm sure what you want to do is most worthwhile, but I'd have to speak with President Newburn first," said Bobby.

"No, no, don't do that!" exclaimed Merry and Bertha simultaneously. "We understand," continued Merry, "that you're an extremely wealthy woman. We're appealing to your sense of responsibility. Uh, actually, you could set up an anonymous fund for Bertha and me to use in our work. I repeat, Mrs. Druse, the wealthy have an obligation that they should not try to avoid."

"Hey, you guys are academic panhandlers. I don't really know what to say. Maybe we could get together for lunch someday next week. But now I really should get back to Mel. He'll think you've waylaid me," and Bobby left the bedroom.

Merry, wordless now, looked at Bertha, a fixed ophidian stare, and Bertha peered into the mirrors of her companion's glasses, seeing not his eyes behind the lenses, but her own reflection on the surface. She nodded almost imperceptibly, and the two of them glided into the bathroom, Merry turning on the light and locking the door behind them.

Merry listened attentively to the whirring ventilator. An exhaust fan, he had read, used to whirr in the gas chamber at San Quentin, sucking the cyanide upward from its acid bath beneath the metal chair to form a lethal cloud around the face of the victim. He had heard that there was an exhaust fan above the electric chair, to draw up the smell of burning flesh and defecation. Yes, and he knew that the ultimate orgasm came at the end of the rope, when it snapped the neck and the condemned ejaculated and defecated simultaneously.

In the antiseptically white room, Merry stiffened slightly and exhaled an almost pained "Oof!"

"Don't stop! Don't stop!" urged Bertha. And Merry renewed his amatory ministration, until, after a very few strokes, Bertha tensed and through clenched teeth made sweet moan: "Errrgh!"

Bertha clasped Merry in her arms, her head against his necktie, her pantyhose clustered about her ankles. Merry, whose characteristic posture was an open S, sat rigidly upright, the lenses of his glasses reflecting the pure whiteness of the bathroom.

When Bertha and Merry returned to the living room, the party was noisier than before, the room more crowded.

Heather Figaro, the senior department secretary, was now the only direct object of Peggy O'Neil's durative verbosity. " . . . and I don't see why faculty should run their own copies. I mean, after all, do you think a person like Harold Bloom spends his time over a copying machine? We should talk to Warren about this. Where's Warren? Isn't Warren coming? Alvin, I could use another very very short drink. . . ."

"How can you be so sure that Eliot meant *anything* in 'The Love Song of J. Alfred Prufrock'? I mean, after all, you're not a mind reader, are you?"

Professor Peggy O'Neil had backed Assistant Professor Mary McPherson into a corner of the room.

"That's hardly to the point," replied an intrepid Ms. McPherson, "especially since Eliot is no longer with us. I assume that the poem is language, and language always has an intention behind it. It's not a natural phenomenon, like an earthquake, the result of physical laws, but an intended human act."

"How can you prove anything's intended? How do you know? I mean, after all, are you God or something?"

"I can't prove—"

"There, you see." And Peggy O'Neil, her restraint exhausted by Mary McPherson's prolixity, pounced. "That's the trouble with you true believers: you can't prove anything, and yet you talk about the meaning of this poem and that author's intention. After all, you really should, you know, read Derrida. I mean, after all, if you haven't read Derrida you can hardly claim to understand the instructions for assembling a barbecue, let alone a difficult poem like 'Prufrock.' I mean Alvin has read Derrida, and he's not even an English prof. He's a physicist, you know. "

attitudes

"I have read—" interjected Mary McPherson.

"Let me just give you some advice." Peggy O'Neil came close to Mary McPherson, almost nose to nose. "If you want tenure in this place—and I really hope you get it, I really do—if you want tenure, you've got to play the game according to the rules. I think you're very bright. I mean I can tell you have a good mind. So don't go around arguing positions that went out with the Edsel. I mean you've got to convince people that you're up to date, with it. You simply must read Derrida, for instance."

"I have read—"

"And don't sound so positive when you talk about meaning. I mean you don't *really* know what 'Prufrock' means, yet you talk as if you've got it all figured out. You don't think Eliot knew what he meant, do you? I mean just how much can anyone know about meaning?"

"I think—"

"Speaking of 'Prufrock,' I want to talk to Warren about the undergraduate program. We're just not giving those people enough background in modern poetry. Where's Warren? Isn't Warren coming? He must be coming. He wouldn't miss the annual get-together."

Jerry Gelb had captured Bobby while Mel occupied himself with the roly-poly surliness of Bridget Heiman.

Jerry looked austere, Puritanical. His sharp features were those of, perhaps, a Jonathan Edwards, or, more properly, a Ralph Waldo Emerson, whom Gelb would have resembled strikingly if Emerson had worn a beard.

"This is the first departmental party that I've attended," said Bobby. "Usually Mel either goes alone or stays home. I thought it was about time I came out of hiding. Mel's colleagues are quite a bunch, aren't they?"

"Dear lady," Jerry said, "the pleasure is ours, all ours. We've been so fond of your wonderful husband, and now to meet his charming wife, to call both of you friends, is almost more than one could have hoped for."

" . . . my next book. I told Alvin that he'll be neglected while I work on. . . ."

"Could I get you some refreshments? Would you like another drink? I'm so fortunate to have you to myself for a few moments," oleaginously crooned Jerry.

"I'm just fine," said Bobby. "Not another thing. Thanks, anyway."

"Uh, I understand," said a hesitant Jerry Gelb, "that you have quite a close relationship with President Newburn."

"I know him. I see him every now and then. I don't know that you could call our relationship 'close.'"

"But you do have the chance to talk with him. You have access to him that faculty members don't. If you were to ask to see him tomorrow, would he take time for you?"

"I guess so. I'm sure he'd see me if I had a good reason."

"That, dear lady, is my point," said Gelb. "President Newburn would have time for you, but faculty members can't get to him. Now I don't mean that he isolates himself. After all, if one faculty member could see him, then all of them would want to. He's a busy man. He can't let the camel get its nose in the tent. I'm not criticizing him. He's a great leader. But give faculty members an inch and they'll take a mile. Hahaha. So don't tell the president I was criticizing him. On the contrary, I know how hard his job is, and I wouldn't do anything to make it harder. I'm President Newburn's greatest admirer."

"So?"

"As you might know, Dean Amore is looking for an assistant dean. Uh . . . actually, I think I'd be very good in that position. I've had my fling at scholarship and teaching. Now I'd like to try administration. A word or two from you to the president. . . ."

Professor Gerald Gelb, author of *The Fruits of Learning: Peacham's "Garden of Eloquence" and the Development of the Renaissance Sensibility,* grasped Bobby's hand, raised it to his hirsute mouth, and kissed it.

" . . . *New York Review* is hokey, just a commercial rag. I mean they didn't even review my last book. I wouldn't mind another falafel. Adam! Adam! Is there any more. . . ."

Adam Adam's response, however, was not to Peggy O'Neil's request for falafel. Loudly calling for silence, he announced: "Dean Amore just phoned. He told me that Warren Burden is dead."

Mel was stunned. He was vertiginous. "Oh God," he muttered, "I've killed Warren."

"What was that?" asked Bobby.

"Nothing. Just talking to myself," said Mel, his voice trembling.

"So who'll replace Warren?" said Peggy O'Neil. "Adam, is there any more falafel? I love it."

> From: PONeil@cdu.edu
> To: Blum@yale.edu
>
> Dec. 9, 2000. Last night Warren Burden, our chairperson, died. I don't know the details yet. I think you knew Warren, didn't you? Well, as far as I'm concerned, if you've endured one department chairperson, you've endured all of them. It makes no difference to me who succeeds Warren. And I'll never be considered for the chair. I'm too outspoken and honest. I wouldn't kowtow to the administration.
>
> Well, I think we're doomed to four years of malapropisms and truisms. I think Bush just won the presidency, courtesy of the Supreme Court. One of my colleagues, Mel Druse, is a big Bush supporter. Do you know Mel? He's a strange guy, a real stuffed shirt. He married the widow of a Nevada casino magnate. I've heard she's worth four or five hundred million, but the Druses don't know how to enjoy their money. I don't think they travel much, and Mel

drives a dirty old Chevrolet and Bobby, his wife, drives a big red Buick.

I'll see you in a couple of weeks at the convention. Are you staying at the Hilton? We should get together for lunch one day. Let me know your schedule.

From: Blum@yale.edu
To: POneil@cdu.edu

Warren Burden's passing is certainly no loss to the profession. He was a third-rate scholar at the very best. As for Mel Druse, yes, I know him slightly—and I don't want to get to know him better.

But think of this. Anyone who could spend years studying Vanbrugh is just cracked enough to be enthusiastic about Bush. Have you run across this one? "If you don't stand for anything, you don't stand for anything! If you don't stand for something, you don't stand for anything!" Anyone whose brain is that scrambled is a menace to this nation and to the world.

See you in a couple of weeks.

4. Rolaids; or, the Enigma

On the drive home from the party, Mel kept glancing in his rearview mirror, looking for the police that would undoubtedly be following him. The burst of a siren drained him, made him limp, and he pulled to the side of the freeway and stopped, but the Highway Patrol cruiser, lights flashing and siren wailing, roared past him. For several minutes, he sat, slumped against the steering wheel, sobbing. But with a tremendous effort of will, he made his way down the freeway, to the correct offramp, and ultimately to Dimple Dell Drive.

When he was within sight of 1415, his address, he saw headlights turning into his driveway, and again he went limp and pulled to the curb. When the garage door opened, he could see that the car was Bobby's red Buick, not a police cruiser.

In bed that night, Mel's sour stomach churned, and his throat burned from the acid that he had burped up and then nauseatingly had choked down again. He knew, he was absolutely certain, that the stabbings in his solar plexus were not a heart attack, for the pain did not radiate to his left arm or to his neck and jaw, but as the agony increased, he stumbled from bed, groped his way to the bathroom, turned on the light, fumbled in a drawer, withdrew a tube of lipstick, threw it angrily to the floor, groped further, withdrew a nearly depleted pack of Rolaids, popped two of the lozenges into his mouth, chewed them and swallowed their gritty chalkiness, sensed almost immediate relief, sighed, turned out the light, fumbled his way back to the bed, flopped into it, and pulled the covers up around his shoulders.

Mel was groping in a fog of awareness. He now understood death—the end, curtains, the undiscovered country from whose bourn no traveler returns, the sadness, the terrible sadness of stepping into nothingness. What dirge would play him out of life? The insistent repetition of Philip Glass's "Requiem"? "The Swan of Tuonela"? Largo from "The New World Symphony"? Goin' home, I'm just goin' home.

He shifted restlessly, easing the pressure on his aching right shoulder.

Suddenly he was awake. Olivier, as Archie Rice the entertainer, had said to his daughter, "Look at these eyes. There's nothing behind them." Mel shifted again, so that in the moonlit bedroom he could dimly see his own reflection in the mirrored door of the closet. What was behind those eyes he was gazing into?

His own mood, his own awareness fascinated him. He now was not sad, but simply hollow. The thought of nothingness left him in a void, a black hole in which he barely heard strange sounds that might be voices or, on the other hand, might be music, or perhaps the soughing of winds from eternity.

Never before had Mel felt so empty. His own nothingness was a strange consolation.

The last thing in Mel's consciousness before the blackness of sleep was the image of a gurney with someone strapped to it, an IV leading from each arm. .

When he was awakened by Bobby's stirrings, glorious sunshine penetrated the drapes in the bedroom, making them appear to glow from within, as if by their own source of radiance. Mel, pursuing a zigzag course to full wakefulness, stared at the radiant drapes, began to feel the warmth of the sunshine, and realized the deep, almost despairing melancholy that had followed him from what had been a dreamless sleep.

His stomach was still sour, and again he began to feel the searing pain of acute indigestion. Clambering from bed and staggering to the drawer in the bathroom, he found one last Rolaid. Popping it into his mouth, he chewed and swallowed, and the pain in his solar plexus was somewhat relieved.

He had showered and shaved. Christiane Amanpour and Wolf Blitzer were talking seriously about the most current world crisis. His stomach was in a state of profound unrest, but had not yet marshaled its forces for a complete revolution.

The fragrance of Musk aftershave somewhat soothed Mel, as it always did, and Christiane Amanpour, with her exotic accent cheered him slightly. He found her so completely undesirable that his admiration for her had an uplifting purity. Mel could imagine a tussle in the back seat of his Chevy with Judy Woodfruff, but nothing more than a kiss on the cheek for Christiane.

Poised before the set, dressed and ready for the day, Mel absorbedly watched Christiane Amanpour, her voice cheering him slightly, though conveying no information. But Bobby called from the foot of the stairs, "Your tea's ready," and the enchantment was broken. Mel's day had begun.

attitudes

On the drive to the university, Mel, as usual, had tuned his radio to the all-news station, and isolated words and phrases occasionally penetrated his consciousness. . . . *Iran . . . pork bellies Rumsfeld . . . AIDS . . . Preparation H . . . stalled vehicle at Oakmont.* . . . Often he drove this route by psychic automatic pilot, amazed when he reached the offramp for the university and sometimes passing it in his absorption. The commute was a time in no time which, on occasion, resulted in "Eureka!" but most frequently more inextricably entangled him in a snarl of his motives and resolutions. When he attended professional meetings, associates from "college towns"—Madison, Iowa City, Urbana—asked him how he tolerated the freeways, and he always answered, "The commute is my time to think. I'm sealed in my car and have an hour or so to work out problems and take stock of myself. Oh, I enjoy the radio, too. Some awfully good stuff on PBS, you know." In fact, to relieve himself of the intensity of his frustrating self-absorption, he often tuned to the "oldies but goldies" station and sentimentally sang along: "*Oh, it's a long long time from May to September.*" Then, too, he enjoyed, with a sense of guilt, the lurid escape into pop psychology, Dr. Aileen Necropolis leading her callers, with slick sympathy, into more and more details about the infidelities of the their husbands or lovers, into more and more explicit accounts of their own fantasies, but always stopping just short of the most toothsome details.

"I wonder," said Mel to himself, "if they'll be waiting for me when I get to my office."

On this dyspeptic morning, stop-and-go, the air heavy with exhaust, Mel perversely would not escape, would not flip the dial to "Grab your coat and get your hat, leave your worries by the doorstep," the familiar lilt of which would have disentangled him. Grimly he accelerated and the braked and then accelerated again. His only relief from the smoldering hostility of his reverie was the flare-up when some asshole, who really had nothing to gain, tried to cut in front of him, usually a jerk in a Porsche or Corvette.

A glance in the rearview mirror. He saw that no police car followed him. Plainclothes in an unmarked car?

On this morning, Mel did not overshoot his offramp, and the lights were in his favor.

He waved to the guard at the campus entrance and headed for his parking lot.

When Mel saw the lot was blocked off for resurfacing, he muttered a heartfelt "Oh shit!" and began to search for a place elsewhere on campus. Dean Amore, old lover boy, of course, would always have a parking spot reserved for him, regardless of the exigencies, and President Newburn, that pompous prick, he wouldn't have to spend his morning searching the campus for a parking spot. But faculty didn't matter. They'd probably grin and make bad jokes when Mel was arrested. The university was becoming like an industrial concern: Amore, Newburn, and their ilk were executives, with all the executive perks—private dining rooms, inviolable parking spots, bathrooms with showers—and the faculty were the mill hands. That mighty symbol of American enterprise, the River Rouge plant, fuming, glowing, and clanking on the banks of the Detroit River, it was the condition after which the likes of Newburn and Amore aspired—the university as an assembly line, grinding onward, semester by semester, producing . . . well, producing . . . yes, producing the likes of Miss Kimberly Grundschuh, whose nails were impeccably manicured, whose shoes and purse were Gucci, whose auto was a Porsche, whose honey-blonde hair was perfect, whose major was international marketing ("Because I like to travel and meet people"). Mel had a wry vision, and he smiled for the first time all morning. The campus had sprouted smokestacks that belched clouds of sulphuric brown crud into the atmosphere; the university had become clangorous, its machinery grinding and pounding; it had developed a hellish glow, its furnaces raging. Into the academic River Rouge plant walks Kimberly Grundschuh with her manicured nails, and after four years, she emerges—like a Ford subcompact—diploma in hand, mortarboard securely pinned at a flattering angle, Gucci shoes and shapely legs below the sedate hem of her academic gown; the emerges, smiling, bemused, vacuous. She pauses. Her engine comes haltingly to life and then warms up. The gear lever slips into "drive," and she glides off into the future. She is the reason for the whole enterprise headed by President Harvey Newburn with the assistance of Dean Lester Amore and the practical wisdom of Chairman of the Board of Trustees Donald Schwann.

Mel found a spot in a student parking structure on the opposite side of campus from his building and started the trek to his office, walking faster than he really wanted to, striding along as though eager to get at the business of life, the quest for and dissemination of knowledge. Now and again he nodded a "good morning" to a passerby, but rigorously kept himself from gawking to the left and right in a survey of the coeds who sauntered reluctantly toward their classes or brightly toward the Union Building to play psychological grab-ass with the frat boys who congregated in the coffee shop.

Into Mel's tunnel of vision, approaching him, came none other than the impeccable Kimberly Grundschuh, two books and a loose-leaf clutched against her right side and a king-size chocolate-chip cookie, on which she nibbled, in her left hand. Mel tacitly registered approval of her perfection: the handbag slung over her shoulder, the matching shoes, the mauve skirt and sweater, the liquid hair, the pink lips and nails. She was, without doubt, a ten.

At the socially appropriate distance, Mel smiled, nodded, and rendered a crisp "Good morning, Miss Grandschuh," intending to stride resolutely onward, but Miss Grundschuh braked and threw the gear lever into "Park," her engine idling.

"Professor Druse, I was just at your office. I wanted to tell you why my paper on 'Venice Preserved' is late."

"Ah, yes," replied Mel, with a twinge of guilt. "I was concerned last night when I found that your essay wasn't in the stack"—which he now carried in his briefcase and which he had not examined on the previous evening. "You know my feelings about punctuality."

"Oh, Dr. Druse, you know I really do work in your class. I mean I'm getting an awfully lot out of it, and I don't want you to think I don't care because I really do like the class. I think the Restoration is a really neat period, all of the wit and all that."

"Yes, well, it's delightful and challenging if you'll really apply yourself."

"But I do apply myself, Dr. Druse. The only thing is, I've had a rough time this semester, you know. Dad wants me to be active in Tri Delt because I'll make lifelong friends that can really help me. And Mom is just going nuts about the new house. I mean, you can't imagine how much time it takes to decorate, and she wouldn't do a thing without me. It's my home, too, you know."

"Of course. Of course," said mellowing Mel. "But when you entered the university, you committed yourself to the life of the mind. That takes priority."

"Oh, for sure. I mean, I couldn't agree more. But . . . I'll really settle down. I can get the paper to you tomorrow morning. Okay?"

The "Okay" was so meltingly dulcet that it softened even the stern resolve of Professor J. Melongaster Druse, and with a firm "Tomorrow morning, then," he continued toward his office.

Well down the hall from the door to the English Department main office, Mel detected the rank odor of a pipe and knew that Waldo Clemens was on the shuffling prowl for someone to talk to—a soul who would listen to his account of the weekend trip to the desert to hunt for gemstones. "Most people don't take enough time to appreciate the desert, but if you look, there's life and beauty. You've just got to take your time and keep your eyes open. You know, Betty and I made a great discovery. The desert really is more than two monotonous expanses on either side of the freeway." At least Waldo, single-minded as he was conversationally, talked about something other than departmental scandals and the latest fiat from Dean Amore. In fact, Mel suspected, Waldo

attitudes

probably wasn't aware that five years ago Amore had replaced the "real" dean, affable George McTavish, whose Christmas parties had been so seasonably and sentimentally mellow.

In the main office, Departmental Secretary Heather Figaro and her two underlings (whose names Mel had not yet mastered) were drinking coffee and deliberating the possibility of decorating for the Yuletide.

Mel chirped an affable "Morning all," picked up his mail, and made his way to his own office. He fumbled for his keys, inserted the proper one in the slot, and found that the door was already unlocked. Mel knew, sinkingly, that the police had searched his office. Probably cops were in his office, just waiting for him to appear. But no one was there.

Plopping his briefcase in a chair, Mel grabbed his cup (bearing the witty motto "Don't let the bastards wear you down") and headed for the coffee room. Arriving at the coffee-maker, he was about to pour when he noticed that the cup, richly caffeine-brown on the interior and around the rim, was still half full from the day before. He paused and looked for a receptacle, made a move toward the wastebasket, reconsidered, and took the cup back to his office.

On the coffee table, where the dispirited African violet had lately spent its drooping existence, he found—and he was paralyzed, the cup suspended at a tilt in his hand—an ebony figure.

It was about two feet high, in dark wood, glossy and suave. It was a woman, with hair dressed high, like a melon-shaped dome. At the moment, she seemed like one of his soul's intimates. Her body was long and elegant, her face was crushed tiny like a beetle's, she had rows of heavy round collars, like a column of quoits, on her neck. He stared at her: her astonishing cultural elegance, her diminished, beetle face, the astounding long elegant body, on short, ugly legs, with such protruberant buttocks, so weighty and unexpected below her slim long loins.

Mel was immobilized, catatonic. He stared at the grotesque goddess, his trance broken by the trembling of his hand and the slopping of the stale coffee into the table. The beetle-faced, huge-buttocked figurine was now standing in a muddy puddle.

The goddess's ebony sheen became an anthracite shimmer, amorphous, the swirling entry to a black hole in space. His hand trembled more and more violently, until he grasped it with the other, to keep the remainder of the stale coffee from slopping onto the table. The beetle-face, the melon-head, the macropygianness shimmered and swam before him. For the first time in his life, he felt as if he might faint. A tide of nausea made him gasp, and the dyspepsia recurred, a belch sending a gush of acid upward, to burn his throat and choke him. He gagged and gasped, his left hand clutching his right ever more tightly. His only consciousness now was that he might black out, that a stroke was imminent, that his heart could pound no more thunderously without bursting, could wrench itself no more violently without failing.

He staggered to the swivel chair behind his desk and flopped into it, trembling. Cold sweat ran down his forehead and dripped from his nose. He could feel the clammy wetness of his shirt. He needed badly to piss and sensed a dampness at his crotch.

To escape this horror. To clamber back into the quotidian. That was what he needed. Short of medication. Which he had no idea where to obtain. A shot of thorazine. Student health service. Just across the street. Crazy professor dashing in and asking for a shot. No. No.

There were other ways. A stack of mail was on his desk, placed there, probably, by Heather Figaro as an excuse for her daily snoop. On the freeway, Mel had been self-indulgent, preferring vitriol and anger to mellow music or the news, but now the situation was frantic, a stroke or heart attack possible, and he was keenly aware of his mortality.

He did begin to pull himself together, choosing the soporific of mail over a desperate foray to the student health service.

The first item in the stack was a memo from Dean Amore, reminding faculty of what Amore called "The Life of the Mind Series"—luncheons followed by faculty talks about strictly intellec-

attitudes

tual subjects. Mel grimly grinned. The dean's memo was a help at this desperate hour. Even now—especially now—Mel was a connoisseur of the grotesque, and the thought of Kimberly Grundschuh, who had committed herself also the life of the mind, wrenched a tight-lipped, crooked smile from him and pulled him back a few light years from the black hole into which he had nearly spun. Kimberly and Lester. Kimberly and the ebony goddess. Those images were vivid enough to calm him appreciably.

He pawed further through his mail, his heart thumping less desperately, his trembling almost subsided. The ads for textbooks he threw summarily into the wastebasket; the weekly *Campus Life* he automatically set aside for later; the manila intercampus envelopes he piled on the far corner of his desk; and the first class mail he readied before him, to be opened and perused. After all, the quotidian, the routine of his life, was the best medicine. Not that he achieved total relief, an obliterating narcotic flash, but he was able to climb, via the aluminum stepladder of routine, a few rungs closer to nirvana.

With characteristic wit, Mel had often, in a mock-indignant tone, protested television's neglect of the professoriate. There were cop shows and cowboy shows and doctor shows and lawyer shows and private investigator shows, but the medium had overlooked the drama of the professoriate.

Our hero arrives at his office. He fetches his mail and his matutinal cup of coffee. He sips his coffee and reads his mail. To a knock on the door, as the tension grows, he responds, "Come in."

To a knock on his door, Mel responded, "Who is it?"

"It's Kate," came the ineffably sweet voice. "Are you busy? I can come back later."

"No. No. Just a minute."

The scenario continues. The drama becomes more tense. The professor must pull himself together and prepare his dignity, his wisdom, his manner. As the director had said, the scene must be just right.

The professor wipes his face with his handkerchief. He quickly opens a letter and poises to read it. He glances about. He officiously says, "Come in."

The doorknob rattles, and the sweet voice says, "It's locked."

The professor mutters an "Oh shit!"—which, of course, ruins the scene and necessitates a retake.

Mel admitted Kate. She paused. "Am I disturbing you?" she asked.

"Not at all. Not at all." Mel needed someone, especially Kate, just now.

"You're not ill?" asked Kate.

"I'm fine," said Mel. "Just a bit at loose ends. Couldn't find a parking spot this morning. My lot's being resurfaced."

Mel placed himself professorially behind his desk, and Kate glided into the visitor's chair facing it.

The problem now, as Martin Scorcese would recognize, is how to begin the first really dramatic episode in the professor's story. Mel, of course, an expert on the momentous inconsequentiality of Restoration literature, appropriately ad libs.

"Well, my dear, what's on your mind this morning?"

"Ah," said Kate, "must there be something on my mind? I was here early for a meeting with Les—Dean Lester Amore—and I just wouldn't disappear without at least saying 'Hello.'"

Mel relaxed. An almost miraculous drug had taken effect. Mel said, "Of course, you're welcome." And the anthracite shimmer was utterly supplanted by the glow of glowing Kate. "Would you like coffee?"

But the word "coffee" had triggered the ebony glow once more, darkness visible, and the outline of the goddess wobbled, like an anti-matter will-o-the-wisp in his consciousness, completely absorbing him for he knew not how long.

"Are you sure you're feeling alright?" asked Kate, her breath blowing the dark ignis fatuous from the swamp of Mel's awareness.

attitudes

He forced a smile and a reply. "To tell you the truth, I had a rough night. The falafel didn't agree with me. I had an upset stomach. Still do."

"Poor dear," crooned Kate, enigmatically, half ironically, half tender sympathy. The ambivalence was, however, infinitely attractive to Mel, and for the first time, he really noticed Kate. She wore a slate-gray wool skirt and vivid red silk blouse. Her necklace was some kind of understated exotica, large parti-colored beads, obviously handwork and probably from Africa. Her perfect legs were crossed; her perfect shoes were minimal straps of black leather. Almost imperceptibly she oscillated her foot, keeping time to mystic, unheard music. Her smile was elfin, winning.

She was for the moment the all of Mel's lambent attention: a golden glow that was healing and yet, somehow, virginally sensual. He felt an impulse to hug her close in an embrace that was, certainly, male-female and yet pure, not rank and randy.

" . . . wonder if I really should." Kate had been speaking, but she paused.

Coming back to the scene, Mel responded, "You wonder if you really should what?"

"You weren't listening, were you?" said Kate. "I was telling you that Dean Amore wants me to accept a position in the development office, but I wonder if I really should. What do you think?"

"Les Amore, yes, he wants you—he wants you to take a position in the development office. Yes, I see, the dean is offering you a position."

Kate's smile hardened almost imperceptibly. "The dean told me—he was quite frank—that I could never get a faculty position and that I might have a future in administration. What do you think?"

The ebony aura began to glow. The amorphous goddess shimmered darkly, her grotesque form bleedingly outlined black on black, transfixing Professor J. Melongaster Druse. She wrapped her scrawny, ghostly arms around the neck of Dean Lester Amore. Amore was as inscrutably primitive as the goddess.

"What do you think?" asked Kate.

"What do I think? About what?"

"Should I accept Dean Amore's offer?"

Mel pulled himself up in his swivel chair and with enormous effort focused. "Les is a very powerful man around these parts. No telling what he could do for you. Yeh, I think I'd give it a try. After all, the university is really on the move now."

"Well, that's exactly what I thought. But I wanted your opinion."

Kate fished in her purse for a roll of mints and offered Mel one. He took it gratefully, saying, "I wish it were a Rolaid. My damn stomach is hell this morning."

"I was waiting for you to mention the gift," said Kate, sucking discretely on her mint.

"What gift was that?" asked Mel.

"The statuette, the fetish, the African goddess—whatever she is."

As the ebony glow spread, Mel felt vertiginous, slightly nauseated. Surrounded by an anthriciate aura, the goddess shimmered a slow-motion hula, snakelike, heavy.

"Were you surprised?" asked Kate. When Mel did not respond, she asked more loudly, "Were you surprised?"

"Surprised?" Mel slowly shook his head, not in response to the question, but as a reflex, to regain his balance. "Surprised? Why should I be surprised?"

"Didn't you noticed that this statuette is exactly like the one Warren kept in his office?"

"Yes. It's the same. Yes. I noticed that. I thought it was Warren's. It must be Warren's. But the police are holding Warren's as evidence."

"For evidence of what?"

"For evidence in Warren's murder. He was murdered last night."

attitudes

"My goodness," said Kate, "where did you get that idea? Warren died of a massive heart attack. When he fell, he apparently hit his head on the credenza, but that was just a bump, not enough to kill him.

"Your goddess is just a cheap doodad. I got it at Pier 1 Imports for seven ninety-five. There are dozens of them on the shelf. Warren made such a big thing of his goddess, even talked about donating it to a museum someday, but, you know, I think it was just as phony as the one I bought for you.

"But look at your African violet. It's drooping so badly that I've decided to take it home with me for some TLC. Once I revive it, I'll bring it back."

"Yes, bring it back," said Mel.

> From: KGrundschuh@cdu.edu
> To: JGrundschuh@mdc.com
>
> Wednesday Dec. 13, 2000. I probably won't be home this weekend. I've got to work on a paper for that creepy Profesor Druse. I told him I'd have it for him tomorrow but tonight is the awards dinner at Phi Nu Chi and I'm the emcee and Thursday we're having a get-together with the UCLA Phi Nus and Friday is always my night off. I've spent three hours on the web looking for a paper on—get this!—Congreves use of litotes and hyperbole. For your info that's understatement and overstatement. See all the neat stuff I'm learning. When I'm talking to Orentals about internatianal trade I can hit them with litotes and hyperbole. That should wow them. I'll get the paper to the profesor on Monday and turn on the old Grundschuh charm. He'll eat it up. Boy I sure do look forward to Christmas break!

From: JGrundschuh@mdc.com
To: KGrundschuh@cdu.edu

Daddy and I are so proud of you. We were at CDU before Professor Druse came, but we had to put up with plenty of others just like him. Just grit your teeth and do what you have to. The semester is nearly over, and that will be the end of Professor Druse. A week in Aspen will be good for all of us. Daddy and I are rejoicing. Mr. Bush will be our president. In case, you hadn't heard, that Gore person conceded the election earlier today. The future is bright.

From: KReese@cdu.edu
To: BReese@ned.com

God, I'm devastated! Gore has conceded the presidency to the Yellow Rose of Texas—that's what Gore Vidal calls Bush. We're in for four years of smirking muddleheadedness. Good Lord, in November he said (and I quote), "The legislature's job is to write law. It's the executive branch's job to interpret law." The man doesn't have a high school student's understanding of American government.

Tomorrow I'll send you the stamp collection. I know it means a lot to you, and, honestly, I could never get interested in philately. I really do appreciate your fairness and decency through all of our troubles. I know that we just didn't mix during our three years together, but I still think of you as a good friend. And you'll notice that I'm still a Reese nominally, if not legally.

attitudes

To: KReese@cdu.edu
From: BReese@ned.com

I don't think of you as a good friend. I think of you as my life. Kate, I can't get over you. We could work out a life together if we tried. You always refused counseling. When we met and during the first months of our marriage, you were my lover. I remember those wonderful days and weeks. But you withdrew. I couldn't reach you. You said something I'll never forget: "I'm getting to depend on you. I won't let that happen." Let's try again. You name the terms.

5. Sodium Thiopental

Mel washed his Valium tablet down with a quick swig of diet Dr. Pepper and then sat down at the kitchen table, where a volume of *Encyclopedia Americana* was open before him, and beside it, six other books. He was absorbed in his research.

So the inmate was strapped to a gurney, technicians inserted catheters into his right and left arms—or into *her* arms, because Mel could not forget the execution of Carla Faye Tucker when George W. Bush was governor of Texas. First, as much as five grams or five thousand milligrams of sodium thiopental are administered, a lethal dose that knocks the convicted out within five or ten seconds. Next comes a paralyzing agent, pancuronium bromide, that stops the function of the lungs. Finally, just to make sure, but not in all states, the convicted receives a dose of a lethal chemical, potassium chloride, which interferes with the electrical signals that regulate the heart.

No worse, really, than what happens when a dentist extracts an abscessed wisdom tooth—except you never wake up. No pain. Just the thought of that undiscovered country from whose bourn no traveler returns.

In California, you have the choice of lethal injection or lethal gas. So the pellets of sodium cyanide are dropped into a bucket of acid, creating hydrogen cyanide, the famous prussic acid that played a part in . . . what tale? Was it Sherlock Holmes? No matter, really. Exposure to three hundred parts per million was, as the book put it, "rapidly fatal"—death by asphyxiation because the gas combines with the enzymes necessary to cellular oxidation.

On TV, Mel had watched the old film "I Want to Live," with Susan Hayward as Barbara Graham, whose death in 1955 was the result of hydrogen cyanide combining with the enzymes necessary for cellular oxidation. The guards strapped her into the chair in the gas chamber, and one whispered to her, "Count ten, and then take a deep breath." Mel wondered if that was official advice or just the guard's attempt to be kind.

In the Druse kitchen, the afternoon sun slanted through the windows and splashed in a bright puddle on the kitchen tile. Mel was about to start taking notes in a yellow pad when he heard Bobby's "Anybody home?"

She glanced at the materials on the table: the encyclopedia open at "gas chamber"; Koestler's *Reflections on Hanging; Execution Through the Ages; The Executioner's Song; In Cold Blood; The Supreme Penalty; A Student's Guide to Capital Punishment.* "God, what morbid stuff." She flipped the encyclopedia closed.

"I'm going to do a paper on capital punishment," said Mel. "Yes, that's what I'll do, a paper on capital punishment, something about the death penalty in Restoration literature. I need to write a paper. And, you know, I've been thinking about the paper on Vanbrugh. That's two papers to work on."

"Capital punishment is morbid, it's barbaric, and in my opinion," said Bobby, "abortion is as bad as capital punishment. Both of them mean taking human life unnecessarily, and, good Lord, if human life isn't an ultimate value, I don't know what is."

"Yes, it's in the same category as capital punishment. When I finish the paper on capital punishment in Restoration literature,

I'll do one on abortion in Restoration literature. And," perking up a bit, "I'm going to finish my paper on Vanbrugh."

Bobby filled a glass with ice cubes, fetched a bottle of Jack Daniels from the cupboard, poured herself a liberal slug, sat down next to Mel, lit a Marlboro, and attempted to change the subject. "You're wandering around like a zombie. You don't have any energy or enthusiasm. You can't spend the rest of your life in a fog."

"I'm not in a fog. Who said I'm in a fog?"

"Maybe you need some help. You know, it wouldn't be a bad idea to talk to our doctor about a good psychiatrist."

"I'm not crazy," said Mel gravely.

"Of course you're not crazy. But you're upset. I think that Warren's death and becoming department head. . . ."

"What about Warren's death? Why should Warren's death upset me?"

"Well, naturally it had to be a shock to you."

"I don't like to talk about Warren's death," said Mel flatly.

"You see, that's what I mean. You've been through a lot. I think you need help. But those blue pills aren't going to solve your problems. Why don't you talk to someone?"

"Don't you understand," said Mel intensely, "that I can't talk to anyone? Don't you understand that?"

"What I don't understand is why you can't talk to anyone. I suppose it's hard to bare your soul to a stranger, but a psychiatrist is a professional. And, after all, you don't have anything to hide."

"I have nothing to hide. That's right. I don't have anything to hide. But I can't talk to a psychiatrist. I can't talk to anyone. Don't you understand that? Don't you know that I killed Warren?"

"God, Mel, you are crazy. Warren died of a heart attack."

"But I caused it. I hit him over the head. Kate knows that I did."

"He had an injury on his head, but it was minor, not life-threatening."

"But I caused his heart attack. I killed him."

"Damn it, Mel, you've got to get some help. You're driving yourself—and me!—crazy."

"I've gotta go now. Kate and I have a lunch date. I'll be back by about three."

Bobby was gone, and Mel was left to his own resources. He took a swig of Dr. Pepper, an elixir that seemed to transform him. Pouring the remainder of the soda down the sink and throwing the can into the recycle bin, he marched to the bathroom. In an act of defiance, staring destiny straight in the eye, he flushed the blue pills that remained in the plastic tube down the toilet. He now had a department to run, Hook, Mathis, and Gaylord to straighten out. He had to persuade Waldo Clemens to take early retirement. He had to prevent Potty Tinker from accepting the offer from Pepperdine. And he had the work on Vanbrugh to complete. As the blue pills swirled down the commode, Mel felt the starch unruffle his collar, he looked down to see the crease in his trousers sharpen, and his shoes took on a gleam.

Donning tie and coat, he strode determinedly out the door, unhesitatingly mounted the Chevy, and resolutely headed to the university.

Arriving at the university, striding down the hall of the Humanities Building toward his office, Mel resolved to go immediately into action. He would confront Hook, Mathis, and Gaylord. No more avoiding issues, which was, of course, Warren Burden's way of keeping peace in the department.

In the English Department main office, Mel greeted Heather Figaro with a courteous but not chummy, "Good afternoon, Ms. Figaro."

Her response was courteous but not chummy. "Dean Amore wants to see you right away."

* * *

Finding Dean Lester Amore preoccupied with a stack of papers, Professor J. Melongaster Druse stood attentively before the expansive mahogany desk, stood in the position known militarily as "at ease," legs spread, hands behind his back. For some minutes Amore did not acknowledge his visitor's presence, but continued to process the documents before him, making brief notes on them and sorting them into the proper disposition baskets on his desk.

At last, Amore looked up and ordered Mel, "Have a seat. I'll be with you in a minute."

Good soldier that he was, Mel came briefly to attention and then sat, relieved, in an easy chair in front of the deanly desk.

Amore continued his obviously momentous work. A knock on the dean's door, and Arlene McDonald-Ishimura poked her head in to ask, "Can I bring you a cup of coffee, Professor Druse?" Mel declined.

The last document in the pile having been disposed of, Dean Amore turned to Mel. "Ah yes. How long have you been at the university, Mel?"

"Twenty-one years this fall. I came in '81."

"Twenty-one years of service to students and to your scholarly field—you must have a great sense of fulfillment."

"Yeh, I guess. . . ."

"And now your career has taken a new tack, into administration as department chair. You have another ten or fifteen years to go before you retire. What a marvelous opportunity. You must feel young again."

"Well, I suppose. . . ."

"I'd like to see you leave a real mark on this university, a permanent monument to your influence and service."

"Les, believe me, I feel exactly the same way, and the first thing I want to do is clean up the English Department. I'm disgusted, absolutely disgusted."

"Oh? What's the problem."

"I guess you haven't heard about Hook, Mathis, and Gaylord Learning Consultants."

"No, I don't think I have. So?"

"That's Jim Hook, Howard Mathis, and Freddy Gaylord," explained Mel."

"So they have a consulting firm. What's wrong with that? I'm happy to see a little entrepreneurial spirit in the humanities, to tell you the truth."

"But they're selling hokum—world literature through sleep learning. 'Awaken the slumbering giant.' Really embarrassing stuff like that. And I think they're advertising on the radio."

Dean Amore was grinning broadly, but his voice conveyed the levelheaded, rational sincerity which was necessarily his pose in dealing with faculty. "Do they claim a connection with the university in their advertising? That would be very serious."

"I don't think so. Not in their brochure. I haven't seen it yet, but Freddie told me about it."

"I'll certainly look into this matter, and you'll hear from me. But I want to get back to your future here at the university. Of course, all of us know how important you've been. Years before I arrived, you were carrying the ball. Aren't you the senior person in English?"

"No, Waldo Clemens came five years before I did."

"Yes, Waldo. Waldo is pretty much out of it now, isn't he? But, again, I want to stay on the subject of your future, not your past. You could do so much for this place."

"Believe me, I'll try. If you'll back me, I'll shake the English Department up. I don't think that most of my colleagues are . . . are . . . active enough."

"Really, Mel, I don't know what we can do about that situation, and maybe in the long run it doesn't matter if no one in the English Department does much—as long as they all meet their classes, of course.

"Mel, I'd like to talk to you about my vision of this university—its destiny. If you're familiar with sociobiology—Tinbergen, Lorenz, that bunch—you know that we're genetically programmed to play games. We're like ducks. They don't always dive for fish. They just like to dive. We're like baboons. We play games to establish hierarchy and dominance. So there's not a thing we can do about it: our genes make us into game players. And that's just where the humanities come in; they satisfy man's craving for play, for games.

"But, of course, humans aren't just game players; they're also builders and makers. The practical arts—agriculture, carpentry, medicine—arose from genuine needs for survival, and so did the sciences: mathematics, biology, physics. These are fields with a purpose.

"So you can divide the whole university up into the fields that are essentially game playing—literature, music, the fine arts, drama—and those that are essentially practical. Clearly, we need both; both represent basic human needs. But I'd argue that the game playing fields will pretty much take care of themselves. It's the purposive, practical fields that are the destiny of this university, Mel. There's no doubt about that. And I'd like to think that you're a man of destiny."

"Yes, but what about Hook, Mathis, and Gaylord? Max Schinken calls them Hook, Crook, and Schnook. We can't let them get away...."

"Good lord, man, forget about them. Wish them well. If they can make an honest—or dishonest—dollar without bothering us, well, that's the American way, isn't it?" And summoning all of his deanly intensity, leaning forward and looking directly into Mel's eyes, Lester Amore said, "I want to tell you where your real future lies. It's not with play—the arts and humanities—but with purpose: the sciences and social sciences, engineering, medicine, psychology, sociology, mathematics. As I said before, sociobiology tells us that humans are programmed to play, but they're destined to achieve, to cure diseases, to build edifices, to govern, and, yes, to fight if need be. And the destiny of this university for the next decades is on the side of purpose, not play. If you don't believe me, just read the interview with Donald Schwann that was published in the *Times;* look at the president's last 'State of the University' message.

Mel squirmed, as if his underwear were too tight, chafing his privates unbearably, but that was the sort of feeling Dean Lester Amore was skilled at evoking.

Mel stared at his own image in the broad mirror that hung behind Dean Amore's desk. "To tell you the truth, Les, I really don't know what you're getting at," Mel said, with some effort distracting himself from his own image in the mirror.

Amore's smile was enigmatic, multiply ambiguous: at once a grin and a sneer, its ostensible purpose friendliness, its deep structure pure hostility, the will to win, for the smiler relished his image as the toughest sonofabitch on this or any other campus.

Amore began again, talking slowly and precisely, as though he were addressing a child: "The days when we could afford literary twaddle are over. The university is simultaneously entering an era of financial crunch and commitment to excellence. Something's got to give, and we've decided—the administration and the board—that purpose takes precedence over play. In fact, I wrote the philosophical statement behind our ten-year plan, 'Project for a New University Century.' I'd like to read you some excerpts.

"'The academic and fiscal policies of this university are adrift. Conservative faculty members have criticized the administration's policies. They have also resisted the isolationist tendencies among their colleagues. But no one has yet confidently advanced a strategic vision of the University's role in the world.'"

Dean Amore looked up from the document and stared briefly at Mel. Then he continued, "Mel, this is the age of neo-conservatism. You know that a brilliant group of so-called neo-cons now control the United States government. We intend to apply the same philosophy to this university. Let me outline our specific recommendations.

"First, we need to increase our spending on scientific research significantly. By the way, that means that the telic, practical fields will take precedence over the arts and humanities. Second, we need to strengthen our ties with other institutions that share our values. For instance, the Plato Foundation can become a powerful ally. Third, we need to promote the cause of a practical, purpose-driven university among other institutions of higher learning. Fourth, we must take the responsibility for preserving and extending our ideals throughout the world.

"That, in a nutshell, is the destiny of this university, and I want you to be a part of that destiny."

"It sounds to me—if you'll forgive me for saying it . . . you understand I know nothing about sociobiology . . . I think . . . don't you think?—I mean literature and the arts . . . they're not just play, are they? I mean, neo-conservatism . . . I mean I just read Alan Bloom's book . . . comes right out of the humanities. Why did the Plato Foundation choose that name?"

Mel was completely entangled in his own syntax and his fear of Amore; he was virtually catatonic, inwardly raging. There was no answering the Dean, no rebuttal, no dialogue; Amore did not speak in the ordinary sense; he pronounced. And Mel had heard his latest pronouncement.

"I know, Mel," said Amore, with admirable forbearance, "that it will take a while for you to understand all of this, but ultimately you'll agree with the wisdom of the master plan. And how do you fit? I have chosen two roles for you. In the first place, I've worked out some new courses that I want the English Department to start offering on a regular basis: business writing, technical writing, and document design—courses that have an important function within a purposive university."

"Document design? Business writing? Technical writing? Where will we get the staff?" Mel was stunned.

After a long pause, Dean Lester Amore firmly answered Mel's question: "You already have the staff! It's your job to reallocate priorities. No more Henry James seminars with only three students! No more junior-level modern poetry courses with only ten students! I do keep track of the numbers, you know."

***

Mel was well along on his second double martini, the cool fragrance of gin calming him, restoring a bit of his *élan vital* after the session with Dean Amore that afternoon.

"In fact, it was a hideous day," he said to Bobby, who sat knitting in an easy chair across from his place on the couch. "First there was the business about Hook, Mathis, and Gaylord, utterly humiliating. And Max let me down; I thought he'd be as outraged as I was. And Amore didn't give a damn. That guy has no scruples whatsoever. His only criterion is what's good for Lester Amore, the sonofabitch. He wants me to preside over the dismantling of the English Department. Well, you know where he can go."

"The university is amazing," said Bobby. "For years I was an outsider; in fact, the place and its people frightened me. Since I've become an insider of sorts, I'm more and more appalled by the shenanigans of the whole bunch. I agree with your opinion about Lester Amore—and then some." She took a liberal sip of her Jack Daniels.

"Yeh, Amore gave me all this bullshit about destiny and so forth. He sounded like Hitler, to tell you the truth. *Das Schicksal des Volkes der Universität.* He said I had two roles to play in the future."

"What's the other one?" asked Bobby.

"What do you mean?"

"The other role. He wants you to 'reform' the English Department. And what else?"

"To tell you the truth, I don't know. He didn't say and I didn't ask him. All I wanted to do was get out of his office as quickly as possible. You know, I think he's a goddamn Nazi."

"Mel, you schmuck," said Bobby, "I know what your other role in the future of the university is."

"Yeh, I bet," said Mel.

"Yeh, I bet," echoed Bobby.

"Okay. Okay. So what's my other role."

attitudes

"To get money out of me for the new science complex."

From: Amore@cdu.edu
To: Firestein@ssu.edu

Feb 16, 2001. By now you have received my letter, but I'd like to share some thoughts with you that I wouldn't want to become a part of the deliberations regarding my candidacy for the presidency of SSU. You and I are among those lucky academics whose philosophies (and politics) come from our work at Chicago with Leo Strauss, so you understand what my long-term goals at SSU would be. (By the way, I think that we neo-cons, as we're called, are at long last gaining the power we deserve. Yesterday President Bush sent the name of Wolfie—our old pal Paul Wolfowitz—to the Senate for confirmation as assistant secretary of defense.)

Granted, SSU is not a world-class institution. Granted, the faculty is not distinguished. Granted, you're at the mercy of the state legislature for you funding. Nonetheless, I can envision the university becoming the main power in its region. My intention would not be the hopeless task of making the university into a world-class institution. That will never happen. However, with strong leadership and a clear goal, the university could be a significant factor in bringing the whole area into the future envisioned by such realists as you and me and Wolfie. The university should have a subtle but powerful effect on the politics and economics of the whole region. When and if I become president of SSU, I'll realign priorities and faculty interests. We will, in many ways, simply colonize the whole region.

6. Cassoulet; or, Intricate Indecencies

In his tan warmup suit and Nike jogging shoes, Mel was listlessly puttering around the yard, snipping a branch here, pulling a weed there, making, really, no difference whatsoever in the domesticated flora of 1415 Dimple Dell Drive. Mel's clip-snip was answered by snip-clip from the Golden side of the redwood fence separating the two yards, and, of course, Mel asked, "That you, Greg?"

It was Greg, and hence the time for the weekly pot of coffee.

At the Druse kitchen table, Cynthia and Greg and Bobby and Mel sipped coffee and ate Betty Crocker chocolate chip cookies that Bobby had baked that morning.

Assuming his jaunty just-for-Greg-and-Cynthia demeanor, Mel, startling Bobby, announced, "Hey, neighbors, Bob and I are planning a little party for some university folks: Dean Lester Amore (you've heard me mention him, brilliant guy!), the new graduate dean, and some folks from the department. Nothing fancy. Just a cocktail-buffet with some civilized talk. I think you'd enjoy these people, especially Amore. In fact, we've tentatively scheduled the party for October 28th, so put that on your calendar, huh?"

Greg looked at Cynthia. Pause. Cynthia looked at Greg. Pause. Both started at once, "Well, you see. . . ." Pause. Then Greg said, "I think we have something that evening, don't we, Cyn?" And Cynthia: "I think so, but I'll look on my calendar."

"Why don't you run over and look right now?" urged Mel. "You won't want to miss getting together with these folks if you can help it. Amore is fascinating, a brilliant guy, a linguist. He's a personal friend of Norm Chomsky, and you know what Chomsky did to B. F. Skinner."

Presumably the Goldens didn't know what Norm Chomsky had done to B. F. Skinner, but Cynthia did go home to look at her social calendar, and when she returned she said that she and Greg were free on October 28.

attitudes

"Good! Good!" clucked elated Mel. "You'll love every minute of the evening. You'll have to get Amore to tell you about studying relative pronouns in some group of African languages. Fascinating story."

"Well, neighbor, you know what a sawbones's life is like. If I don't have to straighten out some scrambled brains or splice a few wires that night, I'll be there."

A pause in the conversation. Greg helps himself to another cookie. Cynthia freshens her coffee from the vacuum urn. Bobby replenishes the supply of cookies. Mel gazes abstractedly at the ceiling.

"My goodness," says Cynthia, "I've been spending hours and hours at the museum. We don't have funds for an adequate staff, so board members have to fill in. I've been running the front desk three afternoons a week—in addition to board meetings once a month, and they drag on and on and on. Everybody has to have their say about every nitpicking item."

"It's a sad fact," opines Mel, "that culture always takes a back seat to the so-called practical concerns in a society. I'd rather have potholes in our highways than lack of funding for art, music, and literature. My cultural horizons expanded when I saw the exhibit of nineteenth-century California nature painters at the museum."

"That exhibit was four or five years ago," says Cynthia. "Have you seen our current exhibit of 'found art'?"

"No," says Mel, "I hate to admit it, but I've so busy with the work on my article about Sir John Vanbrugh that I've little time for anything else. He was a dramatist. Seventeenth century. You've never heard of Vanbrugh. You know, that's just the point: we literary gents have an obligation to preserve the tradition and to rescue the worthy from oblivion. I'll stick a copy of one of his plays in your mail box this afternoon. You'll enjoy it, I think."

"Cyn and I were in the same sophomore lit class at Berkeley," says Greg. "We both liked Shelley a lot. 'I bring fresh showers for the thirsting flowers / From the seas and the streams. / I bear light shade for the leaves when laid / In their noonday dreams.' That's from 'The Cloud.' I've always loved that poem."

"Yes," says Mel in his best professorial voice, "the Romantics have always appealed to the undergraduate taste, but many do grow out of this infatuation and begin to appreciate more complex, more nuanced literature. You might try the Metaphysicals—Donne, Marvell—or even more modern stuff—Ezra Pound, for instance."

Mel waxes enthusiastic. "I have a copy of Pound's Cantos that I'll give you. You can keep it." And he bustles to his study and back, book in hand. Placing the volume ceremoniously before Greg, Mel says, "Here's a whole new world for you. I'm anxious to hear your reaction."

"Well," replies Greg, "I'll try to get to it, but with my patients and the staff meetings at the hospital and the doctors' symphony I don't have much spare time. But thanks."

When the Goldens had left, Bobby said to Mel, "So you had a sudden brainstorm. Why didn't you talk to me before you got your party idea going?"

"I didn't tell you about my party," sneered Mel. "Well, now you know about it, don't you?"

In rising from the table, Bobby knocked her chair over. After a moment, Mel heard the front door slam. He sighed. His problems were solved for the next few hours. Bobby would spend the day at the mall, puttering through department stores and shops, buying this and that, and having her beloved hotdog-on-a-stick for lunch.

Singing his "tidey-didey" song (to the melody of "Everybody Loves a Baby"), a compulsive tic that came on when Mel was feeling particularly upbeat, he went immediately to his study to write notes of invitation to his serendipitously conceived party. "Tideydidey tidey-didey tidey-didey tidey-die. . . ." This, for example, to Dean Lester Amore: "Dear Les, Could you and Mrs. Amore join us for a cocktail buffet on October 28 at seven or thereabouts? Dr. Greg Golden and his wife will be with us. You might remember

attitudes

the feature on the Goldens in the 'Modern Living' section of the paper a couple of Sundays ago. I'm sure you'll enjoy getting to know these people. Yours, Mel."

So enormously inspirited was Mel that he resolved to go for broke on this one: he sent an invitation to President and Mrs. Newburn, Newburn the imperious, Newburn the isolated, who was never seen on campus, but, from his office in fortress-like Admin Building, ruled by memo, policy statement, and ukases delivered by the three or four viceroys whom he had anointed, among whom, of course, was Dean Lester Amore.

President Newburn, in fact, strongly resembled Dr. Greg Golden: imperially slim, silver-haired, graceful. On the other hand, Dean Amore, in dim light, could easily have been mistaken for Professor Druse. As Mel perceived them, both the president and the dean were proper, incisive, icy, but Amore had a reputation on campus for being what the students would call a horn-doggler. It had been said that the dean radiated potency, almost an aroma of sexuality, a crackling aura of horniness. Mel readily believed all of the rumors about the couch in the dean's office.

The letter of invitation written—to the new graduate dean and his wife; to the Grupps, utility socialites in the department, always available, unfailingly amusing; to Kate Reese, lovely Kate; and, of course, to President Newburn and Dean Amore—Mel leaned back in his chair, clasped his hands behind his head, and became lost in a reverie concerning the party. What if—just suppose it possible—Amore and Cynthia found elective affinities? What if—and this was not totally out of the question—Cynthia was lured to the university, perhaps as a member of the Dean's Circle, a tonie support group that raised money for the College of Letters, Arts, and Sciences? And what if—stranger things had happened—she was finally lured to the dean's couch? The image of Cynthia and Amore, *flagrante delicto,* on the couch was infinitely satisfying to Mel, and he smiled serenely.

Mel had not been in such a state of fevered anticipation since three years ago when he awaited the publication of his article on

Orator Henley, the fascinating and neglected figure who played such an important role in the development of Romantic thought. (When it finally did appear, Mel had given an autographed offprint of the article to Greg and Cynthia.)

As the sun was sinking in the West, Mel heard Bobby's Buick pull into the driveway, and shortly thereafter the front door opened and closed. "Hey, Bob," called Mel. "Come and talk to me about the party."

Bobby sat on the sofa in Mel's study and lit a Marlboro, violating the sanctity of that haven where Mel cogitated and composed, but at this juncture, Mel did not complain about Bobby's breach of the terms of the household truce.

"Bob, what do you think we ought to serve on the 28th?"

"Doesn't make shit to me," responded Bobby. "I won't be here."

"Won't be here. Where you going?"

"I'm spending the weekend at the Pachenga resort in Temecula."

That was that.

On Sunday, Mel telephoned Kate Reese, explaining that he had mailed her an invitation to a party on the 28th, that Bobby would out of town on that date, and that he would like Kate's suggestions about a caterer. "Oh, certainly," said Kate. "By all means call Jardiniere Catering. They're excellent. And, Mel, I'd be happy to come early to sort of stand in for Bobby."

On Monday, after extensive telephonic consultation, Mme. Devereux of Jardiniere suggested starting with clams on the half-shell and bib lettuce and beet salad with vinaigrette dressing. The main course would be cassoulet. "Cass . . . what?" said Mel. "Ah, oui," said Mme. Devereux, "a rich baked-bean dish with lamb, duck breast, and andouille." "Andoo . . . what?" "Ah, oui. Eet is a spicy pork sausage." "Okay. Of course. Sounds good to me. Cassoolay with andooeel. How about dessert?" "Mais certainement. I would suggest flan with raspberries or strawberries," said Mme. Devereux, sounding much more like Brooklyn than Paris.

attitudes

The Friday of the party, Mel had stayed home from the university. He checked the refrigerator in the garage to make certain that the champagne cooling there had not escaped. He surveyed the pool area, ready to eradicate any trace of green scum. He inventoried the wet bar, making certain that gin, Scotch, bourbon, rye, brandy, tequila, Drambuie, Southern Comfort, and sherry were on hand. He checked the roll of toilet paper in the downstairs bathroom. He filled a crystal bowl with mixed nuts and placed it on the coffee table. He made certain that the proper publications were in orderly display on the coffee table: *Times Literary Supplement, The New Yorker, Harper's, The Atlantic.* And at about five in the afternoon, he popped the top on a diet Dr. Pepper and flopped in a chair, exhausted.

Later, in the bedroom suite, as the whir of Mel's electric razor accompanied his song ("tidey-didey tidey-didey tidey-didey tidey-didey") and the six o'clock news blared from the television, the front doorbell rang.

In his robe, Mel greeted Kate, who glowed into the entry hall and brushed a kiss on Mel's cheek. Effervescent Kate said, "Here I am. What can I do to help?"

"Yeh, well, I think everything's pretty much ready. Jardinere will be here at seven-thirty to set things up for the buffet." And, having done a bit of research, Mel was able to report, "We're having cassoulet. Why don't you grab yourself a drink and make yourself comfortable while I finish dressing? There's chardonnay in the icer."

As Mel was finishing his toilet, the expensively mechanical snarl of Greg Golden's Porsche put him on the *qui vive.* Probably Greg was running to the shopping center on an errand before the party, but the clangor of the telephone following Greg's departure led to only one conclusion.

"Sure, I understand, Cynthia. When he's gotta go, he's gotta go. No sweat. We'll see you in half an hour."

"I'm going down and pour myself a drink," said Mel to himself, and he hurriedly finished dressing and disappeared from the bedroom suite.

Kate was sitting in Bobby's favorite chair, a platform rocker, the orange padding of which was a perfect background for her black satin gown with pearls to underline the simplicity of the sheath. She was perfect, even to her black leather pumps. Mel was certain that her toenails, though impeccably manicured, were not vulgarly enameled in red.

Kate's very presence stanched the searing flow of acids that had begun to bubble up from his innards. She rose and again brushed a kiss across his cheek. Motioning him toward the sofa, she said, "Come and sit with me for a few moments before the party begins."

Mel sat beside Kate on the sofa, and she stroked his hand. "I know you've been upset, but now you should just relax and enjoy the party."

"You know, I'm sure Bobby would have liked to be here, but she has volunteered as a big sister for kids on the Pechanga reservation, so she's in Temecula this weekend."

The chiming of the doorbell ended the conversation. Mel had regained his composure and had prepared his face for whatever face he might meet when he opened the door. It was, as a matter of fact, the bearded face of Dr. Samuel Zucker, the new graduate dean, and his wife. Zucker was a physicist, obviously not of renown, else he would not have chosen the administrative path upward on the academic ziggurat. His wife was a short woman in a gray smock, her arms bulging out at forty-five degree angles from the sides of her rotundity. Hardly waiting for the amenities of introductions, she waddled to the couch and settled into its cushions, couch and Emma Zucker merging into an overstuffed unity. The dean seated himself in an armchair, and Kate graciously took her place next to Emma Zucker on the couch.

Mel explained, "I'm sure Bobby would have liked to be here, but she has volunteered as a big sister for kids on the Pechanga reservation, so she's in Temecula this weekend."

"Most laudatory," said Dean Zucker.

"Indian kids are real cute," said Mrs. Zucker.

The three guests having been settled comfortably, Mel chimed, "Drinks? Mrs. Zucker?"

"Just give me a beer," she replied.

Mel scurried to the garage to retrieve a bottle of Heineken and after removing the cap was about to pour the brew into a mug, when Emma Zucker stopped him: "I'll drink it out of the bottle," she said, her voice a rumble from her depths, more like a gastric disturbance than speech.

Samuel Zucker sipped a Jack Daniels on the rocks, Kate wet her lips with a very mild whiskey sour, and Mel undecorously gulped a Beefeater on the rocks, after which he refilled.

Drinks in hand, the necessity now was conversation.

Mel suavely initiated the sociability. "Well, how do you folks like Southern California?"

"Absolutely fascinating," replied Dean Zucker. "A marvelous change for a pair of Down Easterners like Emma and me."

Mrs. Zucker took a long pull on her bottle of Heineken and asseverated, "I sure won't miss the snow. I always hated winter."

Kate agreed with Emma Zucker. "I wouldn't move back to Ohio for anything. We still have the family home in Columbus. I don't want to sell it, but I don't want to live in it."

The ice, so to speak, having been broken, real conversation could now get under way, the order of topics an inviolable sequence in Southern California: first, the weather; then the smog; next the freeways; finally, the impending earthquake.

Smog had just entered the conversation when the phone rang. Mel answered. "Really! No one hurt, I hope. . . . Thank goodness for that, anyway. . . . You think the car's totaled then? . . . Yes, I bet you are shaken up. . . . Take care of yourselves. See you Monday." Mel remained standing. "That was the Grupps. On their way here, they were hit by a dump truck. Driver ran a light. Their Volvo was totaled, but neither of them is seriously injured. Nancy got a bump on the head, but Herb isn't even shaken."

The doorbell rang again. This time, the person at the door was Cynthia Golden in a svelte golden pantsuit, her golden hair flowing to the chic collar, her footwear golden sandals. Mel paused momentarily to view her and then decorously pecked her on the cheek. "Really too bad that Greg had to miss the party, but, you know."

Directly behind Cynthia were Dean Lester Amore and his wife Donna. "Good to see you, Mel. Awfully good of you to think of us. We've been looking forward to getting to know Mrs. Druse better."

Amore assessed Cynthia. "Won't you introduce me to this lovely lady?"

"Sure, of course," stammered Mel. "Cynthia Golden, this is Dean Lester Amore and his wife, Donna."

Cynthia shook hands and attempted to glide from the entryway to the parlor, but Dean Amore had a gasp on the fleshy part of her arm. "Yes, Les has told me about you and your husband George."

"Greg," said Cynthia.

"Of course, Greg. He's a doctor, isn't he?"

"A neurosurgeon."

"And you live next door to the Druses. Have you thought about becoming involved in functions at the university? I'd like to recruit you and your husband. How about lunch next week?"

"I'm afraid Greg couldn't make it."

"Of course. Of course. But you're free one day, I hope."

"I'll call and let you know."

Donna Amore, her face framed by the precise page-boy cut of her ebony hair, gushed histrionically, "My GOODness, to think I've NEVER met Mel or Mrs.DRUSE. Lester, you NAUGHTY man. Why haven't YOU invited Professor and Mrs. DRUSE to our place?"

With forbearance, Amore explained, "Certainly. Certainly. We should have been more collegial, more sociable. But now we'll make up for past failings. And where is Mrs. Druse?"

"I'm afraid she won't be joining us tonight," said Mel. "I'm sure she'd have liked to be here, but she has volunteered as a big sister for kids on the Pechanga reservation, so she's in Temecula this weekend."

"We're disappointed," said Amore, "but what an admirable thing for her to do."

"The DEAR, SWEET woman. I must get to know her soon."

"When President and Mrs. Newburn arrive, we can eat," reported Mel.

Dean Amore gravitated toward Kate and placed himself on the arm of the sofa. "And how are you this evening? Are you the grace note that our host thoughtfully provides?"

"I'm a kind of substitute for Bobby this evening. I volunteered to help Mel since Bobby's away."

"Ah, so you're—how should I put it?—a family friend, a close family friend?" Amore lightly touched Kate's shoulder, and she shrugged his hand sway.

"Just say a friend of Mel and Bobby. Just a friend of both of them."

Without a trumpet fanfare, august President Harvey Newburn and his wife arrived. The imperial, impeccable Newburn led his wife to a chair opposite the wet bar and systematically greeted each of the other guests. "Les, good to see you." He shook Lester Amore's hand. "Donna, what a pleasure. Haven't crossed paths with you for a month or so." He pecked her on the cheek. "Sam, glad you're getting into the social whirl at the university." He shook Dean Samuel Zucker's hand. "Emma, how do you like Southern California?" Without waiting for her to respond, he shook her hand. "Mel, thanks for inviting us." He gave Mel a hug. "And these two young ladies. I don't think I know them."

Mel did the honors. "President Newburn, this is Kate Reese."

"Glad to meet you. I see you've already captured Les." He shook Kate's hand.

"And this is Cynthia Golden, my neighbor."

"A pleasure. A pleasure," said Newburn as he shook Cynthia's hand. And where, might I ask, is Mrs. Druse?"

"I'm sure Bobby would have liked to be here, but she has volunteered as a big sister for kids on the Pechanga reservation, so she's in Temecula this weekend."

"Admirable," said President Newburn. "I greatly admire people who give of themselves. We're sorry to have missed Mrs. Druse, but there'll be other times. There'll be other times, I assure you."

"Drinks?" asked Mel.

"Diet Cola for Cora, and Scotch on the rocks for me," pronounced President Newburn.

Spectral Cora Newburn, isolated in a corner of the room, sipped her Coke. Harvey Newburn stationed himself in front of Kate. "So what's Les been telling you? I bet he's been explaining our 'Plan for a New University Century' to you. He's a real bulldog when he gets on a subject."

"Actually," said Kate, "we've been talking about the University Symphony. Dr. Amore has explained to me that it's not only self-supporting but even profitable, what with CDs, concerts, and so on."

"That's Les," said Harvey Newburn. "Always has his eye on the practical aspects of the university. I try to convince him that our institution has plenty of room for the impractical."

"And music is impractical?" Kate leaned slightly forward, anticipating a response.

"That's really not what I meant," said President Newburn. "You see, in the university, there are some programs that are profitable and some that aren't. For instance, our chemical engineering department makes enough in grants and patents to pay for all the salaries and then some. On the other hand, the English Department is simply an expense. I agree with Les to this extent.

attitudes

It would be most gratifying if our English faculty were able to raise some money, through consulting or whatever."

Mel restrained himself. He did not begin a discourse on Hook, Mathis, and Gaylord. Instead, he announced, "I suppose if everyone's hungry we can eat. The caterer has everything ready."

With enormous flailing, lurching, and grunting, and with the aid of her husband, Emma Zucker stood up, whereupon she made her way with waddling alacrity to the food. Eagerly lifting the lid of the casserole and peering in, she emitted an ecstatic rumble: "Wieners and beans! I love it!"

* * *

Postprandial coffee and liqueurs. President Newburn stationed himself next to Kate Reese on the sofa, and Dean Amore stood by the unlit fireplace with Cynthia Golden.

"You should join me for lunch at the university," said Amore. "Fascinating exhibit of Native American art at the McCabe Gallery on campus. After lunch, we could visit the gallery. I know you're interested in art."

"Greg and I try to be something more than middle class householders. He's in the doctors' symphony, you know, and I'm on the board of the museum of art. Actually, our lives are very full."

"I wish Dr. Golden were here tonight. I'd like to meet him."

"Greg is never 'here.' I mean, he's so involved with his practice that you can't count on him to keep social commitments."

"When you said, 'Greg is never here,' I think I detected just a slight tinge of bitterness."

"You can't have everything." Cynthia wet her lips with B&B.

Lester Amore's gaze assessed Cynthia from her golden hair to her golden sandals. "How true. How true." Then, after a pause, "Come to the university Monday, Tuesday, Wednesday—any day next week. We'll break bread together and then enjoy the Native American art."

"I'll call," said Cynthia.

***

Mel had bade farewell to the Zuckers, the last of the guests to leave, and Kate was moving toward the front door when Mel sighed mightily and asked Kate, "Why don't you stick around for a while? Let's have a cup of coffee."

Kate returned to her seat on the couch, and Mel brought two cups of coffee, placing them on the table in front of the couch. He sat facing Kate, one leg folded under the other. "My God! what a night. Emma Zucker is a dumpster. She ate enough cassoulet to feed a regiment. And eight bottles of beer. Eight bottles!"

"I understand how you feel," said Kate, "but my heart goes out to that poor woman. Think of how she must feel. She knows that she's a . . . how shall I put it? . . . that she's out of the ordinary."

"Yeh, she sure is," said Mel.

Kate sipped at her coffee. "Let's change the subject. I want to know about you. I've read your book on the fop in Restoration drama. It's a wonderful piece of work. Opened up a whole new area of literary experience for me."

Mel straightened from his sag on the couch and used Kate's opening to begin a disquisition on his work. "You know, right now I'm just completing a paper on Sir John Vanbrugh. Amazing guy. He's the architect who designed Blenheim Palace. In the last years of the seventeenth century, the French threw him into the Bastille. Thought he was an English spy. And he wrote wonderful, witty plays. He's not much known today. I hope to resurrect him. Know what I mean?"

"I think so. Really fascinating," said Kate. "But tell me about Barbara. Tell me how you two met."

"You see, I had gone to Las Vegas to do some research in collections at the UNLV library. After I had the information I needed, I went to the Xanadu buffet. Everybody said it was the best in town. I remember that I had chicken cacciatore. Well, there were no vacant tables, but Bobby asked me to join her. Of course, I didn't know it was Bobby at the time, until she introduced her-

attitudes

self. So we got to know one another," Mel chuckled, "over chicken cacciatore."

"We got to talking, and Bobby asked me if I'd ever been to Valley of Fire. That's a state park north of Las Vegas. Spectacular rock formations. So she said she'd take me to see the park the next day, Sunday. To make a long story short, things clicked with us, and I came back to Las Vegas two more weekends in a row, and then Bobby came to LA, and you know how things develop. We got married in Las Vegas. She came to LA and bought this house. And we were domesticated."

"What's Bobby's background?" asked Kate.

"Oh, she was an actress," said Mel. "Had parts in various stage performances. She married Bert Reddick, the producer, and when he died, she inherited all of his loot."

"Fascinating. I know I shouldn't ask, but I just can't help myself. How much did Bobby inherit?"

"A bundle. A real bundle. Four or five hundred mill. I think the only one who really knows what she's worth is Steve Bloom, her accountant."

"Bobby's funny. She really doesn't care about dough, as long as she has enough to pay for her whims. You know, she collects china. Take a look around the house. Six hutches full of chinaware. And boxes full of the stuff in the garage."

"I'd so like to get to know Bobby," said Kate. Will she be home next week?"

"Yeh, she's coming back from Temecula Sunday."

***

Cynthia had excused herself from the party early, complaining of a headache. Immediately on arriving at home, she poured herself a liberal shot of vodka on the rocks and went to the bathroom, whence she extracted a plastic tube from the medicine chest, shook one tablet out of the tube, and washed it down with vodka.

Next, she went to Greg's study, where she seated herself at his desk.

She systematically went through a stack of papers at the center of the desk, quickly turning official documents over and pausing to examine handwritten notes. These she subjected to the sniff test, a search for olfactory evidence.

She picked up the telephone and dialed the hospital. "This is Mrs. Golden. Will you please page Dr. Golden for me? Ask him to call me."

Cynthia finished her drink and fixed another before the phone rang. Dr. Golden had not responded to the page, the operator informed her. In fact, Dr. Golden had not been in the hospital since about five.

Cynthia went to the bathroom again. Contemplating herself in the mirror, she sensed an otherness, a secret self that thorazine was specifically intended to hide. The face she gazed at was hard, the lips sneering, the hair straw. "Which one is me?" she muttered.

Continuing to gaze at the image in the mirror, she took another pill from the tube and washed it down with vodka.

Freeing herself from her pantsuit, she sat contemplatively on the toilet, listening to the gush and splash of her pee. She contemplated her perfectly manicured toenails and then her perfectly manicured fingernails. She had no volition, no will to move. "Peace comes dropping slow," she muttered. "Peace comes dropping slow."

The snarl of Greg's Porsche pulling into the driveway alerted her. She wiped herself, flushed the toilet, poured the vodka down the sink, rinsed the glass, and went to the kitchen, where she was pouring a glass of tomato juice when Greg entered.

"So how many lives did you save tonight?" she asked listlessly.

"Don't be nasty, Cyn. I have enough trouble with my patients and the hospital staff without getting worked over when I come home."

"Your new assistant—what's her name?—must make life easier for you."

"Judy? Judy's very good."

"I'll bet she's very good. Was she very good tonight?"

"Cynthia, have you been taking your thorazine?"

"Sure. Took two of them tonight."

"And washed them down with vodka," I bet.

"You know what I think, Dr. Golden? Do you remember the old movie 'Gaslight'? Charles Boyer tries to drive Ingrid Bergman insane."

"You're implying that—"

"Not implying, Dr. Golden. I'm telling you—you're driving me nuts. The perfect couple. The Raquette Club. The symphony. The museum. While you're out screwing Judy and any other bimbo you can get to spread her legs.

"I need another vodka."

"Go ahead. Go ahead. You know, of course, that a mixture of thorazine and alcohol can be fatal. But go ahead. It's your choice." Greg moved rapidly to leave the kitchen, but he halted and took a seat at the table next to Cynthia. "I should have known better than to leave the thorazine for you. From now on, I'll give you your pill and watch you take it. I'm going to set you up for an appointment with Charlie Newbold. You need psychiatric help."

* * *

Mimi's was at least two notches above Denny's or IHOP, and several notches below the Ritz-Carlton or Roy's. The waiter had brought the postprandial coffee, so it was time to settle in for a getting-to-know-one-another conversation.

"Barbara," Kate began, "I've known Mel for three or four years, but somehow my path didn't ever cross yours in all that time."

"Yeh, call me Bobby. I gotta tell you, I'm not so hot on the university bunch. They live in Lala Land, and I don't mean L.A.

About a year ago, Mel invited Pottle Tinker and Waldo Clemens to dinner. God, what a night! You know Potty, don't you? Jesus, that 'hrump . . hrumph . . hrumph' drives me nuts. 'I think . . . hrumph . . . I'd like . . . hrumph . . . another cup of . . . hrumph . . . coffee.' And Waldo is gone, over the hill. The dullest person I've ever known. He sucks on that damn gurgling pipe and talks about finding rocks in the desert."

"I'll admit," said Kate, "that Potty and Waldo are something else again, but think of Max Schinken. He's interesting. And a very nice man. And Ken Turing is a lot of fun. And Amore. Amore really bugs Mel."

"Dean Amore is a real power at the university," said Kate. "He's a fascinating person."

"Mel says he's horny."

Kate chuckled.

Leaning forward, and placing her hand over Bobby's, Kate asked, "What would you like to be doing right now, instead of sitting here with me? We can be honest with one another. You know, right now I'd like to be in London, having lunch at the Tate. So what about you?"

"Yeh, I've never been to London and don't want to go. You probably think I'm a slob, but I'll tell you truly: right now I'd like to be at the Southland Super Lanes bowling. I love to bowl."

"No, no, no," insisted Kate. "I don't think you're a slob. I really admire you. You have guts enough to be honest. Bobby, you're one of the few really genuine people I've met since I came to Southern California. Please consider me your friend."

> From: GoldenMD@aol.com
> To: MitsumiMD@msn.com
>
> February 16, 2001. Well, here I go again. You're my e-mail shrink. Or maybe my father confessor—ever since med school at Hopkins. Fred, Cynthia is driving me nuts. Everyone who knows her thinks she's

the perfect wife, she's so bubbly and upbeat all the time. But, let me tell you, when she's at home with me, all of her gold turns to ice. She's a frigid, quibbling bitch who's never satisfied with anything. My God, our house is in a continual state of remodeling. She had the patio repaved with flagstones, and right now the kitchen is torn apart to install new appliances. She got the idea that she needs a stove big enough to cook for an army.

You always had the hots for Cynthia. You have no idea how lucky you are. I wish I'd had sense enough to escape from the charms of the golden goddess.

Oh well, life isn't a bed of roses. Have you thought about joining our group. We need a psychiatrist. We have every other specialty covered. Move into our territory, and you can join the Raquette Club and drool over Cynthia. But come to think of it, the Raquette Club is ladies only.

From: MitsumiMD@msn.com
To: GoldenMD@aol.com

Old buddy, my heart goes out to you. What a tragedy to be married to the hottest female in or from Baltimore. My professional opinion—which I suppose you were asking for—is this: put up with what you have at home and develop other interests away from home. You always have been what we randy young medics at Hopkins called a cocksman.

Anyway, you should judge your troubles in light of what's happening and will happen to America during the Bush regime.

7. Sherry; or, Portrait of a Lady

Chad's thoughts drifted, from the graceful, artful eulogies, to those afternoons in Lewis Lambert's office, when that senior and distinguished scholar, widely known for his definitive study *Strange Voices: The Art of James Branch Cabell,* relaxed and chatted wittily though inconsequentially over sherry. Easy talk and sherry—those would be Chad's memory of his colleague. He looked about for Kate, but she was not in the half-filled small auditorium. Chad had waited in his office for her, expecting to accompany her to the service and then, in a private memorial gesture, to drink a glass of sherry with her, a final toast to their departed friend and mentor.

Next to Assistant Professor Martin Chadwick sat Mel, surreptitiously reading a paperback.

Dean Lester Amore was speaking in his characteristically appropriate way of Professor Lambert's genius for maintaining the highest standards of scholarship while, nonetheless, being human and accessible. "A sociable scholar" was the term Amore used. And Chad nodded in agreement.

His consciousness eddied back to Kate, the third member of an alliance that for three years had sporadically met to rescue academic afternoons from the waste of ennui that four o'clock, the hour between the end of classes and the beginning of evening's rituals (the trip home, dinner, work in the study, the late news, bed), imposed. Chad remembered one afternoon in particular. "She isn't really beautiful," Lambert had said, "not beautiful at all, though something else, of more worth than beauty: she's attractive, certainly one of the most attractive women I've known. When it comes to a choice, attractiveness outdoes beauty every time."

Late afternoon in harvest time, season of mellow fruitfulness: Professor Lewis Lambert, known for his study of James Branch Cabell and also for *Ronald Firbanks, the Conscientious Pixy,* Professor Lambert, ensconced and senior, reaped meticulously during

attitudes

these afternoons with junior colleagues and graduate students. Sherry, declining light, the beginning of an academic year, the careful deference of entenured colleagues such as Assistant Professor Martin Chadwick, desultory conversation (not quite gossip and tinged with literary allusion), the almost deserted campus, the obligatory ivy and books, even the barely audible whirring of the freeway and the oily tinge of exhaust that blew through the open window in the professor's office—the makings of a perfect scene for discussing Lambert's preoccupation: the charming lady.

"You've noticed, Chad, that one of her common phrases, almost a tic, is 'bringing it off.' 'If I can just bring it off,' she says to me repeatedly. Her whole life is devoted to 'bringing it off,' as if everything she does is a plot, all her successes coups."

One day in the spring, Kate had appeared in Lambert's office at the magical hour when the professor ritually poured sherry. She came, of course, at just the right time, when the professor would be most open, most convivial, most relaxed.

She did not enter a room at all in the ordinary sense, but, rather suffused the place of her presence with a bubbly, though not girlish or counterfeit, effervescence, Moet et Chandon quality, Cordon Rouge depth: sparkle, body, fragrance, the promise of slight intoxication. After her perfect rap on the door and a measured "Come" in response, she glowed into Lambert's office at the moment when he was pouring himself what he thought would be a lonely glass or two of "Dry Sack." Whether by intuition or design Kate had arrived on the rare afternoon when Lambert would be hers alone is an unanswered question. But welcome she was, for a late afternoon in spring and "Dry Sack" are to be shared companionably; so much the better, if the sharing is multiply ambiguous, with resonances anatomical: corticular, cerebral, and glandular. So much the better, to sip sherry with a charming lady who might—except for age, honor, propriety, reticence, commitments—have been more than one's good friend and protegé. So much the better, to spend a discrete hour with a friend and admirer than with a graduate student. So much the better, the easy relationship between Professor Lewis Lambert, the scholar in his fifties who for the last decade had taken to wearing richly decorous garb, and charming Kate, the lady of thirty-five or so whose wardrobe always fit the occasion, brown tweeds with a white frilly blouse on this particular afternoon, but denims with red checked shirt or black and pearls on other occasions.

Lambert motioned Kate to a seat, extracted a glass from his desk, and poured the fragrant, dark amber wine. Only after Kate had taken her first sip and smiled approvingly, that winningly elfin smile which was hers exclusively, did Lambert speak. "As I ended my work and prepared for my afternoon ritual, I thought, 'How good it would be to sip and chat with Kate,' and, you see, here you are. Surely you come by design, not chance. You arrival proves to me that history is teleological," jested Lambert in his elephantine way.

"How could I, at the fateful hour, walk past your door? I'm a victim of fate. And anyway, it's been weeks since we've sipped and gossiped. I think that I must have at least three hours of news for you. I had dinner with Marge and Chad last Saturday, the first time I've socialized with the Chadwicks for months. Bertie didn't go with me. You know how he is."

Lambert contentedly sipped, and thought about the mysterious Norbert, whom Kate referred to only as Bertie or Norie. She had spoken of his silken skin and his skill at handiwork. For Lambert, who had never met him, he was primarily a nasally oleaginous voice on the telephone.

The professor groped for the topic that would open this seance up to the sort of magical talk which united the two of them in an almost conspiratorial closeness. The subject that seemed always to work best was the time, two decades ago, when Lambert, then Kate's age, was a blossoming scholar with a beloved wife and blessed son—a first appointment at a "major" university, a first book well reviewed, a first real home, a first painting bought at considerable sacrifice, a first sense that life would now repay those years of struggle and abnegation which Lambert had willingly undertaken and which his wife had uncomplainingly accepted; and then the nights of agony and the weeks of alcoholic blur, the months of utter numbness, because an undergraduate, pampered and mindless, had gunned his Porsche down the wrong side of a campus street and in a head-on collision, just at noon as the carillon began to chime, had killed himself and Mrs. Lambert and the five-year-old David Herbert Lambert. This subject, however, worked best with the second glass, or even the third, so Lambert opened unobtrusively with, "Yes, Chad and Marge, two of my favorite people. And what was the occasion?"

"You see, Lewis, if I can bring it off, I want to publish my book, and I need Chad to help me get the manuscript in shape and to put me in contact with publishers. Chad has awfully good connections that I can use—and, of course, anything that you can do for me. . . ."

"Certainly, certainly, anything I can do. And what's the nature of the book?"

"I call it *Practical Grammar for Remedial Students*."

At which Lambert took a precipitous and liberal gulp of sherry, hoping that the conversation would make a sudden veer. However, Kate burbled on for some minutes about her project, which did, after all, as Lambert could immediately see, perfectly reflect the attitudes and motives of this charming author: the venality of one who had pursued various get-rich schemes, franchising distributorships for plastic containers, among other endeavors; the commitment of a teacher who believed that through language skills the wretched of the schools could become masters of society; the naive reverence for a book, any book; the ambition to become something, in this case, an author.

Kate paused alertly, forcing Lambert to respond. "Yes, ah, let me give your stuff the once over, and I'll see what I can do for you." And Lambert wondered momentarily what his knowledge of modern literature would allow him to do for Kate.

Settling back in her chair, Kate almost sighed, "I knew you'd want to help. You always do, don't you? Now, could I have just another splash of sherry? It's exactly the thing for afternoon, you know."

This afternoon, however, went awry. The talk was desultory, forced. Lambert felt that Kate was lingering in payment of her dues, adroitly sidestepping possibilities for a real heart-to-heart, and, indeed, when she had drained her splash, the disks whirred, the screen scrambled and then unscrambled, and Kate was reprogrammed, ready for the next episode in her scurrying day.

Glowing Kate was, at her best, the romantic flicker of a candle or the sociable warmth of a blaze in a fireplace, but all too often she was the scrambling fluorescence of a computer screen.

Her departure, almost brusque, only assured her continued presence in Lambert's thoughts. She is, he mused, the genius of the right touch at the right time.

Some months earlier, he had contrived an occasion for her to meet *the* Gerald Griffenhagen, winner of the National Book Award for poetry, frequent contributor to the *New York Review,* international man of letters. When Lambert extended the invitation to a small dinner party, Kate had bubbled with enthusiasm. The date was clear on her calendar, and this *was* another of those wonderful opportunities that Lewis created for her.

The guests—Kate, naturally without Norbert; the Grupps, faculty colleagues who were always available for the right occasions; Griffenhagen, of course; and the host—were to assemble at Lambert's apartment for cocktails, after which they would experience Mr. Ling's miracles at exquisite "La Chinoise," where the owner-chef had created a perfect blend of Oriental and *haute cuisine,* a menu justly famous among connoisseurs throughout the United States and abroad.

Lambert had arranged the event for Kate after she had mentioned her desire to meet Griffenhagen during his term as visiting professor at the university. In the two-week interlude between invitation and grand finale, Lambert had grown progressively more apprehensive, knowing the volatility of the lady's commitments. On the night of the dinner, the Grupps and Griffenhagen arrived simultaneously, and one bottle of champagne and then half of another elapsed; the caviar was disappearing; and Lambert writhed, knowing that Kate would phone to make excuses for canceling. However, it was the doorbell, not the phone, that rang, and lovely Kate was there, extending her ineffably sweet greetings and heartfelt apologies for being late. Naturally, Lambert chatted with the Grupps while Kate enchanted Griffenhagen, in minutes changing his usual dour terseness into warmly sociable volubility. It was the first time Lambert had ever heard Griffenhagen chuckle.

It was, of course, unthinkable to tamper with the destiny of Mr. Ling's *cuisine chinoise,* appointed for eight sharp, so at seven-thirty Lambert firmly suggested departure. At which, Kate approached, gave Lambert a moist kiss on the cheek, and informed him that she would have to miss the dinner, as much as she hated, in her own words, "to bug out," but other completely unavoidable obligations had arisen, and she knew that Lewis would forgive her departure, and, anyway, they would get together soon, for she *did* so want just a few friendly hours with him.

Lambert, of course, seethed during the rest of the evening.

Such reminiscing was always painful for him, and he poured himself another large glass of sherry. Did the mysterious Norbert have something to do with Kate's volatility? In any case, Lambert knew the old saw that life imitates art and immediately thought of that superb chronicle of manipulation, *The Wings of the Dove.* Thumbing through the novel, which was on his desk, he found this reading of Kate Croy's motives: " . . . every one who had anything to give—it was true, they were the fewest—made the sharpest possible bargain for it, got at least its value in return. The strangest thing, furthermore, was that this might be, in most cases, a happy understanding. The worker in one connection was the worked in another; it was as broad as it was long—with the wheels of the system, as might be seen, wonderfully oiled."

As he slipped almost into a trance, dusk now deep upon the campus, he read the passage again and again.

Chagrin, punctured ego, cynical philosophy, however, are vulnerable to the right touch. The next afternoon, a messenger delivered a plant to Lambert's office. The card read, "You are an important part of my life. Love, Kate." That was just the right touch.

Summer came. With finals over and the pomp and circumstance of commencement behind him, Lambert's existence became almost somnolent. How he enjoyed the slight melancholy of those halcyon days before summer term: the warm farewells to a few graduating seniors whom he met on campus or who made their way to his office; the necktieless ease of puttering about, catching up on the this-and-that which he had neglected during the semester; reading for the sake of reading.

One Tuesday just before noon, Kate stopped by his office and invited him to lunch, a quite unexpected pleasure. She was particularly lovely, having blossomed forth in an almost old fashioned dress (gingham? crinoline?) of pale green with white frills, fresh and starchy. Her fragrance was soft and understated, a redolence of gardens, not salons. There was something of the dance about her: stockingless (the perfect touch), minimal white sandals. Even with her wardrobe, Kate had a genius for being in tune, vibrating always in just the right key.

In an almost deserted faculty club, Kate and Lambert ate tomatoes stuffed with tuna salad and shared a bottle of excellent chardonnay, over which they lingered as they chatted.

Lambert had recently taken to characterizing his acquaintances according to their manner of locomotion. Assistant Professor Woodsman "slithered" about, whereas Mrs. Bankopf "bustled"; poor old Waldo "lumbered" through life, and Harold "shuffled." Kate "skittered" hither and yon, always on the verge, Lambert felt, of dashing off at right angles into a mysterious orbit, only to reappear, as on this afternoon, unexpectedly. But during lunch and the postprandial sipping, she seemed uncharacteristically at ease, occupied only with this moment, with Lambert's company. The conversation meandered through mutual friends, summer

attitudes

travel plans, laying in young wines as an investment, and the phenomenon that the club had promptly and accurately filled their orders.

It was a perfect luncheon on a perfect early-summer day with a perfect companion, so much so that Lambert was unprepared for two events that would break the spell.

Kate finally did get to the point, for, as Lambert profoundly knew, she always had a point. "Lewis, you know what a terrible situation I'm in. For three years I've been a fill-in on the faculty, and I never know from one semester to the next when the department won't need me. The uncertainty is killing me. I've got to get something permanent. Do you think there's any possibility that I'd be hired as an assistant professor?"

Lambert paused, fiddled with his spoon, and wondered how to avoid commitment. "Well, you know, it's a sticky situation. You haven't completed your doctorate, and even when you do, the department will be unlikely to give you a tenure-track position. You know what Groucho said: he wouldn't want to belong to a club that would accept him as a member. The department has something of the same attitude: we wouldn't want to hire anyone who had taken a degree here. After all, we know how exceptionally fine we are, yet there's always Harvard, Yale, Princeton, and Hopkins. I just can't give you much hope."

The mood was, of course, broken. Kate demolished the fragments. She picked tuna salad from between her teeth with her fingernail.

Simultaneously, Lambert and Kate gulped down the wine remaining in their glasses. Kate wiped her mouth, reprogrammed herself, rose, pecked Lambert on the cheek, told him that she had an appointment with the dean of a local junior college, and skittered away.

Two weeks before the memorial service, which was now concluding, a janitor had found Professor Lewis Lambert slumped at his desk, his face in a puddle of sherry from an overturned glass. He had died, the autopsy revealed, of a massive heart attack. On the screen of the computer by his desk was the beginning of an essay, the first sentence of which read, "In its concern for the grandiose, the literary establishment has neglected its duty to artistic voices that speak in subdued tones, modestly but veraciously."

Chad made his way to the lobby of Preston Hall. There, the mourners, decorously subdued, sipped sherry, nibbled canapes, and obligatorily, of course, reminisced about Professor Lewis Lambert. "The Trout," always one of Lambert's favorites, wafted and fanned its sinuous tail through the currents of elegiac talk; the air was funereally scented with carnations from the one spray that stood on the mahogany table between, on one side, the sherry bottles and goblets and, on the other, the large silver tray of canapes. Chad absently rolled his memorial program into a tight tube as he chatted with Dean Lester Amore and Mrs. Barbara Druse. Then, realizing his gaucherie, he unfurled the mournful banner and slid it carefully into the pocket of his jacket.

Chad, of course, was inwardly squirming, for conversation with the dean was always an intense, losing game, the dean being utterly self-assured, meticulously cordial; a scholar of some renown, an academic with the proper sentiments, an administrator who was quite capable of saying, who did, in fact, say, to a senior professor during an interview, "I understand that you're unhappy with the way things are going. I intend to make you happy again." Such impeccability, along with considerable intelligence and carefully nurtured iciness, does create, especially for untenured faculty, a situation like that when, in company, one's underwear is too tight and clawing at one's crotch is out of the question.

It was Kate who rescued Chad, just at the moment when the impulse to claw himself out of his bind was virtually overwhelming. She glowingly appeared, her smile, her warmth for Chad, her miraculous, "How wonderful to find you here!"

"Ah, Kate," said Chad, enormously relieved, "I'd been looking for you. Didn't know you were here."

attitudes

"I just arrived. I'd planned to be at the services, but at the last minute I got a call from my sister, poor Dora! and had to listen for what seemed hours to her problems. But that wouldn't interest you. Poor Dora! Thank goodness she's in Pittsburgh." apologized Kate. "Dean Amore, hello. I didn't mean to ignore you."

Brightening, the dean took Kate's hand, somewhat lingeringly. Enigmatically he asked, "Have you thought about your future?"

"I have. Yes. I do wish that I could tell you definitely what I want. I very much need a change in my life."

"A change?" the dean asked. "What sort of change?"

"How can I say? I want something more than I have, but I don't really know what I want. If I told you that I want such- and-such, you would begin to program me into some course. Would you think me silly if I said, 'I want what I can get'?"

Chad, laughingly: "Kate is another Henderson, a rain queen. She wants."

A puzzled Kate, canny enough to understand that she should not, did not ask Chad who Henderson might be or what she had to do with rain.

Dean Amore, impeccably dressed in a beige suit with purple tie and matching breast kerchief, again, lingeringly, took Kate's hand and suggested, "when we meet, I hope to point you in the right direcgtion."

Kate smiled at the dean and then changed the subject. "Lewis was our friend and mentor, wasn't he, Chad?" And she radiated gratitude for the past, expressing her sincerity by intonation, slight gesture, and a barely perceptible move toward Chad. "I did love him, you know. He was an important part of my life."

Chad, now at ease, as was everyone who chatted even for a moment with Kate, could be sentimentally wry, a welcome relief from the conventional piety that talk with the dean on this solemn occasion demanded. "I guess I'll give up sherry. If Lewis had lasted another five years, I don't think my liver would have. Still, we had good times together, Lewis and you and I."

"Chad," in a quizzical tone, a new mood, Kate probed, "do you think Dean Amore would offer me the position in the development office?"

With his almost birdlike hesitancy, Chad thought and then answered, "People *do* like your company, you know. Anyway, I've heard that Amore is horny. Maybe he wants to try your virtue."

"Lewis always called you the Dirty Young Man. You are horrible, you know."

"As far as I'm concerned," said Chad, "Amore is an iceberg, but I have a theory about male sexiness: might makes manhood, and Amore radiates power, which women—at least some women—translate into eros. I have trouble seeing him from any perspective."

"Lewis, how we'll miss him.." Then ending the conversation, she told Chad, "Let's get together for lunch before too long—and give Marge my love."

Chad watched her move across the room to where Dean Amore was chatting with President Newburn. He viewed the pantomime as the president greeted her, and he saw Amore loop his arm in hers.

"I do love her," he said, "and so did Lewis. Yes, and she has loved us truly. I'll invite her for sherry next week."

> From: Chadwick@cdu.edu
> To: OConnell@lsu.edu
>
> The MS that you generously offered to read is in the mail. Don't be reluctant to criticize.—I think you've met Kate Reese. It looks as if she's going to become a cog in Les Amore's machine. Old Lover Boy wants her in the development office and, I suspect, elsewhere. I think Amore has made a wise move. Kate is a genius at charming whomever she sets her sights on, so she'll charm bucks out of prospects for the university. But here's the mystery: Kate

is an operator, yet with her charm, there's a real capacity for affection. That's her secret. She's not cold and calculating, but warm and calculating Perhaps you've heard that Lewis Lambert died. He was in love with Kate, and, I guess, so am I. Don't get the wrong idea. I'm not in a red-hot affair, but there's no escaping Kate's mystery. She's inexplicable and irresistible.

FROM: OConnell@lsu.edu
TO: Chadwick@cdu.edu

I'll get to your MS next week. I look forward to learning what you're up to with your work.—Yeh, I met Kate Reese at the Big Convention last December. In fact, you introduced me to her. You're right about her. She has an ineffable luminosity. She's certainly one of the most attractive women I've ever encountered. Be careful, my friend. Somehow I don't think Kate could ever replace Marge for you.

FROM: Chadwick@cdu.edu
TO: OConnell@lsu.edu

Not to worry. Kate Reese is inaccessible.

8. Cigarettes; or, The Inner Sanctum

The bronze plaque on the door read "Lester I. Amore, Dean." And Kate was tempted to knock, for, in spite of her characteristic aplomb, she was still intimidated by Fortress Admin, the impregnable bulwark in which destinies were sealed, but she boldly flung open the heavy oak door and breached the fosse, the anteroom that protected Lester Amore from sappers. On guard was ever alert Arlene McDonald-Ishimura, loyal helot who recently had sacrificed her Dell PC for a Mac, which glowed and hissed at the work station beside her desk.

(Two secretarial colleagues of Arlene had carried on the following witty dialogue:

"Arlene loves her Mac."

"Oh, you know that's not true. Arlene has always been afraid of Mac. This is the first Mac she's ever had in her life."

"Don't you think Ishimura taught her some tricks with his Mac?"

"Heaven's no. She didn't ever touch his Mac.")

Kate knew that she was in a different world when she stepped into Dean Amore's precincts, a sphere of decisions, of the future, of lasers and computers, of "financial synapses" (the new term for "budgets"), hardly the world of the English Department conference room. In short, Kate was uncomfortable, but resolved; a stranger in a strange land, but stalwart.

Arlene McDonald-Ishimura had been the subject of much discussion on campus. No one had ever seen the honorable Ishimura San to whom Arlene McDonald, then forty, had entrusted her fate, but it was said that he was a sumo wrestler whom she had met on a vacation trip to Japan. Arlene herself was a ripe, matronly, plump, bespectacled peach who dripped the honey of sexuality—not beautiful, no; not stylish, no; not wanton, no. But somehow infinitely desirable, dressed conservatively, yet erotically; primly desirable. And, of course, the invidious faculty wondered about Arlene, Amore, and the famous couch. Even a virile young assistant professor such as Chad had been known to say that he wouldn't mind a quick tussle with Arlene, Dean Amore's loyal and invaluable secretary

Via the intercom, Ms. McDonald-Ishimura announced the dean's next appointment, the last of the day: Kate Reese. And Amore went to the door to escort her into his office.

Her stylish beige shoes, her rich leather handbag, her tweedy frilliness, her herbal scent—all of these (and the airiness of her step, the sweet pixyishness of her smile, the richness of her

attitudes

"Good afternoon, Dean Amore," the ballet-like grace with which she took a seat and crossed her long legs) were perfect for an afternoon meeting with the fascinatingly potent administrator.

Behind his desk, Amore sat alert, erect, and immediately performed his cigarette ritual, opening the silver case, extracting a cigarette, snapping the case shut, tapping the cigarette two or three times on it, stowing the case in his breast pocket, puffing on the unlit cigarette, studying it, exhaling clouds of the non-smoke, Kate meanwhile smiling, expectant, awaiting the pleasure of the powerful dean, who, she sensed, created pauses not because he was rattled or unsure of himself, and not because he was a thoughtful person who needed moments to decipher the riddles of human relationships, but because these lacunae, these gaps, like the mirror that hung on the wall behind his desk, made others uncomfortable and gave him the edge. The mirror behind his desk was enormously distracting to those who dealt with Amore on his own territory, for watching themselves rattled them; he considered it one of his cleverest and most successful strategies.

Another of his ploys was scrutinizing visitors from top to toe, as he was doing now with Kate, his eyes lingering first on her girlish breasts and then on the small patch of thigh that her crossed legs revealed.

Kate, however, remained the unabashed pixy, her smile serene and enigmatic, her whole posture gracefully at ease. Amore's gaze had forced more than one female visitor to shield her breasts with crossed arms and to pull her skirt down over her knees, but Kate, the dean realized, would be a worthy opponent and valuable ally, which was precisely the reason for the present meeting: to enlist Kate in his cause.

"Since we met," said Amore, "I've done some inquiring about you."

"I'm flattered that you'd be interested in me," said Kate laughingly.

"Ah, but you're a most interesting young woman. I find you're supposed to be working on a dissertation to complete your doctorate, but no one in the English Department quite knows the status of your project. In effect, you're in limbo, so now's the moment of truth. Do you want the position in the development office. Yes or no."

Her pixyish smile still glowing, Kate asked Amore, "Why me? I mean, why would you go out of your way to get me a job?"

"I think you and I can be frank with one another," said Amore, in dead earnest, his sardonic smile gone. "I find you very attractive. And I want you to do something for me."

Kate's smile transformed itself, becoming somehow knowing. Her eyes narrowed; her lips changed configuration by fractions of an inch; the crinkles around her mouth rearranged themselves minutely. This was not Kate the pixy, but Kate the knowing, clever operator, who would play her hand astutely, reserving trumps for the crisis; it was Kate the card-counter, who filed away in memory the tricks that had been played and thus could guess or sometimes calculate the exact power of her opponent's hand.

"Lester—I can call you Lester, can't I?—"

"Just call me Les."

"Okay, Les. I have no idea what you mean about finding me attractive. I'm glad that you do. Once again I'm flattered. I find you attractive too. Are you flattered?"

"So, then, let's knock this stuff off and get down to cases," said Lester Amore, now in dead seriousness.

"Marvelous. I like directness. I appreciate frankness." And Kate, as if by magic, resumed her pixyish charm, her glowing smile.

"Would you, Les, do one thing now to show me your sincerity? Hang something over that mirror. You've no idea how much it annoys me."

Lester Amore laughed. "You are clever," he said admiringly. "Suppose we both move to the couch—which will make equals of us. You on one end and me on the other."

attitudes

"Agreed," said Kate as she decorously and faultlessly arose, walked the short distance across the thick carpet, and assumed her graceful position on the far end of the deanly couch.

Dean Amore settled on his end of the legendary banc and began the cigarette ritual, but without removing a cigarette, he stuffed the silver case back in his pocket.

"You know Bobby Druse quite well, don't you?" asked Amore.

"We have a standing date for bowling and lunch every Tuesday," replied Kate. "I think I can say that she and I are friends."

"I don't suppose you know that Bobby is a very wealthy woman. I've heard as much as five hundred million."

"Yes, I've heard that myself," said Kate.

Amore automatically fished for his cigarettes, but satisfied himself by clasping his hands behind his head and smiling at Kate. She was an interesting mixture of innocence and experience, of openness and guile, of naiveté and wisdom. One could not determine whether she was extremely bright or merely extremely clever, but, in any case, she had abilities that Amore appreciated more and more as he experienced and thought about them. It was, after all, rare for anyone to get the upper hand in relations with Lester Amore, and Kate, in the past few minutes, had succeeded in making her opponent circle warily, his guard up.

"Suppose you could help Bobby enjoy her money—would you do that? She and Mel don't travel; they don't buy art. Bobby drives that hideous red Buick. Why have money if it's not used for some purpose?"

"Let me be a sibyl," said Kate laughingly. "I should urge Bobby to accompany us to Europe for the summer, at her expense, of course. Over and back on a chartered jet."

"That sounds a bit like Henry James to me. The innocent American discovering the old but corrupt culture of Europe—with Kate Reese and Lester Amore as docents, of course. But it's not quite what I had in mind. I'd like very much to encourage Bobby to donate a substantial amount toward the new science complex."

"Don't you mean that you'd like *me* to encourage Bobby to donate money to the university?" said Kate.

"In fact, yes."

"I'm puzzled. What should be my motive for working on Bobby? Altruistic love of higher education?"

"Well, if you're Bobby's friend, you could do it for her. Don't you think she'd find it exciting to be a mover and shaker in the development of the university?"

"Possibly," said Kate.

"And then, of course, there's your future. The development office is a real power vacuum. If someone like you stepped into that place, it could become a power center. Phil Mardirosian has doddled around for five years without raising any real money. Would you like to be the university's new development officer?"

"I translate 'development officer' as 'fund raiser.'"

"Something like that," said Lester Amore. "The more I think about it, the more convinced I am that you're the perfect candidate."

"I really don't know what to say," responded Kate.

"We'll get together again soon. You have a few days to make your decision." Amore stood up, signaling the end of the interview. "It's cocktail time," he said, as Kate rose from the couch. "Could you join me at the faculty club?"

He approached Kate and grasped the upper, fleshy part of her arm, looking straight into her eyes.

"Another time," said Kate, smiling and staring fixedly into his eyes. "Yes, I'd like to work in the development office."

As she walked out the door of his office, Lester Amore reached for a cigarette, and Mrs. Donna Amore brushed past him into his office.

"GAWD, Lester, is she ANOTHER member of your harem?"

Amore closed the door to his office and hissed, "Jesus Christ, don't you have any sense? You don't need to announce your paranoia to Arlene. That's like announcing it to the world."

attitudes

"Your AFFAIRS are public knowledge ANYWAY. You're SO dense, SUCH a schmuck. Haven't you heard ANY of the WISEcracks about your couch?"

"And haven't you heard any of the wisecracks about your phony hairdo. People call you 'the brunette Carol Channing.' Not just your hairdo. God, I'm sick of your TRYING to ACT sophisticated. I know you got your culture at Texas A&M. Those farmers have a way about them. You should've married one."

"WELL, where did you get YOUR high-and-mighty culture? From that BITCH you called a MOTHER? GAWD, I was so HAPPY when she croaked. Twelve YEARS of putting up with HER. You should've STOWED her away in a REST home instead of letting her LIVE with US. 'Honey doll, where's my pills?' 'Honey doll, could you bring me a cup of tea?' 'Honey doll, I'm constipated.' GAWD. when she CROAKED, I felt liberated."

With icy calmness, Dean Lester Amore said, "You cannot. You dare not speak about my mother that way."

Suddenly the iceberg melted and Dean Lester Amore clasped Mrs. Donna Amore to himself and sobbed on her shoulder, but Mrs. Donna Amore pushed Dean Lester Amore away and spat out, "You're disgusting. DISGUSTING."

> Dear Aunt Lucie,
>
> You promised to send me the pictures of Mom when she was a teenager, but I haven't received them yet. I'm putting together an album of her life and writing her biography, and I need those pictures. Take care of yourself. I enjoyed the oatmeal cookies that you sent. They were just like the ones Mom used to bake.
>
> As for your coming to visit us, you know that Donna and I would love to have you, but right now I'm so tied up with my duties at the university that I couldn't do your visit justice, and Donna is thinking

about taking an extended trip to Europe to study art.

We'll look forward to seeing you perhaps next year.

          Love,
          Les

Dear Lester,

I'm enclosing the pictures of your mother. There are some things about Maybell that you don't know, and since you're working on the memorial album and are planning to write her biography, let me tell you, she was a very popular girl in high school. The picture of Maybell in the mother hubbard was taken her last semester in high school. After graduation, our parents sent her away, to stay with Uncle Jack and Aunt Flossie, in Tuscaloosa. When she came back from Alabama, she didn't wear the mother hubbard any more. Draw your own conclusions. If you want any more details about your mother, call me, and I'll give you as much as I know.

          Love,
          Aunt Lucie

9. Tuna Casserole; or, Behind the Closed Door

Four women, not youngsters, but autumnal. One heard their laughter and the intermittent rumble and crash. On this fine fall day in early November, they were absorbed in one another, unaware that groups to right and left, equally self-absorbed, chatted, laughed, and also listened subliminally to the rumble-crash. Amid others, the four ladies were quite alone.

    Rumble-crash. Rumble-crash. Rumble-crash.

attitudes

Bobby Druse, Donna Amore, Cora Newburn, and Kate Reese were bowling together in the din of Southland Superlanes.

* * *

With a sense of relief one Monday morning, Bobby watched Mel climb into his Chevrolet Lumina and pull out of the driveway. She sat at the kitchen table, sipping coffee and listening to "The Music of Your Life," the oldies and goldies that she had danced to in high school and college.

When the phone rang, she glanced at the caller ID. It was Kate. Bobby concluded the brief conversation with, "Sure. I'll see you about one at Mimi's."

* * *

Their BLTs eaten, the postprandial coffee once again before them, Kate got right to the point. "You know, Bobby, you're remarkable, the most interesting of all my friends. You have potential that maybe you don't realize."

Bobby chuckled. "Yeh, I know I can improve my game. I keep missing easy spares."

"Oh, you and your sardonic sense of humor. That's what I like about you. But you really don't take yourself seriously enough."

Bobby contemplated the diamond ring on her right hand, absent-mindedly memorializing Bert Redd, gone now for nearly twenty years. With her little finger, she twisted the ring so that it magnified and returned the glint of light from a bulb in the ceiling of Mimi's Restaurant.

"You could do such wonderful things, you know." Kate took Bobby's right hand and looked closely at the ring. "See, your ring is just a small token of your potential."

"So what is my potential?" asked Bobby.

"Who knows? But you should explore. What if you could have a big influence on the university? You'd find that exciting, wouldn't you?"

Bobby laughed, loudly, indecorously, causing heads to turn. "God, you mean spend time with Potty Tinker and Waldo Clemens and the other literary lights in the English department? No thanks."

"I'll tell you what. I don't believe in destiny. I think life is a crap game. Sometimes you win, and sometimes you lose, but you've got to throw the dice to find out which. Let's have some fun. Let's get together with Dean Amore's and President Newburn's wives. See what they're like. See where things go. Are you interested?"

"Sure," said Bobby with wide grin. "Let's invite them to go bowling with us."

"Yes, let's," said Kate.

"You're not serious?"

"I've never been more serious in my life."

* * *

Tuesday, Wednesday, Thursday, Friday, Saturday—as the week moved toward its close, Mel became more and more certain that something was up, for Bobby skittered about, leaving this task undone to start on another, which she would then abandon; drinking half a can of cola, leaving the can in the bathroom or bedroom, and absent-mindedly opening a new one; staring at the newspaper without reading, as her morning coffee grew cold and her boiling eggs became hard. Of course, Mel could have asked her what was in the works, but that was not his way. He preferred a Holmesian line of induction based on clues meticulously assembled, and he watched for hints that would lead him inevitably to the dénouement.

Sunday afternoon, over a dinner of potroast and vegetables, with Mel's beloved brown gravy, Bobby said, "I want to talk to you."

"So talk," said Mel, shoveling a chunk of roast into his mouth.

"I'm going bowling with Mrs. Newburn, Mrs. Amore, and Kate tomorrow."

Mel was immobilized, his mouth open, a wad of half-chewed potroast about to drop onto his plate. But he soon realized that Bobby must be joking, and he good naturedly joined in the fun. Occasionally she did have an impishness that he enjoyed. "And, naturally, you'll have lunch at the restaurant in the bowling alley. I bet their cheeseburgers are out of this world."

"I hadn't thought about where we'd have lunch. I'll see what the others want to do. Do you think they'd like Chinese food?"

"Oh sure. After you get through bowling, you ought to take them to the China Kitchen for some egg rolls and chow mein. Nothing like a fortune cookie to top off a good meal and an edifying experience."

"Well, to tell you the truth, I think the China Kitchen is sort of crummy, and since I'm the hostess, I'd like to take them to a nicer place. I'll get Kate to make some suggestions."

"Bobby, there's no chance, is there, that you're not joking?"

"I was going to invite Mrs. Zucker, but I thought maybe that wasn't the thing to do. She'd feel like a bump on a log. I'm sure she couldn't bowl."

"You *are* serious, aren't you? I can't believe this. You really did invite them to go bowling with you?"

"Kate suggested it."

"My God! What will Newburn and Amore think? That goddamn crummy bowling alley. Oh shit! I've never in my life seen anything like this." Mel was ragingly incoherent. He ripped the refrigerator door open, snatched a diet Dr. Pepper, slammed the door, popped the top, and took a deep swig, which calmed him somewhat. "They won't show up. You know that. They'll never go bowling with you or anybody else, not Cora Newburn or Donna Amore. Not on your life. Kate will go, but not those other bitches."

As the large Budweiser clock on the wall at Southland Super Lanes registered high noon, Bobby threw the last ball of the three-game series. Her companions had already changed from their rented bowling shoes into their street wear and were ready for whatever might next eventuate.

While Bobby changed shoes, Donna Amore gushed: "That was such a UNIQUE experience. My goodness, I became absorbed, absolutely ABSORBED, in the game. I had no IDEA how difficult bowling is. My whole ATTITUDE has changed. And we can thank BOBBY for this MARVELOUS adventure."

Cora Newburn—gray-haired, puffy though quite slim, her face splotched—seemed impatient, ill-at-ease; she was fidgety and glanced here and there, as if looking for someone or something. When Donna asked, "Don't you think this was a WONDERFUL morning?" Cora answered distractedly, "Are we going to eat lunch soon? I need a—I'm very hungry."

"Oh yes," said Bobby, "we're on our way to lunch, at 'Les Mille Fleurs.' Kate says it's a very good restaurant."

In a hybrid tone, part abject pleading and part irked annoyance, Cora replied, "I don't want to drive half way across the state just for lunch, and, anyway, I don't like French food."

Characteristically, Kate rescued the situation even before it had become dangerous. "I think it'd be fun to eat here," she said. "Why not go all the way? We've been bowling. Let's eat in the coffee shop right here."

Bobby was elated. "I like the food here. And maybe they wouldn't have let us in at Mille Fleurs—in our bowling clothes, I mean."

Cora was relieved. "I'd just as soon have a BLT right here."

Pleased, displeased, or indifferent, Donna Amore revealed nothing and, uncharacteristically, did not gush.

When they were seated at a table by a window in the coffee shop, a void during which there was no talk, a gap in time be-

attitudes

tween recreation and alimentation, Cora again seemed uneasy, squirming in her seat, glancing rapidly about. "Aren't they ever going to wait on us?"

When the waitress finally arrived, she and Bobby had a reunion of sorts. "Hi, dearie. How'd you do today?"

"Not so well," replied Bobby. "I had a 450 scratch series."

"You can't click every time. Now, what can I get for you ladies, or do you need more time to decide?"

"Does anyone want a drink?" asked Cora? "I think maybe I'd like one."

"What'll it be, dearie," asked the waitress.

"Vodka on the rocks. And as long as you're at it, make it a double."

"Anything for anyone else?"

"Well, Cora," said Donna Amore, "you can't say that I'm a POOR sport. Since SHE'S having a double, I'll have a double Rob Roy on the rocks."

"Just a glass of white wine for me," chimed Kate.

"Anything for you, dearie?" the waitress asked Bobby.

"Give me Blackjack on the rocks," said Bobby.

The drinks having arrived, Kate tasted her wine knowingly, Bobby rattled the ice cubes in her glass and then sipped at her Jack Daniels, Donna ate her maraschino, and Cora, holding her vodka in both slightly trembling hands, sipped eagerly.

The waitress having, in due course, returned for orders, Bobby took her by the hand warmly and attempted to remedy an obvious gaffe. "Gladys, I forgot to introduce you to these ladies. Cora Newburn, Donna Amore, and Kate Reese, this is Gladys. I'm sorry I don't know your last name."

"That's all right, dearie. Happy to meet you. And now can I take your orders."

Cora found she wasn't very hungry after all, but would take another double vodka, just to be sociable. Donna thought a cheeseburger sounded just DELICIOUS, and she WOULD have a Coke with it. Club sandwiches and coffee for Kate and Bobby.

When the orders arrived, Cora gave her second double vodka as much concentrated attention as she had bestowed on the first one; four long sips, and only the ice remained. After having sucked the last tinge of flavor from her glass, Cora excused herself, asking Bobby the location of the ladies' room. "Just through the bar," answered Bobby.

"Kate, what are YOU doing now?" asked Donna.

"Doing? Well, I'm teaching a sophomore survey—you know, as they say, Beowulf to Virginia Woolf—at the university and two composition classes at a junior college. I've been one of those freeway flyers. But Dean Amore has offered me a position in the development office, and I've accepted."

"That's JUST marvelous. So you'll be WORKING with Lester. Yes, Lester DOES know how to PICK the right people for HIS purposes. Congratulations. I KNOW that you and Lester will hit it OFF."

Bobby took the last bite of her club sandwich. "Boy, I must say I wouldn't be enthusiastic about becoming permanent in that English department." But she caught herself and began to backtrack. "What I mean, Donna, is that I'm just not the sort of person who would want to teach of a bunch of bubble-gummers from Beverly Hills."

"Yes, I KNOW," said Donna Amore. "The university has a TERRIBLE reputation. People think it's JUST a social club for rich kids. But that's NOT true. Les has made a REAL effort to bring in WORTHY students from ALL walks of life."

The conversation dribbled on for ten, fifteen, twenty minutes. Cora Newburn's chair was still empty.

"I wonder if she's alright?" said Kate.

"Maybe she's SICK," said Donna

"I'll go and see." And Bobby rose from the table and headed through the bar for the ladies' room.

Cora was sitting at the bar, a large drink-on-the rocks before her. Bobby hesitated, embarrassed, watching Cora gulp at her drink, and then returned to the table.

"Well?" said Kate.

"Is she ALRIGHT?" asked Donna.

"I think she's alright," answered Bobby. "She's at the bar."

"We'd BETTER rescue her," said Donna Amore. "She has a REAL drinking problem, you know. I'll get her."

Shortly, Donna returned with a wobbly Cora, who sagged into her chair.

Signalling the waitress, Donna ordered a cup of coffee for Cora, and long minutes of silence were broken when Cora blurted slurrily, "Ya know somethin.' Harvey Newburn is a pompous jerk. You don' know what it's like being married to a big president. Big deal."

"I think we'd BETTER go," said a concerned Donna.

Bobby and Kate both gazed at a point far off in space, light years from the table in the coffee shop of Southland Super Bowl.

"Ya know what? Ol' Harvey made me come bowling. Yep. Ol' Harvey, the Big President, says to me, 'Cora, there's gold in them thar bowling alleys. Bobby Druse is worth four hundred, maybe five hundred million.' God, Bobby, are you really that loaded?"

"Right now I don't think I'm as loaded as you are," said Bobby.

"Well, lemme tell ya, sweetheart, ol' Harvey thinks he can tap you for five or ten mill or so. Yessir, ol' Harvey's hot on your trail. Don't you wanna put a couple million into the new science complex. Ol' Harvey'd make sure your name was on one of the restrooms. Just think of it: the Bobby Druse Memorial Ladies' Lounge." And Cora spiritedly began to hum an off-key version of "Pomp and Circumstance."

In a hissing whisper, Donna said to Cora, "I think you should just shut up. You're DRUNK." And then to Bobby and Kate: "Let's get her out of here."

Bobby on one arm, Donna on the other, Cora, loudly singing ("Land of hope and glory . . ."), made her way to the big red Buick in the parking lot of Southland Super Bowl.

When the Buick pulled into the driveway of 1415 Dimple Dell Drive, Mel was in his study, having returned from the university early, fearing the absolute, ultimate worst in regard to the bowling party, but, impelled by morbid curiosity, not wanting to miss a single excruciating moment of the humiliation that was in progress.

Meeting the ladies at the door, Mel was shocked to see Cora Newburn standing limply between Kate and Bobby, who supported her on each arm.

"She's had a heart attack!" flustered Mel. "I knew something would happen. Get a doctor. Is Greg home? Call Greg."

Donna, an Amazon generalissima at rigid attention, arms staight along her sides, bosom outthrust, chin folded in, head held high, announced, "She is NOT having a heart attack. She has had TOO MUCH to drink."

With a good deal of bustle, Cora was deposited on the living room couch—the same couch, of course, with which Emma Zucker had merged and on which Mel had sat with Kate when the door closed on his guests from the party. Half lying, half sitting, one leg on the cusions, one heel on the floor, Cora drunkenly hummed her paean to the academy.

And then she barfed, copiously, unwrenchingly. Wiping her mouth with her hand, she hummed on.

"Oh, goodness!" said Bobby, rushing from the room.

"Oh, dear!" said Kate, turning away.

"Oh, my GAWD!" said Donna, immobilized.

"Oh, shit!" said Mel, forgetting himself.

Bobby returned with wet towels, and, cradling Cora's head, began to soothe her and wipe her face. "There, there," crooned Bobby, "you'll feel better now. We'll get you upstairs so you can rest."

Bobby urged Cora to her feet and led her haltingly up the stairs to the master bedroom.

Mel, left with Kate, Donna, and the soiled couch,

was in a dilemma. Should he wait for Bobby to return and clean the couch? If so, what to do in the meantime?

attitudes

He solved the problem by inviting Kate and Donna into the den. Can I get you anything? Coffee? Tea? A drink?"

But Kate had to rush off. She and Norbert were entertaining that evening, and Kate had to prepare.

Donna wanted nothing but, obviously, to escape. When Kate had departed, with Mel's profuse apologies for the mess, Donna told Mel the story of the luncheon at Southland Super Bowl, and also that Cora, in the back seat of the red Buick, had pulled a silver flask from her purse and had drained it in one long pull.

Bobby descended the stairs, joining Mel and Donna. "I've gotten her cleaned up, and she's in bed now. I think she'll be alright."

"I've GOT to go," said Donna. "What'll I DO with Cora? She CAME with me."

"You go on," said Bobby. "Poor Mrs. Newburn doesn't feel like going anywhere yet. We'll get her home."

Mel and Bobby bade farewell to Donna Amore. Once again the door closed, and once again Mel flopped on the couch.

"What a mess," disconsolately. "What a lousy mess!" emphatically. "What a goddamn mess!" enragedly. " Now what're we supposed to do with that lush upstairs? Why'd you let her get drunk? Oh shit!"

With icy calmness, Bobby responded: "I want to tell you two things, and I want you to listen. In the first place, don't ridicule Mrs. Newburn. She's a sad person, and she doesn't need someone taking cheap shots at her. In the second place, don't blame me for everything. Don't blame me for anything."

"Don't blame me for anything," echoed Mel in falsetto.

"Ah, shove it!" said Bobby.

Mel grabbed a copy of the *Times Literary Supplement* from the coffee table and began to leaf through it. He was keenly aware, however, of Bobby's phone call.

"Hello. This is Professor Druse's wife. Could I speak to President Newburn? . . . It's very important. . . . I know he's busy, but his wife isn't feeling well. . . . She's at my home. . . . Yes, I can hold."

Mel groaned inarticulately and threw his newspaper on the floor.

"Hello, President Newburn? This is Bobby Druse. Your wife is at our place, and she's quite ill. . . . I see. . . . Well, quite a bit, actually. . . . Yes, of course. . . . We'll expect you, then. Goodbye."

"So what's the deal?" asked a subdued Mel.

"President Newburn knows that his wife has a drinking problem. He'll be here in about an hour to pick her up."

Humbly, contritely, Mel uttered an emotive "Oh shit!" He picked the *Times Literary Supplement* up from the floor, reassembled and straightened it, replaced it on the coffee table, and sat in the posture of "The Thinker" on the couch. The radio, which Bobby had turned on, was playing

> *I must have that doggie in the window,*
> *The one with the waggily tail.*
> *I must have that doggie in the window.*
> *I do hope that doggie's for sale.*

And Mel could hear Bobby in the kitchen, getting dinner.

When the doorbell rang an hour later, Mel had prepared his face again to meet whatever face he might meet, and the face he did meet was that of President Harvey Newburn.

Unctuously, in a sick-room voice, in the tone reserved for conversation around the mortally ill, Mel, taking President Newburn's elbow, said, "She's upstairs."

"Professor Druse," said a stentorian President Newburn, "I'm grateful to you for taking care of Cora. You understand that she has a little problem. Every now and then she forgets herself and has one or two too many, and she just can't handle the stuff. I'll collect her and take her home."

Cora, however, was not yet collectable. Her parts were so utterly strewn as to make pulling them together, for the time being, impossible. When Harvey Newburn tried to awaken her, first with an authoritative "Cora, it's time to go home!" and then with an equally authoritative shaking, he found that all of his puissance availed naught. Trying to lift her was like managing a hundred and twenty pounds of Jello. With a sigh, he let her sink back into the bed and uttered an authoritative "Oh, shit!"

Mel, who had hovered behind Newburn, suggested a cocktail, and Newburn eagerly accepted.

In the den, martinis in hand, the professor and the president, equally ill at ease, danced a stiffly formal give-and-take of

"Well, the new student center is nearly complete. An attractive building."

"Yes, indeed. I had to scramble for funds to build that one, but I, so to speak, captured my man. Hahaha. As you know, George Billington—he's the oil man—put up the three million for the center."

"The campus is looking good. I've noticed a lot of planting and landscaping."

"Oh, to be sure. To be sure. Mrs. Stackpole, the widow of Roger Stackpole (he was the banker), gave us the money for the landscaping. I worked on Clotilda Stackpole for three years to get that half million. Drank tea until it was running out my ears. She has a cocker spaniel. 'Sweety' she calls it. Damn thing bit me twice and used my leg for a fire hydrant."

"Well, we faculty members always wonder what the future holds. Where do you see the university going in the next decade?"

"We need a new science complex. I've started to make contacts. Wonderful opportunity for givers. Three buildings. Each one needs a name. What a great memorial, to have your name on a building."

Bobby now made her first appearance. Courtly, handsome, impeccably dressed Harvey Newburn rose when she entered the room and graciously kissed her cheek.

"Awfully good of you folks to take care of Cora. Certainly decent of you. I'm afraid I'm interrupting your evening. Now I've imposed on you good folks enough. I'll see if Cora can function well enough to get to the car."

"Maybe," said Bobby, "you'd like some dinner with us. We have plenty. Then your wife could rest a little longer before you take her home."

President Newburtn authoritatively accepted the invitation.

When Bobby put the dinner on the table, President Harvey Newburn exclaimed, "Tuna casserole. I love it!"

> FROM: PresNewburn@cdu.edu
> TO: Betty@Smurthwaite.com
>
> You must be surprised to hear from me. It's been a long time since we've gotten in touch. How long? Ten years? Twenty? I often think of you and of the good times we had at Dartmouth. The biggest mistake in my life was marrying Cora instead of you. Cora is a lush, a sloppy drunk. She disgraces me again and again. What are you doing? Is Hal still in the plumbing business? Do you have kids? Let's keep in touch.

> FROM: Betty@Smurthwaite.com
> TO: PresNewburn@cdu.edu
>
> It's a real shocker to hear from you. . I'm so sorry to learn that Cora is having problems. She and I were good buddies, actually roommates, at Dartmouth. Yes, Hal's business in thriving, and we have three kids. Two daughters are still in high school, and our son, Hal, Jr., is a freshman at Dartmouth. Harve, I can't resist. There was no way that I thought about spending a life with you. We didn't really date. The three of us palled around, but other than that—nothing. Take care of Cora. She's worth your love

and concern. And, as I remember you, I wonder if you haven't been a contributing factor in her alcoholism. Sorry to be so frank, but that's the way I am. Cheers!

10. Crêpes; or Men, Women, and Monsters

Heather Figaro had cheerily called, "Goodnight, Dr. Druse," and Mel was alone in the English Department central office, slumped at his desk, in a troubled reverie, musing about the strange new course his life had taken since the momentous party. The African violet on the coffee table was drooping sadly, and Mel dispiritedly poured the remains of cold coffee from his mug into the pot, then flopped once again into the chair behind the desk.

In his position as department head, he was, if possible, even more isolated and alone than he had been as the department specialist in Restoration literature. Before he took the helm, he had, by virtue of his membership in the crew, alliance against the captain, but now that he ruled the bridge, he keenly sensed the loneliness of command, and even more poignantly, he knew that his ship was small stuff in a flotilla, the destiny of which was controlled by the likes of Les Amore, Vice-Admiral Lester I. Amore, with his one-star flag and private gig.

Mel's consciousness bored more deeply into the puzzles of his existence. Ken Turing had told him, "Never look upward toward the top of the Great Chain of Being, because if you do, you always know that you're below someone. If you cast your eyes ever downward, you live with the heartening sense that there's always someone below you." Yet Mel had cast not just furtive glances upward, but prolonged, longing gazes; he was transfixed by the images of Lester Amore, Harvey Newburn, and Donald Schwann. The mystery of hierarchy entranced him, was narcotic. This much he knew: those above him in the Great Chain of Being—stretching even beyond Donald Schwann—were very much like

Dean Lester Amore, unapproachable, controlled, impenetrable and hence mysterious.

Boozy, ashen Cora Newburn; brassy, vivid Donna Amore; waddling, rumbling Emma Zucker; charming, elfin Kate Reese; shining, vivacious Cynthia Golden—they, Mel knew, had spent the afternoon with Bobby, listening to Max Schinken discuss *The Wings of the Dove,* about which Bobby had been enthusiastic, the first time Mel had ever known her to get into "serious" fiction.

Mel, not feeling up to sociability with anyone, had dallied in his office until he was sure that the guests would have departed his home. Gathering up his briefcase and umbrella and glancing about to see if he had forgotten anything, Mel made toward the outer door of the English department central office, meeting Sunshine, the janitor, who was just coming in.

"Evenen, Dr. Mel," said the sunny Sunshine.

"Good evening to you," replied Mel, cordially enough, but without pausing to talk.

"Yah'll have a good dinner, yuh hear. And tell Mrs. Mel I said hello."

***

When Mel arrived at Dimple Dell Drive, he found Kate Reese's silver Nissan sports car in his driveway. And in the living room, on the couch, sat Bobby and Kate, talking.

Bobby had decided that Mel could take Kate and her to dinner at fashionable La Pouce, specializing in crêpes, and Mel was outwardly gracious though his inward reaction was a characteristically Drusian "Oh shit!" for he had wanted to remove his trousers, drink a martini, watch the news, eat some dinner, and then catch a movie, any movie, on cable TV; that is, Mel was not exactly anti-social in mood, but highly asocial: he wanted peace, quiet, and solitude.

Kate, her sensitive antennae ever atwitter, knew that Mel was grumpily anti-social and that he exchanged amenities only from a sense of duty, being trapped. He was, then, a challenge to her, as the sullen intricacies of logic must challenge mathematicians for no other reason than that they are there. Kate would make Mel smile, not grudgingly, not woodenly as a social duty, but glowingly and genuinely. Without being sexy in any vulgar sense, Kate could be infinitely seductive, her aura not the rank effluvium of, for instance, Marilyn Monroe, but a subtler, finer emanation, alembicated femininity.

"We were waiting for you," said Kate. "After all, Bobby and I feel incomplete without you."

Kate had shifted slightly as she spoke, sinking more deeply into the luxuriance of the couch. As if she were controlled by a rheostat, she began to glow a bit more brightly, to smile more radiantly. The vulgar term is "turning on the charm." Kate did not "turn on" the charm; it was a part of her and, hence, sincere, spontaneous, uncalculating. Just as one feels that a great prizefighter is spontaneously pugnacious or that a great thinker is spontaneously inventive—for certainly Ali and Einstein did not spend their lives calculating—so Kate was simply by nature charming, and if this charm, this reflexive way of dealing with the world, brought its rewards, well, then, did not champions always receive their trophies and prizes?

"How'd the afternoon go?" inquired Mel.

"Oh, Max Schinken is so—" bubbled Kate. "But let Bobby tell you."

"Yeh, Max is great," said Bobby. "He knows just how to talk to a non-literary bunch like us, without making us feel stupid. A non-literary bunch like most of us, I should say. Kate is literary in the official sense. But I think everyone enjoyed the afternoon. Emma seemed to appreciate the lunch. Dora looked better than I've ever seen her—more color, less puffiness. I think she's feeling better. At least I hope so, poor soul."

And Bobby talked on, chattingly, pleasantly. She was genuinely fond of Emma and Dora; hence, they worried her—both with compulsions, which, as Bobby commented, were ruining their lives and would ultimately kill them.

"Kate and I are starved," said Bobby. "You're elected to take us to La Pouce for crêpes."

"I will not run, and if elected I will not serve—or something like that. But if I am really elected," said Mel, brightening with a sudden idea, "we'll ask Greg and Cynthia if they want to join us."

* * *

"The spinach and feta crêpe is superb," said Kate; "I can recommend it."

The five of them sat at the table with its checkered cloth, in La Pouce with its quaint décor, and subconsciously heard the discrete baroque music that bubbled quietly in the herbally fragrant atmosphere, as they sipped a California zinfandel chosen by Kate, who was too independent to be intimidated by the Gallic ambience of the restaurant. If Kate had been dining at the popular and chauvinistically named Café California, she would have ordered French wine.

"This zinfandel is different," said Cynthia. "I respect the native wines. Anyway, we didn't want to turn the evening into a wine tasting, did we? For the price, you can't beat this Heritage zinfy. It's always a safe bet. That's why people who don't know much about wine stick with it."

"Last night Bertie and I shared a bottle of Gemello merlot. Gemello is our great unsung winery, don't you think, Cynthia?" said a smiling Kate with infinite sweetness.

"Oh, Greg and I have tried Gemello now and then, but we've found their reds to be a trifle rough, too oaky, really. We think Chateau Lafitte is doing a marvelous job, especially with whites," and Cynthia, smiling, was no less sweet in tone than Kate.

"When I was in Germany I drank a lot of wine," said Mel, as he stuffed a hunk of kielbasa and egg crêpe into his mouth. No one really heard Mel in any case, for Greg was obviously preparing to speak, and everyone looked attentively to him.

"Cyn and I don't make a big thing about wine, but we know what we're drinking, and I think you'd be impressed with the selection we've laid in over the last ten or twelve years. But all this wine talk—it gets to be one-ups-man-ship. It's *the* subject in the doctors' lounge at the hospital. Lord, the members of the doctors' symphony talk wine instead of music."

"Yeh, I agree with Greg," opined Mel. "All this wine talk gets to be a pain in the. . . . I mean, in the department you'd think oenology was a branch of literature, the way my colleagues talk about it. Yeh, I agree with Greg. It gets to be downright pretentious."

"We could use another bottle of wine," suggested sweet Cynthia. "What would you recommend, Kate?"

"I think we should leave the choice up to you. Anything on the list that you and Greg have in your collection?" Kate reached across the table and briefly touched Cynthia's hand.

"There's a Moose Leap chardonnay that might be drinkable," suggested Cynthia. "We had a red. Why don't we try a white?"

Bobby, with an edge of impatience, said, "Why don't those of us who want more wine just order a glass? I've had enough, myself."

"Actually, I'd like a beer," said Mel.

"Well," said Cynthia, "Greg and I would like some more wine, and we really don't want to run the risk of a house wine. I'm sure Kate would help us with another bottle."

"Actually, no," said Kate, "but you guys go ahead. If you want more wine, by all means, have it. Enjoy yourselves."

Golden Cynthia hardened slightly. "We hardly need more wine. We thought others might enjoy a glass or two. We don't want to be party poopers. If no one else wants more, neither do Greg and I."

Having shoveled the last of his crèpe into his mouth, Mel, as he chewed and swallowed, branched the conversation by some fifteen or twenty degrees. "Greg, I hear there's a lot of alcoholism among doctors—alcoholism and drug addiction. How many of your colleagues are lushes or addicts or both?"

Greg, who had been slumping a bit at the table, having forgotten for the moment that he was a physician—not professionally at this time, but socially, anthropologically—pulled himself up, smiled indulgently, and undertook patiently to answer Mel.

But Mel, with a glazed stare toward Greg, had drifted into a reverie. He was back in his office at the university, thinking of Dean Amore. "You asshole," he muttered.

Greg asked, startled, "What? What was that?"

"Just clearing my throat," replied Mel.

"As I was saying, the notion that doctors. . . ."

But Mel was staring at golden-haired Cynthia and for the first time noticed her cabbage breasts and her coarse straw-blonde hair and grainy complexion. Her underwear, Mel knew instinctively, would be black, and not fresh. The luxuriance of her cheeks had become angular; the ripeness of her lips, a vivid scar; the wondrous blue eyes, gimlet squints. Cynthia was, as a matter of fact, frightening.

Mel had never before seen Kate overdone, plastered with makeup, mascara, lipstick—even perhaps false eyelashes. But now she was grotesque, the effluvium of her cheap perfume as heavy as the oily fly spray that he remembered from his youth. She seemed, as Mel stared at her, both feline and rankly sexual.

"Are we ready for the check?" asked Bobby, obviously bored by the wine talk that Cynthia and Kate were still carrying on and by the lecture on medical responsibilities that Greg was delivering for Mel's benefit.

Mel started, sat up straight in his chair, and shook his head, like a retriever just coming out of the water. No one was talking now, and Mel noted that Kate's right hand lightly rested on Greg's arm.

"I want a little goddamn courtesy. You give me a little courtesy and we'll get along fine. You don't give me courtesy, I'll make

attitudes

sure you're out on your ass. You got that, baby. Nobody screws around with Herbie."

* * *

That night, with Bobby breathing softly and regularly at his side, sleeping, as she always did, peacefully and almost silently, Mel contemplated the Great Chain of Being. In his groggy fantasy, massive links of gold, self-illuminated, glowed in the profound blackness of time, from any vantage point extending infinitely upward and downward, world upon world. If the chain were infinite, then there could be no higher or lower, just above and below, up and down. No matter how many links you climbed up the chain, a naked mortal straining both muscles and will to pull yourself one link more and yet another link, you gained no altitude, never got higher.

Mel absorbedly, in the trance of consciousness just before sleep, watched himself struggling upward on the golden, glowing chain. He was naked, his flabby pectorals and biceps barely outlined, his penis hardly discernible, retracted almost completely, his bald head reflecting the auric glow of the Great Chain.

The last thing in Mel's consciousness before the blackness of sleep was bit of an image, not even an idea, but a sense of profound sadness.

11 Bach and Spaghetti

Dean Lester Amore nodded at acquaintances who passed him on the stoa of Schwann Hall, where the School of Music held concerts and the School of Performing Arts staged dramas. Before entering the hall, Professor Pottle Tinker greeted Amore. "Hello . . . hrumph . . . Les. Didn't know . . . hrumph . . . you were a fan of . . . hrumph . . . Bach."

Oh, yes. Yes. I have the Glenn Gould CDs—Bach's toccatas. Wonderful background music."

"Background music. I . . . hrumph . . . have never heard . . . hrumph . . . the toccatas in an elevator. Hrumph. I think . . . hrumph . . . Bach is a good deal more . . . hrumph . . . than background music."

"Ah," said Amore, "you must excuse me, Potty. Here's one of my guests." And Amore swept Cynthia into his arms in a hug and kissed her cheek. "But where's Greg? I was expecting both of you."

"Greg always has an emergency. In fact, I think I know the person he's treating tonight."

"Oh, a friend? Someone close to you?"

"Not really a friend. And certainly not close to me. But where's Donna?"

"She had to beg off. One of her headaches. She's not awfully fond of music. Maybe the thought of Bach caused her problem. But now you and I can kick up our heals. By gosh, this is like old times when I was an undergraduate, dating a beautiful girl for a free concert and then buying her a hamburger and a Coke afterward. But tonight I'll do better than a hamburger. I know just the place for a late supper."

As Amore and Cynthia made their way toward the first row of seats in the auditorium, pairs of heads here and there came together and inaudible conversation took place.

Settled next to one another in their seats, Amore let his right leg rest against Cynthia's left leg, and he glanced at the swath of thigh he could see between the hem and her skirt and her knees.

He leaned close to her, feeling her breasts with his right arm. "Quite a treat tonight," he whispered. "All organ music. A trustee bought the organ for the university, and this is the inaugural concert."

The organ, throbbing, rumbling, and singing through six Chorale Preludes, was indeed background music for Amore, his awareness focused on the woman beside him, golden Cynthia. He could not, of course, directly look at her, but when he focused on the far corner of the auditorium, she was in his peripheral vision.

attitudes

He watched as her breasts rose and fell almost imperceptibly with her breathing, and he focused on her when she uncrossed and re-crossed her legs.

The coda for the evening was the mighty Toccata and Fugue in D Minor. Lester Amore was rapt, following the insistent theme with its infinite variations, the finale of the last few bars so perfectly and quietly resolving the ambiguities developed through the body of the music. With the rest of the audience Lester and Cynthia rose to applaud and cheer, "Bravo! Bravo!" He hugged Cynthia closely and then loosed her to continue clapping.

* * *

Candlelight and wine, arias and melodies from Italian operas, a bottle of pinot grigio.

Cynthia held her glass before the candle, the flicker refracting through the wine. "I guess I should feel guilty, but to tell you the truth, I have no ayenbite of inwit," said Lester.

"What's that, what you don't have?"

"Oh, I'm just being ostentatious. It means 'prick of conscience.' It's a fourteenth-century translation from the French. And please don't ask for more knowledge about it. For some reason I remember it from the medieval history class I took as an undergraduate at Berkeley."

"Say it again. I want to add it to my collection of mental odds and ends."

"Ayenbite of inwit. Ayenbeeta."

"Ayenbite of inwit. Prick of conscience. I have it. I'll drag it out at appropriate moments."

Cynthia smiled and place her hand atop Lester's. "But tell me about the Dean's Circle. That, after all, was the main purpose for our meeting. Lovely of you to throw in the concert as lagniappe."

"Lawn what?"

"Lagniappe. L-A-G-N-I-A-P-P-E. It's something thrown in for good measure. In New Orleans, if you buy a dozen donuts, the baker might throw in a thirteenth as lagniappe."

"Another item for my mental bin of odds and ends. How's this: 'I'm enjoying myself, and as lagniappe, I don't have ayenbite of inwit'?."

"Brilliant. Bravo. Now, about the Dean's Circle."

"That cursed university casts its pall over my whole life. Here I am. A perfect evening with the most beautiful woman I've ever known. And the university intrudes. Can't we talk about something else for now?"

"Just give me a hint, and then we can change the subject."

"The Dean's Circle," said Dean Amore in his most deanly voice, "is a support group for the College of Letters, Arts, and Sciences. To be candid, the main purpose of the group is to raise money. There. Now you know."

"So, then, what benefit would I gain from joining?"

"You'd get to know interesting people. You'd get season tickets for football and membership in the faculty club. You'd become an integral part of the university community.

"God, Cynthia, that's my sales pitch. I don't want to sell anything tonight. I'll invite you as a guest to the next luncheon meeting of the group. I want to enjoy this rare moment. Might call it a romantic moment? The music. The wine. The candlelight. I'm enjoying myself. You're so different from Donna."

Cynthia was silent, gazing at the red and white checked tablecloth.

Lester continued. "Donna is vivid. Yes, that's the word. She's vivid. Some people find her almost overwhelming."

"And Greg is a doctor. Not only in the hospital, but at parties and in the bedroom. I think he's a brilliant doctor. But he's always a doctor. The tribal shaman with knowledge beyond the ken of ordinary mortals. Day after day, life is quite literally in his hands. He makes me feel like one of his patients."

Lester raised his glass. "Well, let's drink to one another."

attitudes

Cynthia and Lester clinked their glasses and drank the last of the wine in them.

***

"Well, did you have a LOVELY evening with Dr. and Mrs. Golden?"

Lester Amore, sitting next to his wife on the sofa, answered, "Dr. Golden wasn't there. He had an emergency."

"How convenient for you. The concert ended at nine. What did you and Mrs. Golden do between then and now. You know, it's one a.m."

"We went directly to a motel and climbed in bed for a hot tussle."

"You wish! It'd take you more than one evening to thaw that iceberg. Let me tell you what you did. You went to Luigi's for a late supper. You ogled one another over spaghetti and wine. You drank a toast to each other, and then you parted. No, that's not right. You drove the Golden girl back to her car and saw that she was safely tucked in and buckled up. You gave her a modest kiss on the cheek and watched longingly as she drove off."

"Well, if I didn't make out with Cynthia, how about you? Do you want to climb in bed for a hot tussle?"

"Jesus Christ, you're disgusting! You think I'm going to be a surrogate Cynthia?"

"You really don't have what it takes to be a Cynthia anything. Let's be honest. You don't like me, and I don't like you."

"Right on!"

"Look, Donna, we can be civilized about this. You want to go your way, and I want to go mine. We can split the sheet without a war. We don't need lawyers to get involved. I have a suggestion. Major Kohn is the university mediator. We could ask him to help us work things out."

"What, have a damn army officer settle our differences. You're nuts."

"He's not an army officer. Major is his first name. He's a retired professor of psychiatry."

"You're nuts. Have one of your cohorts from the university mediate? Not on your life. You'll hear from my lawyer. In the meantime, why don't you pack up and get the hell out of this house."

* * *

Greg was in bed, reading a paperback. On the bedside table was copy of *JAMA*. When Cynthia entered the bedroom, Greg put down the book and looked at his watch. "Do you realize it's after midnight? What in the world have you been doing?"

"Oh, after the concert, Les and I went directly to a motel and made passionate love."

"Uh huh. Yeh. And he proposed marriage. When are you eloping? Here's your thorazine. Take it and come to bed."

Greg watched Cynthia undress. As she was stepping into the bottoms of flannel pajamas, Greg said, "Forget the pajamas. Come to bed."

Cynthia donned the flannel lowers and uppers, brushed her teeth, washed her thorazine down with a glass of water, and climbed into bed, her back to Greg.

12. Cherries

"Poor Sunshine. That guy must wince every time he opens an office door in the English Department. First he finds Lewis cold as a mackerel, and then he practically stumbles over Warren—lying there cold as a mackerel.'"

In the departmental coffee room, Professor Max Schinken was having his midmorning cup and chatting with Professor Kendall Turing. The "Sunshine" whom Schinken had mentioned was the janitor who had had the misfortune of discovering Professor Lewis Lambert at his desk, dead from a heart attack, and Professor Warren Burden on the floor of his office. Sunshine, who had earned this sobriquet because of his unfailingly cheerful attitude toward life and people, deserved better.

Professor Pottle Tinker's ample belly preceded him into the coffee room. When all of him had arrived, he poured himself a cup and took a place at the table with Schinken and Turing.

"What do you . . . hrmph . . . think about . . . having Mel . . . hrmph . . . Druse as your new . . . hrmph . . . chairman?"

"Frankly, my dear," said Turing, "I don't give a damn. Tomorrow I'll be back at Tara wif dose darkies strummin and dose banjos hummin, and who gwine be sad, Marse Tinker, when de shrimp boats be a-comin up de bayou and we cookin up dat gumbo and we be lookin foh de new boss who be a-comin wid his tambourine to make us happy and gib us darkies a whole day off so's we kin dance and sing. And Marse Boss, he be a jolly fella wid his tambourine. Fack is, Marse Tinker, I be thinkin Marse Boss Druse he jest maht be nothin but a nigger lahk you 'n' me, cuzz he be workin fo dat ol' Dean Amore, and dat ole debbil, he be de goldurndest meanest ol' bassard eber put his cloven foot down inside any which unibersity nowhere. Why dat Amore, lemme tell you, man, he be so mean dat he celebrate when some poh sinner get de lecric chair or de needle.

"You've got to hand it to Amore: he takes action. On Friday Warren croaks, and Monday morning the dean announces his appointment of Mel," said Turing in propria persona.

"Amore's playing games with Newburn," said Max Schinken. "Both of them want the credit for getting Bobby to come up with some real mazoola—if she ever does. So Amore foists Mel onto us. Well, I can think of people in the department who'd be worse." And Schinken grinned with an impish maliciousness which he obviously enjoyed.

"Hrumph . . . I can't imagine who . . . hrmph . . . however, there's nothing we can . . . hrmph . . . do about administrative decisions. We're . . . hrmph . . . at the mercy of Newburn, Amore, and that . . . hrmph . . . bunch of . . . hrmph . . . crooks."

"Potty, you should have learned by now that the academic world is made up of two sorts: those of us who devote our lives to the truth and beauty of literature and all of those others," explained Turing. "We literary ladies and gents are less mendacious, more witty, less randy, much wiser, less bibulous, more loving, less selfish, more reliable, and in general better looking and more pleasant to be around than the others. Just think of us and our colleagues: aren't we the noblest goddamn creatures you've ever encountered?"

"And of the 'others,'" added Max Schinken, "the very worst are administrators."

***

An inveterate mutterer, senior departmental secretary Heather Figaro, sitting at the desk where, like Cerberus, guarding the portals of the Department of English, had been listening to the witty exchange of the three learned doctors and accompanying their remarks with a *sotto voce* commentary: "They don't know the half of it. I'm going to have to put up with that stupid Dr. Druse. I'll be at his beck and call. Well, I'll tell you this for certain: he's not going to run me ragged. I can get another job. The chairman of Philosophy has been after me for a month to shift to that department. It's not as if I didn't have any options. The way that Dr. Tinker keeps clearing his throat drives me just wild. I wish Dr. Turing would wash his hair. It always looks greasy. Dr. Schinken is awfully nice. He takes me to lunch every semester."

"I didn't catch what you said, Miss Figaro," remarked Mel Druse as he walked abstractedly into the precincts of the English Department central office.

Heather Figaro blushed and answered flusteredly, "Oh, I was just talking to myself."

"Tell Professor Schinken I want to talk to him." And Mel disappeared into the sanctum of the chairman's office, of late occupied by Warren Burden.

attitudes

"See what I mean?" muttered Heather Figaro. "Professor Schinken is just over there in the coffee room. Professor Druse could have looked for him there. But no, he'd rather make me into an errand girl. Well, he'd better realize that I have more important things to do than page his cronies."

Nonetheless, she stuck her head into the coffee room and sweetly informed Max Schinken that Professor Druse would like to see him.

Sitting behind his desk—until recently Warren Burden's territory—Mel looked haggard, rumpled, as if he had not slept or as if he had slept the torpid, leaden sleep of too much alcohol. His characteristic rosiness was ashen, corpselike.

"What's up, Mel?" asked Max Schinken, taking a chair. "You look awful. Are you feeling okay?"

"I don't feel all that well, to tell you the truth. Warren's death . . . and Bobby. . . ." said Mel vaguely. "But I'll be alright. I want to take hold of this job—get the department going. And, frankly, Max, I'm pissed, pissed as hell."

"Oh?" And Max awaited an explanation.

"Have you seen this?" With a slight tremble, Mel handed Schinken a brochure.

Max read aloud: "'Arouse the slumbering giant! Through sleep learning force feed your subconscious the tastiest morsels of world literature. Polish the rough gem of your culture while you slumber.' What in the world is this hokum?"

"Take a look at who's putting it out."

"'Hook, Mathis, and Gaylord Learning Consultants, Incorporated.' That wouldn't, by any chance, be our colleagues Jim Hook, Howard Mathis, and Freddy Gaylord, would it?"

"I'm afraid so," said Mel. "And they're advertising on the radio, that station that plays the oldies but goldies. Bobby listens to it all the time."

Max Schinken chuckled with deep satisfaction. "Hook, Schnook, and Crook, that schmuck Newburn probably bought the program and turns it on every night when he goes to bed.

'Arouse the slumbering giant. Force feed your subconscious the tastiest morsels of world literature.' Oh, brave new world that has such creatures in it." Schinken's chuckle turned into an outright laugh, at the end of which he wiped his eyes and blew his nose.

"I can't have this sort of thing going on in the department. What about our dignity, our professional integrity?"

"Well," said Max Schinken, "I believe in the free enterprise system. As long as Hook, Mathis, and Gaylord don't conduct their business on university time or premises, I guess they have a perfect right. . . ."

"But what about the ethics? Sleep learning and that kind of thing?"

"It's strange to bring up ethics in regard to this institution or this profession. What have ethics to do with our professional lives? Most of us fill our years with incessant twaddle about subjects that matter to no one, even to ourselves."

"You're saying that literature is unimportant?" Mel was a bit more alive now, becoming once again his old defensive self. His color was better, and he seemed less limp.

"I'm *not* saying that literature is unimportant. I'm saying that the things we say about literature are unimportant—finally inconsequential. The best judgment I can give of our activities in general is that they are relatively harmless, a non-malignant way for a few exotics to pass their years without disturbing the course of history. We are, after all, Mel, totally irrelevant to everyone but ourselves. Engineers build bridges. Doctors treat cancer. Architects design buildings. Even astronomers capture the interest of the general public. But I ask you this: what intelligent layperson would have the slightest interest in the topics we deal with? The scholarly journals—the English department equivalents of *The Journal of the American Medical Association* or *Architectural Digest* were arrayed in a rack behind Max. He grabbed one and read the table of contents: "Guillaume de Machaut and the Consolation of Poetry," "Adulteration or Adaptation? Nathaniel Lee's *Princess of Cleve* and Its Sources, "The Ethics of the *Lettres morales* and Rouseau's Philosophical Project." I bet your neighbors in Huntington Beach would give up watching "Law and Order" to read that fascinating stuff. In many ways, we're as hokey as Hook, Crook, and Schnook. In the context of our profession, I don't see that Jim, Howard, and Freddy are doing anything so heinous."

"Of all the people in the department," Mel choked out, "I thought you would understand. What are we going to do—turn the whole department into some kind of *National Enquirer,* trying to make everything easy and popular? I'll be honest with you. All this bullshit that some of our colleagues talk about soap operas being the Shakespearean drama of our age—I mean that sort of stuff *really* worries me. I'll bet you not one student in five thousand at this university has ever read 'The Way of the World,' yet we talk about 'The Way the World Turns' or whatever the name of that crummy soap opera is. Max, if we don't hold the fort, the Huns and Vandals will burn the library at Alexandria and there just won't be any more culture—except soap operas, reruns of 'The Love Boat,' and Barbara McPartland romances. I intend to fight for culture and academic integrity."

"Oh god!" sighed Max Schinken in a general, resigned sort of way. "I'll talk to you later. At the moment I'm on my way to discuss Keats' 'Ode on a Grecian Urn' with my sophomores—a bunch of premeds, future dentists, computer jockeys, and Tootsie Rolls. Don't get yourself all worked up, Mel; there's no way you can reform the department, let alone the world. At our time of life, as undistinguished professors in an undistinguished university, the Path of Least Resistance is the Yellow Brick Road. Take care." And Schinken left Mel's office.

The office, though Mel had occupied it but briefly, had begun to take on a Drusean personality. In the wastebasket, nestled among crumpled papers and torn envelopes, was a Diet Dr. Pepper can, and the struggling African violet that through the years Mel had intermittently watered, just as it grew sere unto death, was on the coffee table where Warren Burden's African goddess had once stood.

Mel slumped backward in his swivel chair and stared at a picture on his desk, a somewhat blurry likeness of his father standing before the family business, "Druse Plumbing and Heating."

Mel gazed at the picture of his father, the plumbing contractor from Helena, Montana whose aspirations always exceeded his reach, who dreamed of wealth, respectability, and political clout, but who spent his life—and his family's small fortune—in the grand gesture. Mel remembered accompanying his father to the bar in the Montana Club, where George Druse had insisted on buying drinks for the house, Mel huddled in a corner, sucking on a Coca-Cola in its greenish Mae West bottle, listening to his father's boomingly hearty voice, watching his sire slap backs and assume thoughtful stances before delivering opinions on Montana politics, the future of the mining industry, the current state of cattle ranching, the possibilities of making Helena into a winter and summer tourist resort unparalleled in the nation.

George Druse was bright enough, but thwarted by life at every turn. His plumbing business supported the family adequately, though not opulently, and the money that could have gone for vacations, new furniture, that could have been put away for Mel's college expenses or for his parents' retirement was spent on grand gestures such as buying drinks at the Montana Club or purchasing a new Lincoln Continental.

The Lincoln—that sleek, purring, padded, plush machine with its dulcimer horn—a 1959 model, pale green and glistening: its smell when his father brought it home, the newness a bouquet that Mel would never forget, an aroma of lacquer and solvents and fabrics, the most American odor in those years when the new car was the family event, every five years or two years, or even annually—a Chevy or a Ford, or (one step up) a Dodge or Mercury, or the doctor's Buick, the banker's Cadillac, and even beyond these, the slightly exotic, daring luxury of the Mercedes or the Jaguar. George Druse had always been a "Ford man," driving Mercuries and Crown Victorias—a little classier than Chevys, not as tinny as Plymouths.

attitudes

The sound of the band practicing outside his office did not register on Mel's consciousness. He was in a state of mana, the object his past, those years of growing up in Helena, Montana.

At MacDonald Pass on Highway 12 between Helena and Missoula, it snowed every month of the year, even in August, slight flurries, but enough to dust the ground briefly.

Summer of 1959, in the Lincoln, George, Myrtle, and their son Mel had vacationed in Montana. From Helena, they drove to Great Falls, where they took overnight lodgings—with kitchenette—and strolled down the main street as their evening's entertainment, the three of them strangely alone, looking at the goods in the J. C. Penney window.

From Great Falls to Conrad and Shelby and Cut Bank. That is the High Line, windswept, arctic, isolated. For little Mel, the name Cut Bank was legendary. "I just heard on the radio that the temperature in Cut Bank is sixty below, with wind chill factor." "It got so hot and dry in Cut Bank last summer that we had to slaughter our cattle because there was no water or feed." "On Saturday night, Cut Bank is nothing but a pow-wow for a bunch of drunk Indians." "Listen, you don't know what a steak is until you've had a T-bone at the Wagon Wheel in Cut Bank."

The Druses stayed at the Shady Grove Motel, "Strictly Modern." They had a shower, a gas heater, and kitchen facilities. The units were separate, cabins, white cottages with green trim, standing in a grove of poplar trees.

The "Motel" part of the name was, of course, more charming and wistful than practical, for travelers usually did not stay at the Shady Grove. The inhabitants were fairly permanent construction workers, a retired bachelor or two, a child bride and her sideburned man living on relief checks, and probably a mysterious stranger who came and went at all hours and kept quite to himself. A housetrailer on cement blocks attested to the semi-permanent nature of the inhabitants.

The interior of the Druse "unit" was knotty pine, and the gas heater, for cold evenings, was dark reddish brown, the vent pipe curving through the wall instead of ascending through the ceiling. There was an enamel sink and, above it, cupboards with curtains strung on a wire. The gas range was a black Monarch. Two straight chairs and a wooden table, plus a bed and a foldaway for Mel, a nightstand, the bathroom partitioned into one corner—that was it.

As the heat cooled toward evening, George, Myrtle, and Mel sat under the poplars with the owner, a lady about the parents' age, and talked about the old days of hope and bonanza.

From Cut Bank, the Lincoln chugged them through Browning, where they stopped long enough to visit the Museum of the Plains Indians, and then on through Glacier Park, hurriedly, for George was uncomfortable with mountain scenery and reluctant to disembark from the car for views or hikes.

Flathead Lake was their destination, and they arrived there the evening of the third day of their trip. They had a rustic cabin—a vacation retreat owned by a friend of George's—on the shores of the lake, and a motorboat too.

Mel was ecstatic. The lake might as well have been an ocean, the boat a liner. Yelping and dashing about as his parents unloaded the car and settled into the cabin, Mel dabbled his hand in the lake and pulled it out as though it were burned; even in August, the water was so cold as to be a shock. And so crystalline.

The week that his family spent on Flathead Lake was, as Mel remembered, the only completely happy, peaceful time in his childhood. George became the perfect father and husband, taking his son out in the boat to fish for lake trout, treating Myrtle as if she were a person, with mind and feelings.

A ripe bumper crop of Bing cherries overflowed crates and baskets in the fruit stands along the highway—three pounds for a buck, the blackish red cherries, almost as big as plums, warm from the sunshine, bursting with juice. Mel ate them by the sackful, lying under the trees on the patch of grass that stretched from the cabin to the lake's shingled edge. In the cabin he had found heaps of comic books—Superman, Captain Marvel, Spider Man,

attitudes

Wonder Woman—so in the shade, he ate cherries and read comics to his heart's content, the lake slapping languidly at the boat which was tethered to a makeshift dock.

A knock on his door brought Mel back from Flathead Lake to his office.

Miraculous Kate had appeared at just right moment. In the security of Mel's office—the door locked—Kate had no need to ask for a splash of sherry. Mel took the bottle and the glasses from the bottom drawer of his desk and poured two liberal slugs.

"Kate, I don't know what I'd do without you." Mel wiped his eyes and blew his nose.

"You know," said Kate, "that you can call on me whenever I can help you."

"My God! Do you have any idea what Amore wants me to do? He thinks we're going to teach business writing and document design—whatever that is. Well, he has another think coming. What'm I going to do, tell Potty Tinker he has to teach business writing?" Mel snickered, "I'll turn the document design course over to Waldo."

"Mel, Mel," said Kate soothingly, "you get too upset about things."

"Too upset? My God, what am I supposed to do, turn this department into a . . . into a . . . secretarial school?"

"I have some advice. Would you like to hear it?"

"By all means. By all means."

"Just put the dean's mandates on the back burner. And turn off the burner. Lester Amore is a volatile soul. He's very impulsive. A month, two months from now, the whole business will be forgotten, and you and your colleagues can go your old ways, teaching literature to undergraduates, directing doctoral dissertations, and writing papers about literature. I'm certain that nothing can change the English Department, not even the mighty Lester Amore."

"But Les doesn't even care about Hook, Mathis, and Gaylord. They're disgraceful. Les just grins. The guy has no standards."

"Maybe not, but he'll be president of the university."

13. Tea; or, for Two

"God, this place smells expensive," said Bobby. "Target always smells like popcorn."

"Well, you deserve to treat yourself," said Kate, critically examining a smartly tailored woolen suit.

"You won't believe it, but this is the first time in my life I've been in I. Magnin's," said Bobby.

"Look. Don't you think this Irish wool is beautiful, so soft and rich? The burgundy and gray are understated, yet alive. Why don't you try this suit on."

"How much is it?" asked Bobby.

"What do you care?" answered Kate.

"I just hate to be taken for a sucker."

"Just feel this material. Look at the detail of the tailoring. This is really elegant. Try it on," urged Kate.

"Well, I suppose it wouldn't hurt to see how it looks." And Bobby stepped into the dressing booth.

She emerged something of a new woman, the shift from blue jeans and western shirt to rich woolen having changed her appearance remarkably. She scrutinized herself in the full-length mirror, turning this way and that, frowning and then smiling, quite absorbed in the transfiguration.

"It fits perfectly," said Kate. "And let's get a blouse to go with it. And some shoes. Cowboy boots and Irish wool suits don't go together."

* * *

When Kate and Bobby, laughing and chatting, walked in the front door at 1415 Dimple Dell Drive, they found Mel absorbedly working a crossword puzzle and sipping a diet Dr. Pepper. Seeing Kate, Mel arose from the couch to greet her, but immediately realized his mistake, for he was trouserless. Kate turned her back and apologized, and Mel grabbed his trousers from a chair and hastily put them on.

Zipping his fly and cinching up his belt, a restrained but stunned Mel remarked to Bobby, "It looks to me as if you've had a busy day."

"Oh, Kate and I went shopping, and I bought a few things. And then we stopped by her place, and I changed clothes. How do you like my new suit?"

"Just fine. Just fine. What've you done to your hair?"

"Kate talked me into trying a new style. She said that bouffant isn't popular any more. Kate would like a glass of wine, and I need a stiff Blackjack. Could you get it for us?"

Absorbedly watching the two women as they sipped their drinks and chatted, Mel had the strange sensation that it was Cynthia, not Bobby, who was talking to Kate. The soft, light brown curls, the swath of thigh beneath the rich wool of the suit, the shapely legs terminating in new and obviously expensive shoes, the manicured nails—these were not bowling Bobby, she of tuna casserole and gelatin salad.

Kate turned away from her absorption in Bobby to ask Mel, "What do you think of your wife?"

What, after all, could Mel answer, other than, lamely, "Oh, she's just fine"?

Kate's smile was self-satisfied, but not smug.

Mel answered the ding-dong of the doorbell, and Greg Golden, out of uniform, in a beige jumpsuit and loafers, entered, asking if he might borrow some tarragon for the bouillabaisse that he and Cynthia were preparing for a potluck to be attended by the "Pill Pushers," a group of golfing doctors. He nodded at Kate and the other stylish lady, who rose, kissed him on the cheek, and disappeared into the kitchen.

"That was Bobby!" exclaimed Greg.

Having returned with the bottle of tarragon, Bobby paused before Greg, almost posing, awaiting his response.

"You're lovely," said Greg, "absolutely lovely. That new hairdo has done wonders for you."

Bobby dropped next to Mel on the couch. She was now all softness, velvety Bobby. "I don't think anyone has ever before told me I'm lovely. And, yes, I have changed—thanks to Kate. She has taken me in hand. Today she supervised my transformation, including a new hair style and a professional make-up job. Kate is a genius. She's my guardian angel."

"Well, I've got to run." And Greg left, thanking the Druses for the tarragon.

"God, life has really become a circus," remarked Bobby. "Most of the day today shopping, and tomorrow is the '100 Club' spring luncheon. And then Mel and I have been invited to a Board of Trustees retreat in the mountains this weekend."

"But how exciting!" said Kate. "You've really gotten into the middle of things at the university."

Mel could not restrain himself. "Sure she has. They're after her money. They want to suck her in and then clean her out, the jerks."

Kate smiled tolerantly, benignly. "You're a horrible cynic, Mel. Of course President Newburn wants donors, that's only natural. Where would *you* be without the money that people donate to the university?"

"But you say you're going to the mountains for a retreat with the trustees. I'd love to get to know Donald Schwann. I chatted with him at the luncheon the other day. That man is so powerful, so fascinating. They say he has pulled the strings for at least two presidents. I wonder what he's like."

"For one thing, he's rude," said Bobby.

"But don't you think that people like him, with so much wealth and power, function differently from us normal folks? Of course, Bobby, you have wealth, but you don't use it the way Schwann does his. Oh, I'd give anything to spend some time with him."

"Go on the retreat with us, then," suggested Bobby. "I'm sure Harvey Newburn would be happy to welcome you as our guest.

Anyway, you're now part of the university administration, aren't you? I'll call the president's office right now."

"Now, my dear," said circumspect Mel, "we don't know what the situation is. The university has taken over 'Rustic Lodge,' and there may be no rooms left."

"Then Kate can take a room at a motel in the village."

"Bobby dear, you're kind and thoughtful, but I couldn't horn in like this," said Kate.

"Ah hell, Kate, you're not horning in. Come along with us. Be at our house Friday morning at nine. The university's sending a car and driver to pick us up."

"Well, if you think it would be all right. . . ."

"Of course it would."

And Kate scurried off, excusing herself with a confused statement about guests whom Norbert had invited for dinner.

When the door closed behind Kate, Mel immediately removed his trousers and draped them over the back of a chair. In shirt, tie, shoes and socks—and boxer shorts sagging nearly to his knees—he looked quite inappropriate for Dimple Dell Drive or for his wife, out of place, alien.

* * *

A log crackled and blazed in the huge fireplace, its warm fragrance radiating through the reception hall of Rustic Lodge.

Leather upholstered couches and chairs, heavy oak tables, deer and boars' heads; heavy beams, uncovered and unpainted, supporting the steep roof, and natural stone walls rising some twenty or thirty feet—the place was reminiscent, Kate remarked to Bobby, of Valhalla; it was Wagnerian in scope and feeling.

The trustees and a few carefully chosen guests, President Newburn and his court of vice presidents and deans, and some token faculty members chatted stiffly during the cocktail hour. Seeing Kate talking with a lady, Dean Amore glided up and took the charming lady's proffered hand, waiting for an introduction to the companion.

"How are you, Dean?" said Bobby, and the identity of the stranger registered at last on Lester Amore.

"Mrs. Druse! Bobby! How good of you to join us this weekend. Did you find the day's program informative?"

"Yeh, I guess so," said Bobby.

"And Kate, I'm surprised to find you here."

"Bobby and Mel were kind enough to invite me. I hope I'm not intruding."

"Oh, not at all. Not at all." And, to Bobby, "Where's Mel?"

"Somewhere . . . he came down from our room with me. Oh yeh, there he is by the window." And Mel stood, drink in hand, gazing out onto the moonlit swath of glittering snow surrounded by giant pines.

"Well," said Dean Amore, "why don't we freshen up our drinks and join Harvey and Don."

Replenished glasses in hand, the threesome sidled up to Donald Schwann and President Newburn, who, it was apparent, were heatedly discussing Coach Bender, whose first season at the university had reaped five wins and six losses.

"Let's send the sonofabitch back to Indiana," said Donald Schwann. "People don't come to the games to see the university lose. Half the goddamn doctors and dentists in the area are alums, and they want a winning team. How much do you think we're going to get out of fans that we let down?"

"Don," said Harvey Newburn, "I couldn't agree more, but, on the other hand, we don't want to seem brutal. I'd say that we ought to let Bender have one more season, with the understanding that he must develop a winning team, or else."

The chairman of the board glared at the threesome who tacitly begged entrance to the territory staked out by the mighty, and Harvey Newburn glanced a smiling presidential glance at both Bobby and Kate.

"Mr. Schwann, I'm one of your many secret admirers. Ever since that *Newsweek* story three years ago, I've been fascinated by the growth of Schwann Industries," bubbled Kate.

Schwann moved next to Kate and, putting his arm around her shoulders, said, "Little lady, I'd like you to be my pardner at dinner tonight."

"Uh, Don," said President Newburn, "the seating has been arranged. I think Bobby was supposed to sit between you and me."

"Well, then, unarrange it. Re-deal the place cards."

Mel now joined the group, shaking hands with Schwann, Newburn, and Amore.

"I've been rereading *Moby Dick,*" he said.

The group was waiting, expectant.

"It seems to me that Ahab is the perfect symbol of the American: maimed, questing, skeptical, and finally tragic."

There was a silent pause.

"In *Billy Budd* one finds a glimmering of hope, a sense that God has not deserted the universe, but in *Moby Dick* Melville is giving us his final dark vision of the human condition."

"You're an English prof, aren't you?" asked Donald Schwann.

"Yes," said Mel.

"Well then, maybe you can tell me this. Why do kids keep saying 'ya know'? My daughter can't say five words in a string without 'ya know.'"

"Well, you know, that's not really my field."

"Not your field?" said a bristling Donald Schwann. "If the English language isn't your field, what the hell is?"

"I'm in literature," replied Mel.

"So you don't care whether kids butcher the language. That's not your concern; you're in literature. You know, I don't think my daughter has ever used a comma in her life, and the other day, she spelled 'typewriter' t-i-p-e-r-i-t-e-r. That's just too damn much, you know. If you fellas at the university would do your job, maybe the king's English would survive for another generation."

Rubicund and trembling slightly, Mel uttered incomprehensible syllables, flecks of saliva bubbling at the corners of his mouth.

Bobby put her arm around his waist and said, "Oh, Mr. Schwann, I don't think you really understand what Mel does. He doesn't teach spelling and punctuation and that sort of stuff. He's an expert in literature."

"So what does an expert in literature do?" asked Schwann.

Amore interceded. "Every great university has a strong humanities program. This is a great university, so we have a strong humanities program. The most important part of the humanities is the study of literature. Mel studies literature, so he is one of the most important parts of the humanities." And Dean Amore smiled tolerantly, even a bit smugly.

So potent was Amore in both manner and matter that even the mighty Schwann was held at bay. He grumbled a "Yeh, yeh" and directed his attention once again to Kate.

The bong-ding-dong of chimes announced that dinner was served.

* * *

In the icy moonlight on the terrace, Kate shivered slightly and pulled her sheepskin coat more tightly about her. Donald Schwann thoroughly licked a cigar, pulling it lewdly in and out of his mouth to insure its moisture, bit the end and spat the tobacco flecks on the wooden flooring, then lit his huge smoke with a flaring wooden match, sucking voluptuously to assure satisfactory combustion.

"Are you cold, little lady?" asked Schwann.

"It's so beautiful out here tonight," bubbled Kate. "I've heard about silver snow, but now I'm seeing it. Look how it glistens. And smell the pine. This place, right now, is magical. Don't you think this is something special?"

"Yes I do, little lady," replied Schwann. "I don't very often have time to look at the scenery. My life is too busy. In the spring

attitudes

when the leaves come out and the daffodils bloom, I'm jawboning bankers; in summer, when the whole world's green and growing, I'm arguing with labor leaders; in fall, with harvest and the golds and reds, I'm talking to engineers and architects about building a new plant; in winter I'm. . . . Well, this winter night, I'm with you."

Kate came nearer to Schwann. Both were silent, the aroma of Schwann's cigar filling the conversational void.

A meteor streaked across the sky, and Donald Schwann stroked the back of Kate's head.

***

Cora Newburn and Mel sat before the fireplace in the reception hall, Mel savoring Grand Marnier and Cora sipping tea.

His speech a bit slurred, Mel said to Cora, "Do you ever feel left out of things? You know what I mean?"

"I think so. Yes, I feel left out. The university is Harvey's whole life."

"You know, Cora, that's okay. I mean, what's a president for if it isn't the university? See what I mean?"

"I think so."

"But Bobby isn't a president. She isn't even a faculty member. And all she thinks about is university university university. Who's that she's talking to over there now?"

"Ben Hadley. He's a trustee. President of the Food Friend supermarket chain, among other things."

"I'm going to have another slug of Grand Marnier. Join me?"

"No . . . no, I don't think I should."

Mel went to the bar and returned with a Grand Marnier bottle and a second glass. "Have just a touch," he urged.

For half an hour Cora and Mel worked diligently on the liqueur, until finally, shaking the bottle over his glass, no drop came.

"Let's get out of this damn mausoleum," said Mel, even more slurrily. "To tell you the truth, I can't stand to watch all these pompous asses wander around."

A loquaciously cheerful Cora replied, "Old buddy, you can't even imagine what it's like to be married to one of them. Boy, is ol' Harvey ever pompous!"

"Look, I'll lift us another bottle of Grand Marnier from the bar, and we'll go up to my room and have a nightcap."

"To hell with the Grand Marnier," said a reckless Cora. "Grab a bottle of bourbon."

Cradling the whiskey beneath his jacket, Mel led Cora up the long staircase to the second floor of Rustic Lodge and, fumbling momentarily for a key, admitted her to his room. She settled herself in an overstuffed chair, and Mel went about opening the bottle and securing glasses. "There's no ice machine in this damn place," he said.

"Just open the window and get some snow from the sill," suggested serendipitous Cora.

Mel laughed heartily. "We'll have bourbon snow cones!" he said.

Refreshments prepared, coat and shoes removed, Mel arranged himself comfortably on the bed.

"God it's a relief to be away from that bunch!" sighed Mel contentedly.

"How can you talk like that?" responded Cora. "After all, that's our 'University Family.' One big happy family—that's what we are. Who's the Big Daddy, Mel: Harvey or Schwann?"

"No two ways about it, Cora. Schwann's the Big Daddy. Harvey's just an uncle. Uncle Harvey."

"And Amore?"

"Oh yeh, Cousin Lester. Yeh, he comes to visit in a big black Caddie, a couple of bodyguards with him. Buys the kids ice cream. He's our goddamn skeleton: the family Mafioso. Worked his way up from hit man to godfather. He's just waiting to bump Harvey off. What do they call it? 'The kiss of death.' You remember Al

Pacino, how he gave his brother the kiss of death. Oh, Harvey Newburn," intoned oracular Mel, "beware Saint Valentine's Day."

***

"Don't you think it's hot in here?" whispered Lester Amore to Bobby. "Let's go out on the terrace for a breath of air. Do you have a coat?"

Amore fetched his coat and Bobby's from the cloakroom and helped her into the rich gray woolen wrap that she had purchased, on the spur of the moment, especially for the retreat at Rustic Lodge.

In the cold moonlight, Lester Amore fumbled for his cigarette case.

The shock of the icy air made Bobby shudder slightly, and with a jovial laugh, Amore huddled her in his arms, closely. "Brrrr. We need body warmth," he joshed. "What a marvelous sight. The snow. The pines. The crystaline air. The fragrance. And," even more jovially, "the company!"

Dean Amore touched Bobby tenderly on the back of her neck and inhaled mightily. "This air is like champagne," he softly said. "Doesn't it do something to you? The whole scene—the snow, the moonlight, the pines, the glow of the fire in the lodge, the togetherness—all of this makes me feel young again. I guess the reason I've given my life to higher education is that, upon occasion, I can recapture the feeling that I had when I was an undergraduate at Johns Hopkins, the whole world before me, every day an adventure. Do you know, Bobby, people like me are perennial undergraduates. We never get over our enchantment with the sense of the university, and so we stay on. Don't you think that most of us could be Donald Schwanns or Ben Hadleys if we wanted to? Of course we could. But we're sentimental, idealistic fools, given to the idea of the university (that's Newman, you know) and to learning and the hope that we see in our students, in youth, the next generation."

"Mel spends an awful lot of time with students, you know. I don't think they really appreciate him, but he gives a lot for his students."

"Yes. Yes. I'm sure he does. We all appreciate Mel. One of the stalwarts of the university. I realize that while I was straightening out the mess in Wisconsin, Mel was plugging away to make *this* place work. Yes. Yes. We appreciate faculty members like Mel."

Bobby and Lester were silent, listening to the sound of the glee club, now performing in the lodge.

> The girl of my dreams is the sweetest girl
> Of all the girls I know.

Dean Amore seemed entranced.

> And the moonlight beams
> On the girl of my dreams.
> She's the sweetheart of Sigma Chi.

He put his arm around Bobby and began to sing:

> To the tables down at Morie's,
> To the place where Louie dwells,
> To the dear old Temple Bar we love so well,
> See the Whiffenpoofs assembled
> With their glasses raised on high,
> And the magic of their singing casts its spell.

He clasped her to him, and with his left hand clutching her buttock, he pulled her face to him with his right and planted an ardent kiss on her ear, for she was struggling and had turned her head.

"Christ, Bobby," he gasped, "don't fight it."

And then, an agonized "Oof!" for Bobby had jammed an elbow into his solar plexus, that seat of all passion.

attitudes

She ran from the terrace into the chattering warmth of the lodge.

***

Ever alert, President Newburn saw her enter; ever sensitive, he realized that she was distraught; ever ready for opportunity, he rushed to her and, taking her hand, asked if something were wrong, though, of course, he did not use the subjunctive.

"I'm just fine," said Bobby. "I'm tired and want to go to my room. Where's Mel?"

Scanning the hall, neither Harvey Newburn nor Bobby could spot Professor J. Melongaster Druse, and Bobby stood in indecision.

"I'd like you to meet more of the trustees," said President Newburn. "Let me get you a cup of tea, and I'll introduce you to some people."

"That's okay, Harvey, some other time, but I just want to go to bed. If only I could find Mel."

"I hate to see you leave the party so early," said President Newburn, "but let me walk you to your room. Maybe Mel has gone up already." And Bobby, once again on Harvey Newburn's arm, went up the long staircase.

When she opened the door of the Druse quarters, both she and Harvey Newburn recoiled slightly.

Mel, a bottle of bourbon in his hand, was flopped on the bed, and Cora, a glass at her mouth, was sprawled in the chair next to the bed.

Seeing Bobby and President Newburn, Mel, with slurred conviviality, invited them in. "Cora and I were just talking about the fucking university. Come in and join us. Have a drink."

***

The reception hall was deserted. The fire was glimmering its last flickers.

Harvey Newburn and Lester Amore sat at opposite ends of a huge, leather-covered couch facing the fireplace.

You know, Lester," said Harvey Newburn, "I've never liked you, but I've got to put up with you."

"You know, Harvey," said Lester, "one thing I *do* like about you is that there's nothing very much to like about you, so I don't feel guilty about not liking you."

"Well, Lester, we're stuck with one another, aren't we?"

"I suppose so. Do you know how I got my start as a linguist?"

"No, Lester that's a fascinating story I've never heard. But I'm sure you're going to tell me. Does it involve relative pronouns?"

"Actually, the point to the story is a peace-pipe. I was studying the Uto-Aztecan language with a tribe down in Baja, and you know what, those crazy Indians still observed a kind of peace-pipe ceremony. It was very moving."

"Yeh, I bet," said Harvey Newburn.

"You're the eternal cynic."

"Maybe so. But at least I don't get my kicks out of sucking a pipe with a bunch of savages."

"Relax, Harvey. I think you and I should smoke the peace-pipe. We're stuck with one another for a while."

"That's true. So go and borrow a pipe from Alvin Dorsett. That damn guy has given the university over a million, and if he had donated less, I'd have gotten rid of him. He sucks that damn pipe continually. A multimillionaire, and he smokes Sir Walter Raleigh. I think he uses the same pipe cleaner for a week."

"Harve, do you really want to smoke the peace-pipe?"

"Oh shit, Les, what're you getting at?"

"This," said Dean Lester Amore. And from the breast pocket of his suit, he extracted his silver cigarette case. Opening the case, he revealed to President Newburn ten roll-your-owns.

"Harve, why don't you and I seal our relationship with some Mary Jane?"

"My God, Les, I haven't smoked marijuana since I was a graduate student at Yale. But what the hell."

Lighting one of the cigarettes, Harvey Newburn inhaled deeply, let the smoke issue slowly from his nose, and then, in utter contentment said, "Tea. I love it."

14. Roast Beef; or, Plotting

She announced herself into the speaker, the massive gates swung open, and Kate navigated her silver Nissan up the long driveway and came to a stop at the porte cochere. She disembarked, ascended the three stairs to the doorway, and was greeted by a maid in the uniform one would expect of the maid in a Myrna Loy–William Powell movie. "Right thees way," said the maid, and she ushered Kate into the library, where Donald Schwann sat on a massive zebra-skin sofa. He rose, took Kate's outstretched hand, and greeted her. "Howdy, little lady. Here, have a seat," motioning to the far end of the sofa.

Kate surveyed the room. One wall was trophies: heads of a lion, an impala, a bison, and a moose. Two walls, floor to ceiling, were books. The coffee table in front of the couch was a sheet of thick glass resting on the four legs of an elephant.

"Ah, Mr. Schwann, I now know something about you. You are a big-game hunter, and you love to read," said Kate.

"Used to hunt every year. Africa, Asia, the Rocky Mountains. But no more. When I was younger, it was a real thrill to bring down a moose or a lion, but I just don't get a big kick out of it any more."

"But you love books," said Kate.

"Never have been much of a reader. I got all these at a real bargain. Paid twenty-five thousand for the whole bunch. Bought them from the Norquist estate when old Hjalmar died. A fellow told me that some of them are rare, might be worth thousands. I ought to give the whole lot to the university, but then I'd have to redo this room, and I like it as it is."

After knocking twice on the library door, the maid appeared with a cart, conveying champagne and hors d'oeuvres.

"Have some champagne, little lady. And some caviar. I've never liked the stuff myself. Those salty little devils taste like rotten fish to me. A slice of cheddar and a cracker—that's my idea of something to whet your appetite." He poured two flutes of champagne and, offering Kate one, said, "Here's to us, little lady."

Kate clinked her glass with Schwann's, and both drank.

"Mr. Schwann—"

"Ah, why don't you call me Don?"

"Yes, Don, I'd like that. And, please, just call me Kate. I'm not, you know, 'a little lady.'" And Kate smiled warmly, turning, from her end of the couch, to face Schwann at the other end.

"Little . . . Kate, I bet you wonder why you're here. Well, for one thing, you're here to eat the best damn roast beef in America. It comes from my ranch in Wyoming. Grass. Grain. No steroids, no antibiotics. You'll see. You'll agree that it's worth coming just to sink your teeth into that beef."

"I look forward to the experience," said a smiling Kate. "I haven't had beef for years. In fact, Norie and I have pretty much become vegetarians."

"Yeh, Norie. Who's he?"

"He's my companion. Norbert. We've been together for four years now."

"So you're not married?"

"And you? I know that Mrs. Schwann died four or five years ago."

"Yeh, a brain tumor killed Maude. We did everything we could. Mayo Clinic, best doctors. But the damn tumor just kept growing. Good thing is that Maude didn't suffer. No severe pain. She just sort of eased out of it. Lost her mind bit by bit. And then the end."

"Children?"

attitudes

"One daughter. She took a damn degree in social work, and it ruined her. My God, I never see her, she's so busy with what she calls her 'clients.' And you'll never believe this: last year she worked on the campaign committee of that commie fool congressman Dennis Kucinich in Ohio. So Ada and I don't see much of each other."

"Besides the roast beef, why am I here?" asked telic Kate.

"I'll tell you what. Let's get ourselves fortified with some good rare beef and mashed potatoes and gravy, and then we can talk." Schwann escorted Kate to the dining room, a trek from the veldt to Camelot. The dining room was Olde England, lacking only a suit of armor displayed in one corner. A log crackled in a massive fireplace, above which hung a coat of arms, crimson, black, and gold. A massive wrought-iron chandelier with faux candles electrically flickered above the heavy oak table set with pewter plates and mugs.

When Schwann had seated Kate on the side of the table, and he had taken his place at the head, the cook appeared, placing a standing rib roast, still sizzling from the oven, before Schwann, and a maid discretely served portions of mashed potatoes over which she ladled gravy. Green peas and salad (iceberg lettuce, scallions, tomato, and cucumber) appeared as Schwann sharpened a carving knife on a steel, poised the knife above the roast, looked appreciatively at Kate, and began to whack off hunks of rare beef, sliding her plate near to the platter so that he could deposit the beef.

Kate stared at the bloody slab before her. "I wonder, Don, would you be terribly offended if I didn't eat the beef? I'm feeling just a bit woozy. My stomach hasn't been just right for three or four days."

"You're not one of those damn vegans like Ada, are you? You know, it all goes together: vegetarianism, socialism, pacifism. You and I both know that three-fourths of the faculty at the university are vegetarian-socialists. A couple of real intellectuals. Gaffer in Business Administration and Schlotsky in Chemistry.

They talk my language. One of them ought to be president of the faculty senate, but the broccoli-eating pinkos would never elect them."

"Don, I think you have a warped view of the faculty. Yes, some of them go off the deep end, but most of the ones I know are rational. For example, I know Professor Mel Druse speaks your language."

"Does he?. But let me tell you, Bobby is my kind of woman. I mean, she's not some artsy Bryn Mawr grad. Got her education the same way I did, in the school of hard knocks."

"When she married her first husband, she was working on a master's in computer science. I think she's a very bright person."

"But not artsy-fartsy," concluded Schwann. "And now, what can I get you to eat? Something that'll agree with your stomach."

"I'll just have some salad and peas," said Kate.

"If I didn't know better, I'd think you were a damn socialist vegetarian. How about a little wine? It's good stuff. French."

"Just a splash," said Kate.

And now Schwann's whole attention focused on eating. He masticated great chunks of beef and shoveled in forkfuls of mashed potatoes and brown gravy. Schwann's singular ability, to which many attributed his success, was single-mindedness, and he ate with the same intensity that he devoted to the affairs of his multiple commercial enterprises.

After apple pie a la mode, coffee. A relaxed Donald Schwann stretched out his legs under the table, nudging Kate's feet. "Sorry. Didn't mean to tromp on you. You want anything else? How about a brandy?"

Kate declined, and Schwann cleared his throat, preparatory to getting down to business.

"I'd like to talk to you," said Schwann. "I want your opinion. You can be frank with me. What do you think of Harvey Newburn?"

"I don't know him very well," said Kate. "He's always been very courteous with me."

attitudes

"You know his wife is a lush, don't you?"

"Yes, I feel very sorry for her. You know, Bobby has sort of become Mrs. Newburn's guardian angel. You might think Bobby's a little rough around the edges, but she's a very decent, caring person."

"I don't doubt that. Not at all. And you and Bobby, you're pals, aren't you?"

"Hmm, you might say that. Bobby and I share several interests, and, yes, I like her a lot. We bowl together once a week."

"So why don't the two of you come and bowl with me some day soon? I have an alley right here. In the basement. One of the few basements in Southern California. Cost me a fortune to build, but I needed a place for my bowling alley."

"I'll talk to Bobby about that and let you know."

"Let's get back down to business. You know Les Amore. What do you think of him?"

"Oh, he's a very intelligent man. And I think he's . . . Well, he's very firm and determined. Uh, I don't really know what else to say. I owe a lot to him. He was the reason for my position as development officer for the university."

Schwann leaned forward and touched Kate's hand. "I think Les would make an excellent president for this university. If somehow we could get Harvey to resign, I think I could get the board to agree on Les as his replacement. You don't happen to know anything we could pin on Harvey do you? Any dirt."

"Heavens no," said Kate.

* * *

"What's that?" asked Mel, though he wasn't really curious.

"Nothing very fancy," said Bobby, "just paht Thai and a scallop curry."

Mel scraped a portion of the paht Thai onto his plate and ladled a helping of curry over it.

"Hell's bells," said Bobby, "I had a plate for salad." "Why don't you start over? You'll lose the whole effect if you mix the two dishes. The paht Thai is very delicate—just a touch of peanut. And I've made the curry quite spicy. The contrast is the whole thing about the meal."

"I don't like to talk about food," said Mel, and he speared a dripping forkful of the mixture on his plate. But he wasn't really hungry, and chewed absently and swallowed with an audible gulp.

Bobby poured herself a cup of tea, stirred in two spoonfuls of sugar, and then sipped silently.

* * *

Mel had come to campus on this Saturday to . . . to . . . well, to come to campus . . . to make sure that the whole enterprise had not evanesced overnight. He had told Bobby that he needed to work in the library, researching arcane sources for his scholarly paper on Vanbrugh, but he came directly from the parking lot to the English department.

In response to a soft rap at the office door, Mel grumbled a "Come." The knock was repeated, and Mel shouted, "Come in!"

Kate glowed into the office and greeted Mel: "Hello. I'm going to give you a treasure." And from her carry-all, Kate extracted a bottle of Dry Sack and two crystal glasses.

Kate rose and decanted two liberal portions into glasses, handing one of them to Mel.

"Let's forget about the past and drink to the future." And Kate clinked her glass against Mel's. Both Mel and Kate sipped the wine.

Kate began, "I was thinking about the afternoon of Warren's death and—"

"I don't want to talk about Warren's death."

"I was thinking about that afternoon and the night of the party."

"I don't want to talk about either one. I'll tell you about my paper on Vanbrugh."

"Be honest. You know you can trust me. What happened in Warren's office?"

"There was all the stuff about Garth Timmins, the dirty fruitcake. And then Warren told me he'd canceled my seminar in Restoration drama. He scheduled me for an advanced composition class, for God sake! What a hell of a thing to do to a full professor. The next thing, Warren would have me doing janitorial work around the department."

"But that's not all," urged Kate. "You and I can trust one another. Just think of me as your sister confessor."

"And I hit Warren over the head with his damn African goddess," blurted Mel.

Kate slid her chair around the desk so that she was seated next to Mel. She took his hand in both of hers and said, soothingly, "Poor dear Mel, you've been through a horrible time, but now it's over. Warren died of a heart attack. The injury to his head was not the cause of his death. Anyway, don't you remember that on that afternoon, I was with you in your office from 5:00 until we left for the party?"

"You were with me in my office?"

"Yes, and no one else was in the department, except you, me, and Warren."

"Yes, Warren. Warren wouldn't—"

"But you didn't talk to Warren at all that afternoon. I remember that you called 'goodnight' to Warren or maybe it was 'see you at the party,' but we didn't go into Warren's office, and he answered something like 'see you later.' Yes, now I remember exactly. You called out to Warren, 'See you at the party,' and Warren answered, 'See you later.'"

"You walked out with me to the parking lot?"

"Yes, and I saw you drive away. We arrived at the party at the same time."

"Yes, I remember. We arrived at the party at the same time."

"Even if people did get suspicious, you and I have a bulletproof alibi."

"We have a bulletproof alibi?"

"Yes, Mel dear, as long as we stick together, we're invulnerable."

"Then I can concentrate on my paper on Vanbrugh."

"In due time. In due time. But, please, for now let's try to make sure that we know about the afternoon of that terrible event. Can we go over what we did?"

"Yes, we can go over what we did? We were together in my office from five until we left for the party."

"When did we leave for the party?"

"I don't know. When did we leave for the party?"

"About seven. We don't know the exact time, but it must have been around seven because we both arrived at Adam Adam's place at eight or so, and it'd take at least an hour to drive from campus to Adam's place."

"Yes, at least an hour to get to Adam's place."

"And Bobby arrived at the same time."

"Yes, Bobby arrived at the same time. That's right."

"The janitor found Warren's body some time after seven. At least that's what the article in the *Times* said."

"Yes, Sunshine discovered the body. Sunshine discovered Lewis's body, too."

"It was the janitor—your Sunshine—who called 911. Warren's was the first office he was going to clean."

"An important point, now," and Kate's tone italicized the seriousness of this matter. "What were we doing for the two hours that we were together, between five and seven?"

"I don't know. What *were* we doing?"

"You were reviewing the manuscript of my book, *Practical Grammar for Remedial Students*. Your comments were very helpful, you know. I've brought a copy of the manuscript with me. You should become familiar with it in case someone doubts our story."

"I'm a professor of English," said Mel, his dignity under siege. "What in the hell do I know about grammar?"

With ever so slight an edge, a barely detectable trace of pique, Kate answered. "It is a vulgar error among the laity to assume that English professors understand grammar. Odious though it may be, you really should be familiar with my work."

"My God, I'm not in the School of Education or the Linguistics Department. Those folks are supposed to know something about grammar. Why don't we say that we were talking about my work on Vanbrugh? I'll give you all my notes and tell you what my thinking is."

"Ah, then, you're putting the burden on me? Is that fair, really?"

"But if you'd put your mind to it, you'd love Vanbrugh. It's a real shame that his plays are never staged. I'll bet I'm the only person in the English department who has read all of the works of Vanbrugh."

"Perhaps you're the only person in the English Department who has read any of them," said cruel Kate. "My tastes are so ordinary, so banal: Shakespeare, Shaw, Wilde. Last year the university staged 'Major Barbara,' and Masterpiece Theater has a production of 'The Important of Being Ernest.' Life is so short, dear Mel. Do I have time for Vanbrugh, considering all of the possible alternatives in the thirty or forty years I have left?"

Mel had never before perceived in Kate this sharp edge, this tinge of acid. Characteristically, of course, she had taken exactly the right tack, and Mel acceded. "Okay. Give me your manuscript and I'll go through it. Won't hurt to learn a little about grammar, I guess."

"Let's change the subject. Bobby, bless her heart, has invited me to a luncheon with Cora Newburn and Emma Zucker. 'Those ladies,' she said, 'need friends.' I have a hunch. I think that Bobby wants to transform them. Reform them? Help them? What's the word? Bobby thinks they need someone, some-ones."

"Do you know that your wife is quite wonderful? If you'll pour me one more splash of sherry, I'll bare my soul."

"I wish that I could be like Bobby. She's smart, she's tough, and she's really too good for this earth. She has a heart of gold. I know that's corny, but it sure is the saying for Bobby. She's a really loving person. And in spite this tragic flaw, she seems to be thriving in the midst of corruption."

Mel was becoming alert. "Yeh, I know Bobby's a saint. What interests me is not Bobby, but you. Why are you doing what you're doing?"

"What am I doing?"

"You know what you're doing. You know all about Warren's death. How did you find out? Why are you covering for me?"

"Do I know all about Warren's death? Am I covering for you? Explain."

"You brought me that hideous goddess. Why?"

"Why do you think I brought it?"

"To shake me. To terrify me. To let me know that you knew."

"Is that your reading of the situation? Maybe I brought it as a token to mark your having replaced Warren. Maybe the chair's office would be incomplete without a pagan goddess."

"And what about that afternoon? You weren't here with me. Were you?"

"Do you believe that I was here with you?"

"No."

"Well, then, I wasn't here. But remember that my presence makes a big difference in your future. How can you be sure that my version of the story isn't the truth? You were—you have been traumatized. Why don't we simply agree that I was with you that afternoon and that we left together?"

"Okay. Agreed. But I don't understand why—"

"Must you understand? Let's do what the philosophers call a 'thought experiment.' You know, one of the classics is looking for proof that you're not simply a disembodied brain, floating in a nutritive solution and controlled by a super computer. I guess no one has ever been able to get out of that one. You exist only as a thinking mechanism having no contact with reality, if there is such a thing as reality.

"See if you can solve the conundrum of this thought experiment. X is a virtuoso in what the social scientists call 'interpersonal relations.' This X has no more motive for what he or she does than a cat has a motive for chasing a mouse; it's just part of the cat's nature. A hungry frog will not eat a dead fly placed before it. Its nature is to catch flies on the fly. Suppose X comes onto a situation, involving Y, in which his or her virtuosity will make a difference. What would X naturally do? However, Y can't believe that anyone does anything without a motive, a balancing of the books: credits and debits, possible gains and losses. How will X and Y work together? How will they cooperate? X is doing what comes naturally. Y is seeking a motive. And this search for a motive brings everything to a dead standstill."

Mel was becoming ever more alert, emerging from the blue swamp. "Well, I can't prove that I'm not a brain controlled by a super computer, but I sure do have the solution to the conundrum in your thought experiment. Just forget motives. Who cares what the motives are? The possible results are what count."

"Bravo!" said Kate, chuckling and applauding. "And since motives don't matter, Y will let X stick with him or her and enjoy the outcome—or suffer the consequences with Y."

"So X and Y will form a bond closer than friendship. They have committed their destinies to one another."

"I guess you could say that." Kate turned in her chair to face Mel. She moistened her lips with the tip of her tongue and leant slightly forward.

After a pause of seconds or minutes or eternity, Mel pulled Kate to him and kissed her ear, she having averted her face.

Kate's only reaction was to rise and move her chair back to its position in front of the desk. She smiled and said, "Our bond is now closer than friendship—our psychological, our spiritual bond, if you will. But it stops short of the physical. We can be co-conspiratorial lovers, but not lovers. We need to keep our relationship 'clean,' don't we? Above suspicion."

And Kate was gone, her mystery lingering with the delicate, herbal scent of her perfume.

She was certainly the most enigmatic human Mel had ever encountered, either inside the literary canon or in the world outside of books. Her coldly rational analysis of her own motives—or motivelessness—was uncanny. Mel's lucubrations were in infinite regress. What was the motive for her motivelessness? Might it be that she was a gambler, following a random, aleatory path through life's mazes, watching the coin come up heads or tails, the thrown dice equaling seven or snake-eyes, the ivory ball bouncing into number 13 when the chips were on 14, and on the next round falling into 00, just the number on which all the chips were played? Could the motive for her avowed motivelessness be a deception, a clever ruse to hide her real motives? But what might they be?

And what about the mysterious Norbert? With acuity honed by his work with literary analysis, Mel unraveled that enigma.

Norbert was Kate's live-in. Everyone knew that, but no one knew or had even seen Norbert. He was, as anyone who had ever read D. H. Lawrence would realize—he was her. . . . . With Norbert to satisfy her . . . with Norbert to give her. . . . Kate's allure—for she was alluring, very alluring—was her genius. Yes, genius. And impenetrable. Yes, impenetrable. That's the word. Just the right word.

Mel stood, preparatory to leaving for home. As he went out the door of the office, he muttered to himself, "Someday I guess I'll understand."

15. Horsemeat; or, a Meeting of the Minds

"I want the horsemeat sandwich," Donald Schwann told the waiter. And to Lester Amore as well as the puzzled waiter, "I've been eating lunch in this joint off and on again for six years now. I always order the roast beef sandwich. And it's always the same. Horsemeat. Just horsemeat. You chew all the juice out, and what you have left is a wad of string to spit on the plate." And loudly to the student waiter, who was now across the Faculty Center dining room, "Think we could get some coffee here?" Donald Schwann drummed his fingers on the table.

"Well, Don," said Lester Amore, "what's on your mind. You didn't invite me to lunch just so you could experience the horsemeat sandwich."

"Lemme tell you, Les, I'm thinking that this university needs a real shaking up. The damn philosophy department is a booby hatch. Harvey had a series of talks—'colloquia,' he called them—for the members of the board. I suffered through two of them, and that was enough. Jesus, that Professor Habergard was enough to addle your brain. A bunch of bullshit about something he called post-structuralism. A bunch of Frenchies. Dairydah, Foocoe, Boredoo. Something to do with Levis. I didn't ever get the connection between blue jeans and post-structuralism. The only thing I got out of the talks was that they're all socialists."

"Don, I'm afraid you're right. Even our American philosophers have forgotten the great Emersonian tradition of self-reliance and entrepreneurship. Rorty and Davidson—they're as radical as the Continental philosophers. Have you read Bloom's *The Closing of the American Mind?* Came out in '88. It's our kind of philosophy. Bloom was a student of Leo Strauss. . . . But I don't want to turn our meeting into a colloquium on philosophy. I agree that our philosophy department consists of a bunch of fruitcakes.

"You know my philosophy. Human beings are meant to work, but they need to play. I know about your private bowling alley, huh?" And Amore chuckled and nudged Schwann's arm with his elbow. "But you don't bowl for eight hours and then work for one hour every day. What I'm getting at is the idea of proportion, the ratio between work and play, and the university should reflect that proportion. In my honest opinion, the university is really out of whack. Harvey's manipulating the budget so that play gets more, much more, than its proportion of funds. My God! he even backed Ludwig, chair of theater arts, in hiring that broken-down ballet dancer to start a dance program."

"Ballet? God, what are we, a bunch of toe-dancers?"

"Don, I'm going to ask you to listen to a brief lecture on political philosophy."

"Damn it, Les, I don't have time for that sort of wishy-washy stuff. I'm a practical man. I want practical ideas."

"Be patient. Have another cup of coffee. If you'll give me five minutes, I think I can show you a philosophy that's not only practical; it's applicable; and if I ever get to be president of this institution. . . . Well, look, I had the privilege of studying under Leo Strauss at Chicago. That man changed my life."

"But—"

"Just a moment, Don. Please listen. You'll be impressed. Strauss believed that all this modern relativism and liberalism is a bunch of crap. If you read the real philosophers—Plato, Aristotle—you realize that the few, the select few, really understand how the world works, really grasp the nature of society. The rest, what we might call the great masses, can be and should be instruments for the practical working out of the ideas of the few. In a nutshell, that's Strauss's philosophy."

"So don't faculty members here understand that philosophy?"

"Don, I ask you to think of the English Department as an example. Take Mel Druse, for instance. The poor guy spends his life teaching literature that no one wants to read, and he probably voted for Gore and Kerry. Waldo Clemens, he's so far out of it that he probably thinks Jimmy Carter is still president. Even Cyrus Noble in poly sci is so into stuff like the reams Arthur Schlesinger pumps out that he turns up his nose when you men-

attitudes

tion Leo Strauss. God, for its lower division U. S. history course, the History Department adopted Zinn's *A People's History of the United States*, and that book is nothing but left-wing propaganda."

"You've got me interested. Did this Strauss fellow write any books I'd understand?"

"Don, I'll send you a copy of *The Rebirth of Classical Political Rationalism*. That's a good introduction to Strauss's thinking."

"How long is it?"

"Oh, two hundred fifty, three hundred pages."

"Yeh, well maybe you could summarize it for me. You know, I'm a busy man."

"I'll do that. But now, to get back to the university, I've urged Harvey to do a factor analysis of programs at the university. For instance, foreign languages. Russian, Japanese, Chinese—these are languages that students can use in the real world. Arabic. But what in the world is the use for Hebrew? And classical Greek? We ought to leave those for Harvard, Yale, Princeton, Hopkins. Use our resources for practical purposes."

"Les, Harvey's the problem. His priorities are screwed up."

"I hate to say it, but you're right about Harvey. He ought to be running a small liberal arts college, like Lewis and Clark or Antioch, not a major research university."

Schwann leaned conspiratorially close to Amore. "Let me tell you a little secret. I just gave five million to the Plato Foundation. I'm on their board. They do good stuff. You know, they publish *The American Entrepreneur*. Someone from the bunch is always on the TV interview shows, O'Reilly, Matthews, Hannity. President of Plato, Lyman Wolfe, is nearly seventy, getting a little dotty. His wife, Dorothea, wants him to retire and finish the book he's been working on for forty years. *The Key to All Political Philosophies*. This would be a wonderful opportunity for Harvey. He'd be just the man to replace Lyman. Harvey could make a fortune in that job—and be a traveling salesman for sanity in politics and economics. Hell, Air Force One has nothing over on the foundation's jet."

Lester Amore slowly turned his water glass around and around on the table. "Mm hmm. Mm hmm. But there's the problem of getting Harvey to. . . ."

"I'll handle that. I think I can convince the Plato board to make the offer to Harvey. It'll be an offer he can't refuse."

"And then?"

"And then our next problem is convincing the university board that you ought to replace Harvey. Of course. . . ."

"I'm flattered, Don. Really flattered that you think I could run this institution, bring it into the twenty-first century. But I wonder about the board and the faculty."

"I've already met—informally, of course—with the other members of the board. They're ready for a change. As far as the faculty's concerned, I've talked with Gaffer in Business Administration and Schlotsky in Chemistry. They'll represent the faculty. They won't give us any trouble. In fact, they're on our side."

"I have a present for you, Les." From the briefcase on the floor by his side, Schwann extracted a package wrapped in brown paper and handed it to Amore.

Amore removed the wrapping that covered a bronze plaque: Lester I. Amore, President.

* * *

"Could you offer a poor wayfaring soul just one splash of sherry?" asked Kate.

Mel extracted the Dry Sack and two glasses from his desk, poured two splashes, and handed one glass to Kate. Mel sighed. "God, what a day. Waldo spent half an hour in my office trying to get me to approve a seminar in the works of Edward Abbey and telling me about the glories of Afton Canyon, the Grand Canyon of the Mohave. Then Jerry Gelb and Bridget Heiman came in to complain about the guest speakers that Peggy O'Neil and Potty Tinker had lined up. And . . . well, I don't want to burden you with my problems. What's new?"

attitudes

"I've heard, from a very good source—"

"I'll bet it was a good source. Either Amore or Schwann—or both."

"Whatever. I've heard that Harvey Newburn is on his way out and there's a good possibility Lester Amore will replace him."

Mel crooned, "Les Amore, Les Amore, über alles in der Welt. God, that means we'll have to say 'Sieg Heil' when we enter the administration building."

"Ah, come on, Mel. Don't be so cantankerous. Les is a smart guy. And Bobby and I have gotten to know Donna."

"She's more than a bit much, isn't she?"

"Oh, when you get to know her, she settles down. She's really quite human. And I'll tell you this: Lester Amore is a pussycat when he's around Donna. Bobby and I are having lunch with her tomorrow."

"Lotsa luck," said Mel.

"You and I are still co-conspirators, aren't we?" said Kate Laughingly. "Well, if, just if, Les Amore gets the presidency of the university, that leaves the deanship open. How does this sound: 'J. Melongaster Druse, Dean of Letters, Arts, and Sciences'?"

Momentarily, Mel had a vision of the glowing golden chain of being, and he smiled. "Yeh, that would really piss Potty and Merry and Bridget and Peggy off. First thing I'd do is bring Hook, Mathis, and Gaylord into line. Get rid of that phony consulting firm of theirs. They could choose, the university or a huckster business. Yeh, Ken Turing, the arrogant jerk. He'd pee his pants." Mel was growing more and more animated. "But why would you—"

"Remember," said Kate. "We don't ask 'why.' We just play our cards as astutely as we can. We've been dealt an interesting hand. Did you know that I had dinner with Donald Schwann? And he's invited me to cruise on his yacht next week with some very interesting people. I wouldn't be surprised if a certain senator were in the party.

"Now, I've got to ask you to be understanding. Don is going to invite Bobby to join us on the cruise, but I told him you are so busy with your administrative duties and your scholarly work that you won't be able to join us."

"Believe me," said Mel, "I can get away. I'd give anything to go yachting with Donald Schwann and his cronies."

"Yes, I can understand, but you've got to trust me. I want you to be the dark horse, the mystery candidate who steps up at the right moment to fill the void. We don't want Don and the other board members to know where you stand. For example, the Hook-Mathis-Gaylord business. Successful entrepreneurs might not understand why you're so outraged. They might even think you've taken a swing to the left, and in Don's circle, the left is death and destruction."

"Yeh, but I know how to keep my mouth shut. Discretion is my middle name."

"Of course, dear Mel. But just this once, trust me. Bobby carries a lot of weight with Don and the other members of the board."

"Yeh, about four hundred million worth."

"Well, that, yes. But Bobby's . . . How should I put it? Bobby's a paradox. She's shrewd and tough and at the same time naïve. I guess what I mean to say is that Bobby is genuine, the real article. It's strange, but Donald Schwann and Bobby are alike in some ways. They're above artifice. I mean, Don is genuine. Between you and me. . . ."

"Between you and me what?"

"Just that Don can be genuine because of his money. Bobby is genuine in spite of her money."

* * *

Bobby and Kate sat in the salon. "I don't know how you got me on this damn boat," said Bobby. "I was seasick all last night, and, Jesus, I'm tired of listening to Ben Hadley and Donald Schwann play one-upsmanship." An octave lower than he usual tone, her eyebrows arched, and her bosom thrust out aggressively: "'Oh, yes, I acquired Puresip Beverages for a song, a real song. And once I cleaned out the management, the outfit is doing nicely.' 'The best deal I ever made was buying controlling share of the stocks in Prism Products. Let me tell you. . . . ' God, don't those guys ever think about anything but their damn empires? And the women." With prissy nasality: "'We dined with Esa Pekka Salonen last week. Such a wonderful conductor. He never misses a beat.' You want to know what I said?"

"By all means," responded Kate.

"He never misses a beat, and no matter how fast the orchestra plays, he can keep up."

"Bobby, you're downright wicked."

"I'm downright bored. Let's go topside where I can have a smoke."

On deck, Bobby lit a Marlboro and gazed at the coastline, a mile or two to the portside. "That must be Ensenada," she said.

"Right. Ensenada," responded Kate.

"Why don't we dock and spend some time on dry Mexican land? I could go for a tamale and a margarita."

"Goodness, I was in Ensenada with Bertie last year. The place is just crazy. Traffic. Noise. If the wind's blowing in the wrong direction, the place smells like a dead fish. There's a cannery just north of town."

"Poor Mel. He looked like an abandoned puppy when Don's driver picked us up. He wanted to go on this cruise." Bobby was grinning as she shook her head slowly and sadly.

"I know he did. But. . . . Well, you and I love Mel, so we can be honest. He's often so single-minded. What I mean is that people don't understand his devotion to his own work. I don't think Donald Schwann or Ben Hadley would warm up to a discussion of Vanbrugh. See what I mean?"

"Sure, I know what you mean. After all, I live with the guy."

Kate was tempted to ask the forbidden question: "Why?" But she veered to the right, thus avoiding a collision. "Men are a problem, aren't they? Bertie and I get along fine until he starts in on esthetics, and then I simply let him rant. You know, a black blob is just a black blob until its framed and hanging on the wall of a gallery. Then it's art. Alright, I'll buy that. But then Bertie really gets on his high horse. The non-artist has no right to judge any work. So if you see the black blob on the wall at the L.A. County Museum, you can't say, 'Gee, that's dumb' or 'Wow, how inspiring.' You just stand in awe, speechless. How do you think Don and his guests would go for an evening of that kind of talk? There is, you know, a good reason for my keeping Bertie and the university completely separate."

Bobby was about to do the unthinkable: to ask how Kate could live in two such different worlds, the university by day and Bertie by night, but Donald Schwann and the Senator appeared on the sun deck.

Bobby and Kate rose, and Schwann introduced them to the Senator.

"The Senator here has done a lot for this nation. He ought to be the next president of the U.S." And Schwann gave the Senator a hearty clap on the back.

"Well," said the Senator, "I can return the compliment. If Donald Schwann had been president, socialism wouldn't have got its nose in the tent like it did under Clinton."

"That's right. And I'd have taken the ax to a bunch of those duds that Clinton appointed. If I ran Schwann Industries like Albright ran the State Department, we'd have been out of business yesterday. Goddamn it! Pardon my French, ladies. Goddamn it, George W. Bush is the best thing that's happened to this country since William McKinley. George wants me to spend a weekend at Camp David. I look forward to that. I can give him soon good advice."

"You should keep in touch with the president," said the Senator.

"Count your blessings. What if we'd wound up with Gore. God, the thought terrifies me." Schwann loudly called, "Steward! Steward!"

The steward having appeared, Schwann asked if his guests would like some refreshments.

"A cold lemonade sounds wonderful," said Kate

"I'll take a Jack Daniels on the rocks" was Bobby's order.

"Same for me," said the Senator.

"That makes three of us," said Schwann.

The libations having been served, Schwann opined, "Drinking Jack Daniels—that's a wonderful test of character. I've never known a Jack Daniels drinker who didn't talk my language. So here's to Blackjack."

Kate having lifted her lemonade in the toast, Schwann realized his gaffe and set out rectify it. "I mean, not everyone drinks whiskey. Some of my best friends are teetotalers."

***

Donna Amore, Trish Hadley, Kate Reese, and Bobby Druse lingered at the table after luncheon.

"Don, Ben, Les, and the Senator are in the salon plotting the next coup, so here we are, alone. We can do our own plotting," said Bobby.

"WELL, I have an idea," responded Donna. "I THINK we should do SOMETHING about Cora. You know, twice recently SHE has gotten blotto and EMBARRASSED everyone."

"So what should we do, have her exiled to Siberia?" asked Bobby.

"There ARE places, you know, where ALCOHOLICS can be dried out permanently, the Betty Ford Center, FOR instance."

"Alcoholics schmalcoholics." Trish Hadley was on her high horse. "What's an alcoholic? That's just a social construction. It's like insanity. There was no insanity until someone invented it. Have you ever visited Hampton Court. Jeezle-weezle, Henry the

Eighth and everyone there drank all day long—and I don't mean water. None of them were alcoholics. There was no such thing as an alcoholic. That's just one of our unfortunate modern inventions. Jeezle-weezle, if you read Foucault, you'll see what I mean. I mean . . . well, jeezle-weezle."

This was Kate's first opportunity to assess Trish Hadley. When Trish entered the dining area, Kate had noted her ankle-length shirt, bold red flowers against the dark blue of the gingham, the white canvas shoes, the blouse that looked as if it might have been crafted in Peru by Incas. Trish's hair was piled in a bun atop her head. Her only makeup was, incongruously, bright green eye shade.

Bobby shook her head and sighed. "Maybe there's no such thing as an alcoholic, but I'll tell you this, there are plenty of drunks. Oops. Sorry. There is no such thing as drunk. Just people who drink an awful lot of booze."

"Poor Mrs. Newburn," said Kate.

Bobby washed her blood pressure pill down with a liberal swig of water. "Gee, I wish we wouldn't call Cora a drunk. We can do better than that. We know that she's very unhappy. Frankly, I think some human warmth, some friends would do more for her than the Betty Ford Center. But that's just my opinion."

***

Bobby lit a Marlboro and took a sip of her Blackjack. The gentle rocking and plunging of the boat as it progressed toward Cabo San Lucas was soothing. When Donald Schwann appeared on the sun deck, she refocused, ready to do her duty as a guest.

"What a beautiful night," she said. "The breeze, the full moon. It's like something in the movies."

"You don't mind if I smoke a cigar?" said the deferential Donald Schwann.

"Not at all. I've been trying to cut down on the Marlboros, but smoking is such a wonderful addiction. A cigarette with cof-

attitudes

fee, with a drink. A cigarette when you're bored or when you're angry. And, after all, just one more won't kill you."

Schwann thoroughly licked his cigar, drawing it in and out of his mouth. He bit off the end and spat the plug into the ocean. Then ceremoniously he lit the cigar with a wooden match and drew in smoke which he then blew out in a cloud that the ocean breeze wafted to the starboard.

"Can I join you?" he asked.

"It's your boat," said Bobby. "Have a seat."

"Little lady, I've had my eye on you ever since we met for lunch last December."

"Whoa there, pal. What's the 'little lady' stuff?"

"Ah. hell, that's just what popped into my mind. No offense."

"Call me Bobby."

"Okay, Bobby. Lester Amore tells me you're a member of Harvey Newburn's 100 Club."

"I am. Why?"

"Well, Les and I would hate to see you. . . . How should I put this? Look, Bobby, you and I are both wealthy people. That means we've got power. You know, power to change things. The only reason I ever wanted money is to create a better world."

"Absolutely. Just think of the all the poor souls who'd be too tired to do their duty if they were up all night coughing. Your All-Nite cough syrup saves this nation millions of lost working hours."

"Goddamnit, Bobby, I don't think that's funny. Do you realize that more than fifty thousand families rely on Schwann Industries for their livings? What would they do without me?"

"Beats me. Go to work for Ben Hadley, I guess."

Donald Schwann sat upright and threw his cigar into the ocean. "You sound like a socialist. You don't want to get that reputation, do you?"

Bobby lit a Marlboro. "Ah, Don, come off it. God, we're supposed to be living the life of Aristotle Onassis on the wine-dark sea, and you want to talk about the nobility of making money.

You know, I've got a lot of dough, and I've been thinking about what I ought to do with it. I sure as hell don't want to spend it. I have a red Buick that I like. I have house that I like. I have a husband that, for some reason, I love. I'm contented."

Donald Schwann was alert, alarmed. "You're not planning to give money to the ACLU, are you? Or to any of these crackpot interfaith alliances? God, that would be throwing money away."

"What I'd really like to do," said Bobby, grinning widely, "is give about three hundred mill to the university and then run the place. You know, President Bobby Druse, leading the university of the future."

"That night not be as funny as you think," said Schwann. "What if Les Amore replaced Harvey Newburn and your husband replaced Les? I've been talking to Kate, you know. Things are brewing at the university."

"I'll tell you the truth," said Bobby, "I couldn't care less what happens to Harvey, but Cora needs help."

"Yeh," said Schwann. "She's a lush. An embarrassment."

"Oh, she's an alcoholic, no doubt. She's addicted. I guess everyone has an addiction. To alcohol, to sex, to power."

"So what's your addiction?"

"Let me think. Since everyone has an addiction, then I must have one. I've got it. I'm addicted to bowling." Bobby chuckled.

* * *

Kate, eyes closed, stretched out in the sunshine, lounging on her deck chair. Schwann gazed at her legs, glistening with sunscreen, at her white shorts outlining the delta, at the blue silk blouse defining her breasts. "You want to know something funny?"

"If it's really funny," said Kate languidly.

"You know Ben Hadley?"

"I've met him. Don't know him well."

"Ben Hadley drives a silver Corvette."

"What so funny about that?"

"He has it programmed so that when he gets within ten feet of it, the doors unlock and the sound system plays 'Hail to the Chief.'"

"That's funny."

Sunday morning. The yacht anchored just off Cabo San Lucas. Kate and Donald Schwann alone on the yacht, the rest of the party having gone ashore. A dulcet breeze. The gentle rocking of the boat. The somnolent rhythm of the wavelets slapping the hull.

Schwann yawned, stretched, and shouted, "Steward, could we get some coffee here?"

"Kate."

Kate opened her eyes and said, "Yes, Donald."

"Kate."

"What is it Donald?"

"Kate, I'm not an old man yet. Sixty-five. Hell, I have twenty or thirty years ahead of me."

The coffee was served, one cup for Donald Schwann, one cup for Kate Reese.

"Kate, I'd like to think I could start a new life."

"Yes, Donald."

"Kate, I've never known anyone like you."

"Really, Donald?"

"Kate, have you ever thought about changing your way of life?"

"Yes, Donald."

"Ship ahoy!" came a call from the starboard side of the yacht, and Schwann's noisy guests climbed the gangway, ready for cooling libations and the voyage northward.

16. Club Soda

"I'll have the horsemeat sandwich."

The puzzled student waiter looked at Schwann and then at President Newburn.

"Mr. Schwann wants the roast beef sandwich. He's a great joker. Ha ha," explained Harvey Newburn. "And I'd like the Chinese chicken salad."

Schwann drummed his fingers on the table and, when the waiter had almost disappeared through the door to the service area, shouted, "You think we could get some coffee here?"

"Well, Harvey," said Schwann, "how'd you like the Plato Foundation jet?"

"Not only the jet, Don, but also the Institute lodge at Park City. I must say, those folks know how to do things. My guess is that they don't have much trouble getting folks to attend their seminars and conferences at the lodge."

"Wait until you see the headquarters in DC. Hell, it even impresses me, and I've seen some pretty fancy places. Camp David. Checkers. Don't compare with the Plato facilities. So what d'ya think at this point?"

"Don, I'm really intrigued. With Plato, I'd have influence. . . . I mean, in the long haul, in the view of history, I might be a massive, anonymous, unknown force as president of this university. In helping to shape the destiny of this university, I'm also preparing the way for what is now unknown—a cure for AIDS, an understanding of the brain, works of art that are now ahead of their time. Our philosophy department—"

"God, you ought to lock that whole bunch up. Put 'em in a dungeon in the basement of the Administration Building. Harvey, I don't think a one of them knows anything about Leo Strauss. Now that's my kind of philosophy, and yours. Les put me onto it."

"Of course, I've read the main Strauss stuff. How could I avoid it, with Perle coming here as a guest speaker and with Wolfowitz nosing around for appointment as a distinguished professor in absentia. I mean, he wouldn't even be on campus, except now and then for a lecture, but the guy has the Eagle Scout complex. He wants all the merit badges."

"Harvey, have you read Plato's *Republic?*"

"I hate to admit it, but, no, I haven't."

attitudes

"I've read an abridged version that gets right to the meat and trims away the fat. Look, here's what Plato says—and he's the inspiration behind the Foundation—the problem with democracy is that a bunch of barbarians—like the Clinton crowd—can take over. The best government has three classes. The real kings, the thinkers and doers who make the decisions and run the industries. Then there's the army. You've obviously got to have an army. And finally, the common people. I don't know how many people rely on Schwann Industries for their existence, but we have a bargain. They give us honest labor, and we give them a decent wage. Harvey, have you read Alan Bloom's *The Closing of the American Mind?*"

"Yes, I've read it. How could I avoid reading it? Everyone on and off campus was talking about it."

"What did you think of it?"

"I've got to be honest. I remember that I was impressed, but right now I couldn't really explain why. All I remember about that book is its title."

"You know, Les told me I ought to read it, so I did, three days ago. All I can remember about it is its title. When I got through reading it, I didn't know what it said. But to get back on track. I've got to be honest with you. If you become president of the Plato Foundation, Cora's going to be a real problem."

* * *

"We're in a rut," said Kate. "Lunch at Mimi's. We ought to be adventuresome, try that new sushi place in Newport Beach."

"I'm not all that hot on sushi. Now if you want to go Mexican or Thai, I'm with you." Bobby ate the spear of dill pickle left on her plate beside the lettuce leaf on which her pastrami sandwich had rested.

"You know President Newburn might leave the university in the next month or so. In fact, I think he's on his way."

"Adios, Harvey." Bobby gave a bye-bye wave.

"I also happen to know that he's going to divorce Cora."

"Years ago, she should have slipped some botulism into his Wheaties or a little cyanide in his brandy. You know, he makes a big deal about his nighttime shot of brandy. What a jerk. How do you know he's going to divorce Cora?"

"Oh, I have my sources. Do you know Vera Barber?"

"Yeh, she's Harvey's secretary, isn't she?"

"Vera and I had lunch the other day, and Vera told me she'd overheard snatches of conversation and had placed certain phone calls."

"Kate, you're amazing. You should be in the CIA."

"Be realistic. Harvey Newburn is going to be president of the Plato Foundation. How could he be the husband of a hopeless alcoholic without staining the dignity of that august, staid, moral bunch?"

"I'm going to tell you something. Ja, Frau Doktor Bobby vill let you know about alcoholism. Kate, not all drunks are alcoholics, and not all alcoholics are drunks. Alcoholism is something you have in your genes. My mother was an alcoholic, but she wasn't a drunk. Her two brothers and one of her sisters were alcoholic drunks, and two of her sisters lived sober lives. I've watched my mother anticipate the cocktails at a party, and I've seen her gulp the first glass of wine at dinner so she could get a second. But I didn't ever see mother drunk. One night, my father came home loaded. He'd had two or three belts at a party, and they done him in. Dad was not a drunk or an alcoholic."

"So is Cora an alcoholic or just a drunk?"

"Who knows. Both Cora and Emma," said Bobby, "are so unhappy. They do need help. Cora must have been a beautiful woman, but now she looks like . . . like . . . well, she looks terrible. Imagine how awful it must be to live from one drink to the next—and to try to make the intervals longer and longer. And I bet Harvey Newburn is a pain in the you-know-what to live with. Kate, try to picture Cora at some function with her husband—luncheon with the board of trustees or a dinner party with the mayor and the governor. Everyone drinking cocktails and wine, and Cora forcing herself to stay dry. I think Harvey does everything possible to keep Cora out of all the pictures.

"And Emma, that poor gal. She told me she's had her stomach stapled, and that's a drastic step to take. She says that after the operation, she lost more than a hundred pounds, but now she's right back where she was. She needs something to live for—other than food. I'd sure like to do something for Cora and Emma. Have any suggestions, Kate?"

"I'm at a loss. What can you do?"

"Beats me. But those gals worry me."

* * *

Kate's living room was understated, but economically elegant—various shades of tan, cream, and beige, with the one daring touch, a brilliantly flowered sofa. On the walls were photographs, attractively framed—a silo standing out against a cloudy sky, a closeup of a perfect apple, a rail fence in a snowy field—but no prints, no ersatz art. Pottery, obviously carefully chosen, stood about, all of it in earth tones, rough textured. One suspected that some of the pieces might be "worth something," purchased as investments.

Coming in from the garden, Kate supplied the finishing touch to the room: a branch heavy with pink roses, in a large earthen vase, which she placed on the coffee table.

She paused to survey the room and then, satisfied with the general effect, went to the kitchen to finish preparing the luncheon.

The doorbell chimed. At the door, Kate greeted Bobby, Cora, and Emma. "Come in, and join the conspiracy," said Kate.

Emma waddled to the sofa, plopped ponderously down into the groaning structure, and sank into the cushions.

"Could I get you something—a cup of tea or coffee, a Perrier?" asked Kate.

"A cup of coffee. I could use a cup of coffee."

The coffee poured and set before her, Emma began to ladle sugar into the cup—one, two, three teaspoonfuls. She stirred delicately, took a sip, set the cup back on the saucer, and poured in cream, stirred again and again sampled the brew, which now elicited a clucking, appreciative smacking of her lips.

After wandering about the room, inspecting the photos on the wall, Cora took a place on a chair in the corner of the room, and Kate brought her a bubbling glass of club soda.

"Bobby and I have business to do with the two of you, but amenities must precede business," and Kate poured another cup of coffee for Emma and a cup for Cora. Bobby asked for tea, which Kate immediately provided. She also brought from the kitchen open-face sandwiches: cucumber with dill and cream cheese, paté with capers, and smoked Scotch salmon with slivers of Maui onion.

Having put one of each of the delicacies on a plate, Emma, before sampling, began with almost a groan, "Ohhhh, I hate this place. I mean this whole area. The freeways. The smog. My God, driving to a dinner party is like taking a trip. It must be forty-five miles from our place to Bobby'S. I wish Sam had never left Brandeis. No one we knew there lived more than five or ten miles from our place." And Emma popped first one sandwich and then another into her mouth.

"I felt the same way when I came here from Ohio via Las Vegas," said Bobby, "but you get used to things. God, I don't know how anyone can stand Las Vegas. That town is a real comment on American values."

"Weren't you in show business in Las Vegas? That's what I've heard," rumbled Emma.

"Show business? Hell, I was a chorus girl at the Xanadu—phony ostrich feathers, sequins, g-string. If you call that show business, then I was in show business. It was a drag that you can't believe. But I made pretty good money—enough to support myself while I worked on a master's at UNLV."

Cora came to life, emerging from her contemplation of the club soda in her right hand. "You married Bert Redd. Harvey told me."

"Yeh, I guess it was the ostrich feathers that got him. They really tickled him. No pun. I'd just as soon drop the subject."

"Well," said Kate, "you have something to tell us, so tell away."

"I don't know how to start. I want to do something with my loot. I'll give the university a healthy chunk of it, but I have another idea. Been thinking about it for a couple of months. Have you guys ever heard of Ely, Nevada?"

"Do you mean Elko?" asked Kate.

"No, Ely's southeast of Elko. Ely's a strange place. Some gold mining in the area and a maximum security prison. The reason I know Ely is that it's fifty or sixty miles north of Great Basin National Park, my favorite place in the world. I've tried to go there every year, to hike and renew my faith. God, I sound pompous. Ely's wonderful. A town of maybe 5,000 and three houses of ill repute. And nothing much more. I think it's just ripe for development. A first-class casino-resort, skiing all winter, fishing and hunting in the summer and fall. And Great Basin National Park just sixty miles down the road. Look, I'll give you guys a stack of info about Ely.

"To get to the point, I'm thinking about moving to Ely."

Silence. Kate pops the last bit of salmon into her mouth. Emma stirs an empty coffee cup. Cora again contemplates her club soda.

"What about Mel?" asks Kate. "What does he think about this?"

"To tell you the truth, I haven't mentioned the subject to him yet. I was hoping the idea might appeal to Cora and Emma. How do you gals feel about taking this flier with me?"

Silence.

***

The conversation with Bobby left Mel stunned. How long had this half-assed scheme been brewing? "She thinks I'm moving to Nevada she's crazy," muttered Mel. He grabbed a diet Dr. Pepper from the refrigerator and took a long gulp, the cool sweetness as it coursed toward his stomach somewhat calmed him. He was about to take a second swig when the curtains of consciousness rolled back, revealing the full monstrosity of Bobby's idea. How could he finish his work on Vanbrugh in Ely, Nevada? "Maybe she wants me to become a croupier. Jesus, I've never seen such complete idiocy. Just when things are opening up for me. This is the end. I'm staying here."

Mel thought about one of his recurrent dreams. In it, Bobby informed him that she was divorcing him or that she was going to New York and he couldn't go with her or that they weren't really married. The dream had always ended happily, a Morphean soap-opera. Bobby had relented, and she and Mel were reunited. But this wasn't a dream. Mel summed up in one word, "Rejection."

By reflex—after all, what else was there to do?—Mel climbed into the Chevy. He would lose himself in his work on Vanbrugh at the university

But the car headed south on 110, toward Long Beach instead of north toward the university. The Chevy purringly made the transition to 405, moving at a steady 65 toward San Diego, carrying the volitionless Mel Druse with it. The car might have chosen another route, through El Monte and to Jack Benny's Cucamonga, but it did not.

His consciousness was in a tight loop, running the same routine over and over again, fruitlessly. *How could she possibly. . . .*

The verdure of signs slipped by, casting a sickly green, moldy patina over the shimmer and glow, and the Chevy maintained its steady sixty-five. *How could she possibly have thought. . . .* It was a cheesy green thought in an odoriferous green shade, fecal, yet irresistible.

attitudes

Martin Scorsese would have been pleased. The effect was perfect: gangrenous background with phosphorescent white striations (the color of unhealthy flesh), gorgonzola in reverse.

The geography began, blessedly, to distract Mel.

"Irvine" in dayglow white against the verdure. Old John riding his horse to death, sunup to sundown, to capture as much of the land as the King of Spain allowed under the patent. "Laguna Hills," Seizure World, all you need from rocking chair to grave, its giant globe attesting the mortality of earthlings. "San Juan Capistrano," where the swallows come back to, the hills behind the mission aridly bronze. *How could she possibly have. . . .* The Chevy rolled on at its steady sixty-five, never changing lanes, unimpeded during the hiatus in freeway traffic.

"Camino Real," the King's Highway. Junipero Serra had tramped this route, bringing Christianity northward. The old Jesuit, with his staff and his donkey, baptizing Indians, sowing mustard seed along the route, planting a golden path that still blossomed during the spring rains. Junipero Serra, the mission builder. He must have been a tough old sonofabitch, this man of God, sternly righteous, his sandalled feet kicking up the dust of California, shuffling northward with the message of the Lord.

"San Clemente," the King's Hideaway. Nixon had walked on the beach with King Timahoe, his Irish setter, when he brought Pat to Casa Pacifica. That would be the great revelation about Nixon—his relationship with King Timahoe. One had suspected the fatherly affection for Tricia, but that was hardly adequate to explain the deep scorn Mel felt for Tricky Dick. Mel could imagine moments of tenderness between the handsome Irish setter and the glowering chief executive, his five-o'clock shadow more sinister than ever.

And then the bald domes of the nuclear plant. The electric lines ran across the freeway, great cables of crackling power, generated by water boiled with incipient bombs. Barry Commoner had once—or many times—asked, with roaring response, "Do you need atoms to boil water?" But the master of King Timahoe had said, "The San Clemente nuclear plant is my good neighbor. It doesn't have loud parties late at night. Its dogs do not bark early in the morning. I am happy to live next door to such a model citizen." The old bastard's balls were already atrophied, or he'd have thought twice about living next door to a glowing nuclear pile. Of course, he moved to New Jersey or somewhere like that. But Tricia and Julie were back there, weren't they? And King Timahoe was getting old. Pat had always been old, even in the tent in Ely, Nevada, when she was born.

The Chevy breezed past the checkpoint where eagle-eyed federal officers scrutinized each northbound vehicle. These feds had been trained as carefully as the golden retrievers that sniffed out bombs at the airport. With one glance, they could determine whether or not an auto had a Mexican crouching in the trunk. A marvelous example of law and order: an immigration checkpoint seventy-five miles within the United States, when the border with Mexico spanned hundreds of uncontrollable miles. Yes, the Beaners who were caught at this checkpoint deserved their fate, which, after all, wasn't so bad: a couple of days in well-fed detention and then deportation. Anyone with half a brain would take another route. And maybe that was the trouble. Only the smart ones got into the U.S., to take jobs away from Americans. The dumb ones got sent back to Tijuana. What a fate. The destiny of California determined by a bunch of smart Beaners.

How could she possibly. . . . The glow, the shimmer, the cheesy greenness. The silver glitter of the Pacific in the noonday sun hurt Mel's eyes, blinding him momentarily when he glanced to his right. The shimmer, the glow, the cheesy greenness, the glitter. *How could she possibly . . .*

Mel became aware, suddenly, that he needed desperately to piss. The agony of his straining bladder was almost more than he could bear and made his teeth ache vaguely. Unfastening his safety belt and shifting gingerly in the seat, he looked down the freeway for the next exit. Perhaps a mile away, there was a green sign, and Mel accelerated toward it.

attitudes

Taking the offramp at sixty-five, the Chevy nearly skidded out of control, but the driver yanked it back on course and braked just in time to avoid crashing through a red and white striped barrier bar.

The dazzling white military hat of the Marine who stepped out of the guardhouse at the entrance to Camp Pendleton preoccupied Mel for a second or two before he lost consciousness.

Weirdly, he was conscious that he was unconscious and that his whole tranced awareness pulsed alternately with black shimmer, golden glow, and cheesy green striated with dayglow white. He struggled to regain rational control, but the gravity of his spinning trance was too strong for escape, and he whirled—shimmer, glow, moldy green, phosphorescent white. *How could she possibly. . . .*

Finally, a strong surge that was like the glitter of the silver-sequinned ocean and then nothing.

A minute, an hour, a day—after the nothingness came a dim, milky whiteness, and sounds. Mel knew that he was lying down and struggled briefly to sit up, but was restrained. He had no energy; the effort to rise had exhausted his volition. He lay, absorbedly aware that the whiteness was becoming a ceiling with fluorescent lights and that the sounds were voices. He was beginning to focus, not his vision so much as his consciousness. The ceiling, the glowing lights, and the voices were the aliments of tranquility, nirvana, and he vaguely wished to remain forever in this state of utter calm, alive, but passive and mindless.

Now an olive drab figure, bending over him, wrenched him from the peace of mindless awareness to an almost alert state. He was trying to assemble fragments, the strings hidden here and there, to be recalled and printed out through a clever manipulation of the operating system that controlled his random access memory.

"Just lie still. Take it easy. You're okay now. I'm Colonel Giannasi, a doctor. You're in the hospital at Camp Pendleton, and you're doing just fine. Your wife is on her way."

Now totally conscious, focused though sagging physically, Mel looked full into the porcine eyes of Colonel Giannasi. "I must've fainted. I remember pulling off the freeway. What happened? Did I wreck the car?"

"You were all steamed up, Mr. Druse—in what we call a pre-stroke condition. Your blood pressure was two-thirty over one-thirty when we got to you. But we have it under control now. You'll do just fine."

With a blank expression and a colorless voice, Mel responded, "I'll do just fine." And he realized that he was receiving a colorless fluid, drip by steady drip, through an IV in his left arm.

"After your wife gets here, we're going to transfer you to the Oceanside hospital."

"To the Oceanside hospital?" asked Mel lifelessly.

"You'll probably be there for a few days, until the doctors can get your blood pressure stabilized. You need to take it easy for a while anyway. You've been through quite an ordeal."

"Yes, quite an ordeal," echoed Mel.

The Colonel left the room, followed by a nurse whom Mel noticed now for the first time, and being alone, with an indefinite stretch of time before him, Mel unconsciously turned to his preoccupation with his own consciousness. It was a strange state he was in now: not groggy, but not keenly alert; mentally clear, but vastly disinterested, detached. The doctor could have announced his imminent death, and his reaction would have been the equivalent of "Hm, that's interesting." So he had been in a pre-stroke state, as the doctor called it. And if he had gone over the edge? If a cerebral vessel or artery had burst? Would he now be a conscious vegetable, aware of all that was going on around him, but unable to respond, the only sign of life his eyes? His aunt had been in this state, and Mel had visited her in the hospital. The stroke had not deformed her sweet visage, nor had it wracked her thin body; except for her eyes, which sought out voices and responded to sounds, she might as well have been carved from marble, could have been the result of the embalmer's art with the mechanical eyes of Dr. Mirakel. How would it seem to be unable to speak or move? Mel's vision of himself paralytic became populated, with Bertha Bankopf and Bridgett Heimann and Merry Woodsman paying their hypocritical respects, Mel unable to respond as they gloated over his total incapacitation. Strangely, this scene, though vivid, left Mel undisturbed; the psychic abrasiveness of the vision did not light the flare of his temper. He remained perfectly serene, icily interested in his new state of affairs. He knew that now, for the first time, he was experiencing Modern consciousness, chemical consciousness, the profound plastic calm induced by Valium or Thorazine. With the intellectual detachment characteristic of seasoned scholars, who view life as a series of interesting texts to be interpreted, Mel psychically stood back and dispassionately, but not uninterestedly, examined his mental state, resolving to use this experience as a metaphor when he was writing the article that he planned on Vanbrugh's "The Relapse": "The consciousness that pervades this masterpiece of seventeenth-century comic drama is completely modern, akin to the chemical disinterestedness induced by tranquilizers." He realized the cleverness of his metaphor, but he felt no glow of satisfaction; he did not smile, inwardly or outwardly; though normally a great admirer of his own wit, now Mel was neither pleased nor displeased. He could say to himself, "Now I know the horror of emotional blankness, and I really don't give a shit." All in all, Mel knew that, given the choice, he would opt for nature's tranquilizer: alcohol, which provided a glow and guilt feelings and often a hangover. That was, he thought, preferable to this synthetic nirvana—but, frankly, at the moment he didn't give a shit.

The unriffled stream of Mel's consciousness flowed on for he knew not how long—until he heard Bobby's voice.

* * *

Settled into a private room of the hospital at Oceanside, Mel dropped into a profound and dreamless sleep in the early evening and awakened, only in the full brightness of morning, to the clank and clatter of food service and the smell of coffee. A nurse, who looked not unlike Heather Figaro, entered his room, bade him an officially cheerful "Good morning!" and asked, "Are we ready for our breakfast?"

Mel had no appetite, no desire, indeed, for gustatory stimulation, but he was thirsty, and the aroma of coffee did stir him somewhat. "Could I have a cup of coffee? Just a cup of coffee."

He was sipping his coffee in the cranked-up bed when two doctors entered the room, a tall one who resembled Harvey Newburn, and a short one who looked remarkably like Lester Amore.

The tall, silver-haired, imperial doctor extended his hand and said, "Good morning, Melongaster. I'm Dr. Ferguson."

For the first time in his life, Mel felt insult without anger, outrage without rage. Not accepting the proffered hand, coolly, suavely he responded, "Glad to know you, Fergie. You can call me Professor Druse."

The bald, brittle doctor cleared his throat twice and, then, without extending his hand, said, "Mr. Druse, I'm Doctor Callahan."

"Happy to know you, Mr. Callahan," said a cool, controlled Mel.

The two medical gentlemen exchanged knowing glances. This would be one of those hard cases that they'd prefer not to encounter. *Professor* Druse would be on his way just as soon as they could make certain that he had no grounds for a malpractice suit, for he was obviously the sort that would have a shyster down on them at the drop of a syringe.

"Yes, *Professor* Druse," said Dr. Ferguson, emphasizing the *Professor* ironically, "we want to keep you here just long enough to make sure we have you stabilized, and then we'll transfer you to a hospital nearer your home. We've contacted your family doctor. Mrs. Druse gave us his name. He agrees that you should stay put for another twenty-four hours, and then we'll see. In the meantime, we're going to do a few routine tests."

attitudes

Dr. Callahan now stepped in front of Dr. Ferguson. With a steely smile, he said, "You seem to let yourself get upset over trifles. You should learn to control yourself. You'll have a stroke, you know. How would you like to be a paralyzed vegetable, *Professor* Druse?" Callahan was bending over, his nose only inches from Mel's.

Ferguson took Callahan's arm, muttered an unintelligible phrase, and firmly led his colleague from the room. Within a moment, he had returned: the regally silver hair, the well-kept slimness, the impeccable tailoring under the white smock, the perfect fingernails. He performed the ritualistic and the routine, listening here and there with his stethoscope, thumping hither and yon, touching this and that with an almost feminine silkiness. Even in his state of chemical equilibrium, Mel could sense that the examination was soothing, soporific, and he felt a neoprene good will toward Dr. Ferguson, who left him with the assurance that "I'll look in on you again this evening."

The disappearance of the medical men left Mel totally indifferent. This passionless lucidity was a completely new state for him, this chemical calm that he was exploring. He was not avidly curious, but mildly interested, and yet the mild interest was enough to propel his rationality, for there was nothing else, no counterforce of emotion, to divert or thwart the gentle flow of his consciousness. Among the academic canards, at which Mel Sneered, was "the disinterested search for truth"; common sense and basic knowledge of human nature belied that one. Yet now Mel had a sense of what such a quest might be: almost an artificial intelligence, running by some sort of unhurried program.

Bobby appeared. Having found a motel room near the hospital and having eaten breakfast, she felt better than she had since she first received the startling news that Mel was in the Camp Pendleton hospital. She had sat by his bedside during the whole night, and now, tired and relieved, the doctors having told her that the attack was controlled, she went to her room to rest, leaving Mel in the bright sunshine with a blank TV screen on the wall before him.

17. Adam's Ale; or, Brief Conjoinings

Harvey Newburn kissed Cora on the cheek, taking the opportunity to smell her breath. "You haven't been drinking." he said flatly. "So, what have you been doing today?"

"I've been talking to a lawyer," replied Cora.

"A lawyer? Why?"

"Harvey, I'm filing for a divorce."

Harvey was momentarily stunned. "What in the world, for goodness sake. . . ."

Cora walked to the window and looked out over the manicured grounds of the presidential mansion. The meticulously barbered shrubs, the colorful plantings of impatiens and begonias, the luxuriant lawn—these all seemed in a way to mean, for Cora, the existence she was resolved to leave behind, the perfect, but perfectly artificial, life of her front-man husband who was now going on to a more perfect, and more perfectly artificial, existence.

"What in the world will you do with yourself?" asked Harvey.

"For one thing, if I can manage it, I'm going to stop drinking. When you kissed me, you noticed that I hadn't had anything to drink today. You're not very subtle, Harvey."

"If you give up the sauce, I'll become a Trappist monk."

"You don't have much confidence in me, do you, Harvey."

"Why the hell should I? Since I made the mistake of marrying you, you've become worse and worse. Goddamnit, you don't know how many times you've embarrassed me."

Cora was calm, almost icy. "Yes, I'm sure our marriage was a mistake. We've never really belonged together. You need someone different from me. Someone more stylish, more intellectual. I know that I just don't cut it."

"So what about alimony? Who gets the coin collection? It's worth a lot of money."

"You need to get a lawyer to work out the details with my attorney. . I won't try to take you to the cleaners, Harvey."

"Maybe this is for the best. What with my new job at the Plato Foundation and—"

"And no longer having to put up with a wife who's a lush."

"You said it. I didn't."

"What if I stopped drinking? Then would I fit your specifications?"

"Specifications? God, you talk as if I'm some kind of nuptial technician."

"But you do have your ideas about what the wife of the president of the Plato Foundation should be and do."

"Okay. I'll be frank. I don't think you'd ever be happy in my new life with the foundation. You weren't happy with life at the university. You should have married a dentist, settled down in a suburban bungalow, raised three kids."

"Your sarcasm is wasted. Actually that life sounds pretty good to me—at least in contrast to the charades at the university."

"Well," said Harvey, "I wish you luck. In a week or so, we've got to clear out of this place so Les can move in. In the meantime, I'm going to stay at the club. You can do whatever you want to. I'll see you in court."

* * *

A full moon cast a silver glow on Wheeler Peak, and Lehman Creek sang its crystal song. Cora and Bobby sat on folding chairs beside the motor home.

"God, this place is beautiful. Let's drink a toast of Adam's ale. Here's to Great Basin National Park." Cora hoisted her glass and clinked it with Bobby's.

"You know," said Cora, "my family were Mormons. No alcohol, no tobacco, no coffee or tea. My father always said, 'The best drink in the world is Adam's ale right out of our well.'"

"Yeh," said Bobby. "For you and me, no more alcohol, no more tobacco—and we don't even have men. Should we take holy orders and spend the rest of our lives in a nunnery?"

Cora chuckled. "Harvey and I just weren't meant for each other. The poor guy wanted a high maintenance socialite, and I just didn't fit the specifications. He'll be happier without me, and I'll be happier without him. I must admit that he was a bit—more than a bit!—shocked when I beat him to the punch and filed for divorce before he did."

Bobby took another sip of Adam's Ale and unwrapped a stick of sugarless chewing gum. "I guess I can live without the Marlboros, but I'm giving this Trident a hell of a run."

"I knew from the first that Emma wasn't going to join us in this crazy scheme. She's happy with Sam, and I guess he's happy with her."

"Mel had a real conniption when I told him I was going to Nevada, but, hell, he can certainly join us, or he can come to Ely every weekend. You know, you and Harvey weren't made for each other, a bad fit. In a strange way, Mel and I mesh. The poor guy can't admit that all that literary bullshit bores him stiff. It's like he's got himself into the game, and he can't get himself out. His ego's pretty fragile. On the other hand, I'd had it up to here and beyond with the hoity-toity, artsy-fartsy life Mel wanted me to live. Now I can be in my world, and he can be in his, and he can join mine anytime the spirit moves him. We're a thoroughly modern couple, aren't we? He has his life, I have mine, and we can conjoin periodically and briefly. Like the Clintons or the Doles."

Cora yawned. "Okay, partner, let's hit the sack. We're going to make it to the glacier tomorrow."

attitudes

* * *

Vera Barber greeted Kate. "President Newburn will be right with you. Coffee? Tea? Cola?"

Kate declined. She wandered about the spacious foyer to the president's office, that theater in which dramas of epic scope were staged. She contemplated the Alson Clark oil, an impressionist rendering of Mount Baldy; to assure herself that it wasn't plastic, she touched a bromeliad, flaring to bright redness at its extremes,; she ran her fingers over the coarse weave of the beige drapes.

Harvey Newburn startled her, approaching her from behind and touching her shoulder. She swiveled quickly, brushing his cheek with her nose.

"Come on in," he said, taking her elbow and leading her into his office. "Tea? Coffee? Cola? Anthing?"

"Not a thing, thanks," as she settled on the end of the sofa opposite Harvey Newburn at the other end.

"I guess you know," he said, "that I'll be leaving the university next month. A new life, new challenges. I'm afraid I'll be a very public figure when I join the Plato Foundation."

"That's exciting."

"You know that Cora and I are separated. I hope she finds happiness. She's been very unfortunate."

"Don't you think that life is actually a throw of the dice? A hand dealt by fate or whatever? I find the gamble tremendously exciting."

"Are you happy now with your position at the university? I remember the first time we met, at the Druse party."

Harvey Newburn moved closer to Kate on the sofa. "How do you feel about a lifetime at this university? Does that prospect excite you? I'll be honest with you. Getting out of academe and into the political maelstrom gives me a new lease on life. The Plato Foundation is a force in the politics of this nation, particularly now with the Bush administration taking over."

"Oh, I envy you. I'll follow your career. You'll keep in touch, won't you? Maybe you can arrange a luncheon with the president for me." Kate leaned toward Harvey Newburn and laughed easily, liquidly.

"Stranger things have happened. Kate, are you busy this evening? I'd like very much to have you join me for supper."

"I'm sorry—May I call you Harvey?"

"Of course."

"I'm very sorry, Harvey, but I'm engaged, irrevocably committed."

"Tomorrow evening, then?"

"I'd love to."

* * *

"My God! What a man won't do for a beautiful woman."

The fire crackled and flared on the gigantic hearth, but the breeze from the air conditioning kept the room comfortable. The faux candles in the wrought iron chandelier above the massive oak table flickered.

Kate laughed. "Am I a beautiful woman? I'd never thought so."

"Well, you're sure beautiful enough for me," said Donald Schwann. "Could we get started here," he shouted toward the door leading from the dining room. The white-clad cook with a tall toque entered, carrying a silver tray on which reposed two tureens. A maid, most maidishly clad, followed with a large bowl.

"So what do we have here?" asked Schwann. "Pierre, you explain."

"Ah, oui." Pierre lifted the cover of one tureen, allowing Schwann to peer in. "Zis is dhal, an Indian dish. Lentils avec carrots, onion, shredded cabbage, and spices." Lifting the lid of the second tureen, Pierre explained, "And zis is my own invention: a tomato sauce with penne. Very nice. Onion, garlic, red bell pepper, cumin, basil." Pointing to the large bowl brought by the maid, Pierre began, "And zis is tabule—"

attitudes

With a wave of his hand, Donald Schwann dismissed Pierre and the maid, and turning to Kate said, "You see, no meat, just vegetables. I didn't think I'd ever come to this. See how much influence you have, Little Lady?"

"Please, Donald, no more 'Little Lady.' Just for me."

"Sorry. I slipped. If I can eat this rabbit food just for you, I guess I can watch what I call you."

"It's so good of you, so thoughtful, so typical, for you to arrange a menu just for me. I'll enjoy every bite."

"If this is the kind of stuff you usually eat, how the hell do you get protein? You don't look anemic."

"Beans, cheese, nuts—lots of foods other than meat give you protein—without the artificial hormones and the loads of antibiotics that you get with meat."

"Maybe I'll become a vegetarian." Donald Schwann laughed heartily and called toward the kitchen, "Think we could get some coffee here?"

"The dhal is wonderful," said Kate, "and I'm glad Pierre served it with brown rice—so much nuttier and so much more nutritious than polished rice."

"Kate, I've been thinking about easing my way out of Schwann Industries—I mean out of the day-to-day operations. I've got some young blood in the company that can keep things going. You know, basically I'm a soft-hearted guy, and it makes me sick to outsource more and more. Hell, seventy-five percent of the stuff we merchandise comes from China. Just in the last ten years, we've closed an auto parts factory in Muncie, a tool and die factory in Sioux Falls, and a computer chip plant in Biloxi. The Chinese make the stuff at a tenth of what the manufacture costs us in the good old U S of A. Nothing we can do about it if we want to stay in business, but I'm going to let the young cowboys in the company do the dirty work. I've had enough of it."

"So what will you do in your new life?"

"In the first place, I want to found a museum."

"Art?"

"You bet! Art! The art of American capitalism. I want people to appreciate the story of our country. I've been thinking about it. A whole section on Henry Ford. A model of the River Rouge plant. And Carnegie. Rockefeller. Right down to Jack Welch and Don Trump. Damn it, Kate, Americans don't appreciate what men like me have done for this nation."

Kate smiled and nodded. "That's a fascinating idea."

"Let me ask you, what would you want me to do? I mean, just give me some ideas."

"Well, if I were you, I'd think about trying to improve this nation's health. You know, for instance, that we have the highest infant mortality rate of any developed nation. That's a disgrace. Just think of the Sloan-Kettering Cancer Institute. No one associates Alfred P. Sloan with Chevrolets and Buicks. His legacy is the fight against cancer."

"See, I've got you interested, haven't I?"

"Oh, I've been interested in you for some time now," said Kate.

* * *

Cora sat on a granite boulder and took a long draught of Adam's ale from her canteen. "My goodness, I can't believe it. Two middle-aged broads hiking up Mount Wheeler. I wish Harvey could see me now."

Bobby laughed and stroked the rough, shaggy bark of a bristlecone pine. "Just think, this tree is nearly five thousand years old. What was happening on earth five thousand years ago? Oh yes, I remember, from my class in ancient history at UNLV. Five thousand years ago two old broads from Babylon were fed up with life, so they bought a wagon and a camel to pull it and took off for Mount Ararat."

Cora laughed and punched Bobby in the ribs. "Yeh, two old broads from Babylon. How high are we now?"

"Hmmm," said Bobby. "The trailhead was at ten thousand feet, so now we must be at eleven or eleven-five. We'll gain some more altitude on the hike to the glacier. People are always surprised when they find out that there's a glacier in Nevada. Actually, it's the southernmost glacier on the North American continent."

"I think we're above it all. All of the hassles down there, down there in Los Angeles, down there at the university. I know it sounds corny, but I feel reborn. You know, when we ate our lunch at Stella Lake, it was like a baptism. I've never seen a more beautiful place—the wildflowers, the reflection of the mountain in the lake, the absolute peace.

"At our last scene, Harvey was bluntly honest and cruel. He told me that I made it impossible for him to move to the Plato Foundation. 'You're a lush,' he said, 'a hopeless lush.' Well, he was partly right. I was a lush. But I don't think I was hopeless. I needed this mountain, Stella Lake, the bristlecones, and the glacier to prove to myself that I had a future. And—forgive some sentiment—your friendship. I owe you an awful lot, Bobby."

"Okay, buddy, time to saddle up and make the trek to the glacier."

Now above the timberline, Bobby and Cora climbed the trail, quartz shards clinking at their every step. Cora could hear Bobby's heavy breathing, almost gasps to fill her lungs with the thin air. When they reached the barrier of boulders just above the glacial cirque, they paused to gaze up at the summit of Mount Wheeler, now defined by a great billow of clouds behind it. Then they climbed over the barrier, Bobby skinning her knees on the sharpness of the quartz, and crunched their way across the icy snow to the far side of the glacier, where they sat, drinking the last of Adam's ale from their canteens and eating handsful of trail mix. In spite of the altitude and snow, they were warm, a bright July sun having heated the boulders on which they sat.

Cora put her arm around Bobby's shoulder. Motioning with her other arm, Cora said, "The other side is the past. Now that we're across the glacier, we're in the future."

* * *

Arlene McDonald-Ishimura wiped her eyes with a tissue and discretely blew her nose. "I've been a slave to that man for five years now. Staying late to serve coffee, arriving early to get his memos out. Weekends. Yes, weekends, with no comp time. Well, I'm not going to work for Vera Barber. She thinks she runs the university. Dr. Amore will be her third president. He wants me to take orders from her. Well, he has another think coming." And Arlene McDonald-Ishimura again began silently to weap.

Kate went behind the desk and put her arms around Arlene McDonald-Ishimura. "I'm sure Dr. Amore appreciates your service and loyalty to him, but, you see, Vera is a real behind-the-scenes power at the university. I think she's the only one on campus who could navigate the whole intricate maze without running into any cul de sacs. President Newburn relied on her, and she'll be essential to Dr. Amore when he takes the presidency. Arlene dear, life is just a poker game, and you make the best of the hands you're dealt. Look, you've been dealt two aces, haven't you? This change in your life has given you freedom, hasn't it? Now you have no obligations to Dr. Amore. And you're an attractive woman. So buck up. Play your hand carefully. After all, you're starting with a pair of aces."

Sticking his head out of the door to the sanctum sanctorum, Lester Amore said, "Come on in, Kate. Arlene, bring us some coffee, please." To Kate, "Would you rather have Coke?"

"Yes, Coke, please," and Kate settled on the far end of the deanly couch.

Amore stirred his coffee, and Kate poured Coke into a glass. "So, Les, to what do I owe the honor of your summons?"

"Kate, Donna is out of town. In Colorado visiting her mother. You know, I guess, that we're separated. I wonder if you'd have supper with me tonight."

"Impossible tonight, I'm afraid."

"Tomorrow?"

attitudes

"I'm tied up from dawn until the wee hours tomorrow."

"Then how about Friday?"

"That'll work. Okay. Why?"

Amore didn't answer, but he gave Kate his knowing assessment, gazing at her feet in their minimal pumps, at her legs so gracefully crossed, at the few inches of thigh below her plaid skirt, at her breasts outlined by the burgundy silk blouse, at her lips slightly parted, at her hair so naturally curled around her face that one could not imagine its having been consciously arranged.

"Why?" repeated Kate.

"Why not?" said Amore.

"There are a lot of reasons why not," said Kate. "What I need is one good reason for accepting your invitation."

"Let's call it my first social engagement as president of this university."

"And who'll replace you as dean of letters, arts, and sciences?"

"Who knows, and who cares?"

"I care." Kate moved one cushion closer to Amore. "I hope that I can use my influence to make sure that Mel Druse gets the deanship."

"Mel Druse? Why in the world?"

"Just because."

"Give me one good reason," said Amore.

"Alright, here's one good reason. Mel and I are co-conspirators. We're a two-person cabal."

"I don't understand."

"I don't either," said Kate enigmatically. "Why do you need to understand? I refuse to delve deeply into my own motives. Don't you think it would be interesting to see what happens if Mel becomes the big dean, just a couple of steps below the presidency?"

"Fascinating. Okay, you're on. I'll see what I can do about moving Mel from the Humanities Building to Bauer Hall of Administration.

"You once explained your philosophy of life to me," continued Amore. "It's a crap shoot, a poker game. That makes sense.

255

You're dealt a hand, and you either fold or you make the most of it. Sometimes you bluff. Take my own life, for example. Donna wants out of our marriage, and so do I. When we go our separate ways, what will I do? Can't you just see me, the austere celibate devoting his life to creating a cathedral of learning, an oasis of sweetness and light here in the smog and traffic jams? I don't see myself filling that role."

"No, Les, I can't imagine it."

"Kate, you and I are so much alike it's frightening. I'm going to be honest with you. I believe you're the only person I've ever met who is as . . . as . . . how shall I put it? . . as single-minded as I am. You know, we both go after what we want."

"Les, the word you're searching for is, I think, 'ruthless.' Are you ruthless? Am I?"

"Let's say 'determined.' For instance, I'm wondering what you'll get out of having Mel Druse as dean."

"Les, you're not a sentimentalist, and neither am I. But I'll tell you this: if I've ever loved anyone, that person is Bobby Druse. As Bobby might say of someone, she's one hell of a broad. So now you've succeeded in prying it out of me, why I want Mel Druse to become dean. Mixed motives. Of course. Mixed motives. Mainly for Bobby. But also just to do it. Just to succeed in a project. That's the kind of broad I am."

"Are you the kind of broad that might want to make an alliance with the president of this university?"

"But I already have an alliance with the incoming president of this university, don't I?"

* * *

A harpsichord twanged out a Bach toccata, the candles cast their golden light on the snowy linen, and a waiter filled two flutes with Champagne. Harvey Newburn took the bottle and read the label to Kate: "Veuve Cliquot Grande Dame, 1996."

"How festive," said Kate, "and, I'll bet, how expensive."

Harvey tasted the wine, uttered an approving "Mmm," and said, "Well, it's a festive occasion, isn't it?"

"Is it?"

"Oh yes. As far as I'm concerned this is my farewell party, bidding adieu to the university."

"Not the least touch of sadness, of melancholy?"

"Not a bit. I can be honest. Just getting away from Lester Amore is one of the great benefits of my new job. Kate, I detest that man."

"And Lester will replace you."

"Makes absolutely no difference to me. As far as I'm concerned the board could name Mel Druse president."

"Have you heard from Cora?"

"No. I understand she's in Nevada with Bobby Druse. She probably doesn't know where she is. She's in Stolichnaya land. When I married her, Cora was a good looking woman. Now she's a bloated, sloppy drunk. I have no sympathy for her."

"Harvey, Harvey. Don't be that way. Cora needs love. She needs a reason to live. To tell you the truth, she couldn't do better than to team up with Bobby. Bobby's a real human being."

"So all I can say is 'Bless her' and 'Best of luck.' I want to put Cora and the university behind me. They're my past, and I'm looking forward to my future. Kate have you ever thought about how exciting it would be have real power? I mean, to influence the course of history. To have access to the people who shape the destiny of this nation and of the world?"

"That *would* be exciting."

"I know how you could become a part of that world of power."

"Let me guess. I could marry you and be your consort in D.C."

Harvey Newburn sat bolt upright, shocked. He couldn't have been more stunned if Kate had slapped him. For several moments he was speechless. "I hadn't intended to be quite so blunt. I know that you're a reasonable person. You could . . . how shall I put it? You could use your considerable skills to become as much a moving force nationally as you are at the university. I wouldn't even rule out the possibility of your running for office, say, the House."

"Kate, you're the sort of woman I need. You've got class. You're smart. And, Kate, I must admit that you've been on my mind since I first met you. I've thought about you a lot."

"Harvey, I'm flattered. I'm almost flabbergasted. As they say in romantic comedies, 'But this is so sudden.'"

"I know. I know. I'm a passionate man. And Cora. . . ."

"Pour me another splash of champagne, and we'll drink to the future. Who knows what will unfold in this fascinating drama?" Kate patted Harvey's hand and drank two swallows of champagne.

* * *

When Kate left his office, Mel turned to his computer and dragged his folder on Vanbrugh out of its depths. He opened a file titled "Radical" and read the first and only sentence: "Sir John Vanbrugh was an architect, playwright, and radical." He stared at this sentence for several minutes and then turned to that panacea for disquietude, computer solitaire. Red queen, black king, black jack, red ten. . . . The beauty of the game for Mel, as he readily admitted (though only to himself), was that he could split his consciousness, part of his attention on the game, the other part mulling over and over again some annoyance or worry or slight or even trauma. Ace of spades up . . . black six on red seven . . . king of hearts over. . . .

The images that ran through Mel's semi-consciousness as he played solitaire were a kaleidoscopic montage. Bobby driving off with Cora in the monstrous motor home. Kate sitting in front of his desk, sipping sherry. Bobby's odor of stale cigarette smoke. Kate's herbal fragrance. Bobby's sagging breasts supported by a brassiere. Kate's pert brasiereless breasts under her blouse. Bobby's flabby thigh revealed when she crossed her legs. Kate's delicately carved thigh showing beneath the hem of her skirt. Bobby's earthy steps in her sandals. Kate's airy steps in her pumps. Bobby's forthrightness. Kate's mystery.

He turned from the computer and opened the top drawer of his desk. There, where he had put it, was a snapshot of Bobby and Kate arm-in-arm. He took a pair of scissors from the drawer and carefully trimmed the photo so that Bobby and Kate were separated. He threw the image of Bobby into his wastebasket and placed the image of Kate near the front of the top drawer of his desk, so that he could contemplate it whenever he opened the drawer. Aloud and in anguish, Mel grimly said, "I want her."

18. Gin; or, The Mission

"Could we have a word of prayer?" said the Reverend Gerald Bunker.

Mel stuttered. "Yes. No. Why? Here? I mean, I hardly think it's appropriate."

"God hears our prayers. It doesn't matter where they come from—a church, a street corner, or a university office."

Mel sputtered. "Not in my office. I mean I don't think. . . ."

"Do you believe in God?" The Reverend Bunker's tone demanded an answer.

"Well, yes," said Mel. "I'm a deist. What was good enough for Thomas Jefferson is good enough for me."

"The claim that our Founding Fathers were deists is just part of the left-wing conspiracy to create a godless nation. Without the guidance of God, our Constitution would never have been drafted."

"Look, I'm not a Constitutional scholar. All I know is that Thomas Jefferson created his own version of the Bible; he cut and pasted to eliminate all of the miracles."

"You must also believe the godless charge that Thomas Jefferson fathered a child with one of his slaves. Dean Druse, right now I'm going to offer up a prayer. You can join me in bowing your head if you so desire."

The Reverend Bunker fell to his knees, brought his hands together under his chin, and intoned a supplication. "Father in Heaven, we ask Your mighty help at this time. In our humble way, we are trying to bring light into the darkness of this institution. Godless Darwinism has deluded the world. We Your servants will carry the war against paganism to the enemy. We ask that You soften Dean Druse's heart and that You open his mind to Your truths. In the name of Your Son Jesus Christ, we pray. Amen."

Reverend Bunker heaved his bulk from the floor and settled it once again in the chair facing Dean Druse, who sat behind a very large, very shiny mahogany desk.

The reverend's visage fascinated the dean. Above the double chin was a smile that never varied, that looked, to Mel, like the satisfied smirk of someone who has just won a poker game by bluffing.

"I have come to you at the behest of Mrs. Emma Zucker."

"Really?" Mel was astounded.

"That dear woman has found Christ. She has been washed in the blood of the lamb. She felt that I could approach you about our conference."

"What conference is that?"

"The First International Conference on Intelligent Design. ID, for short. We're going to invite scholars from all around the world."

"Ah yes, I know that ID is very much in the news, but don't you think you'd be better off at a Christian College? How about Liberty University?"

"No doubt," said Reverend Bunker gravely, "the Reverend Jerry Falwell would welcome us, but we feel we should be less parochial. We need to show the world that ID is not simply a Christian theory. It's an undeniable explanation of how we came to be. You know that if you want to catch mice, you build a mousetrap, and if one part of the trap is missing, you won't catch mice.

Someone designed the trap. Some intelligence, someone, obviously designed the universe."

"God?"

"We don't use that term. It creates too many problems. Officially, we're neutral about God. We just prove that an intelligence designed the universe. If you want to call that intelligence God, that's your privilege. Of course, I personally know that God created the universe."

"Yes, well, I don't know what to tell you right now. I'll bring the matter up with President Amore tomorrow."

"I'm sure the president knows how close I am to Ben Hadley. He's been in my congregation for a decade now. Fine man. Good Christian. In all modesty I can say that Mr. Hadley supports my mission munificently. I know that he'd like very much to have the ID conference held at the university."

Arlene McDonald-Ishimura's voice announced through the intercom, "Dean Druse, Professors Hook, Mathis, and Gaylord are here."

Mel flipped the switch and responded to Ms. McDonald-Ishimura, "Tell them I'll be with them in a moment."

"Reverend Bunker, you know that I'll do everything possible to help you. And please keep in touch."

"I will keep in touch, Dean Druse. In fact, I'll call you tomorrow afternoon to learn the outcome of your conference with President Amore."

Dean Druse stood. Reverend Bunker stood. Dean Druse and Reverend Bunker shook hands. Reverend Bunker moved to the door, opened it, turned toward Dean Druse, and said, "I'll get in touch tomorrow."

Mel plunked down into his swivel chair and let out an audible "Whew!" and an equally audible, "God, what an asshole." The dean flipped the switch on the intercom and told Arlene McDonald-Ishimura, "Send them in."

Jim Hook plopped in the chair in front of the desk, Howard Mathis sprawled on the couch, his head on the armrest at one end and his feet at the other, and Freddy Gaylord perched on the edge of the dean's desk.

"Hey, Mel," said Freddy, "you gettin' any from Arlene?"

Jim and Howard snickered.

"I understand you have a private bathroom with a shower," said Jim. "Where is it? Through that door? I need to take a leak." Jim disappeared through the door to the dean's private bathroom.

Freddy reached over and flipped the switch on the dean's intercom. "Hey, Arlene, come on in. And bring some coffee while you're at it."

"Yeh," called Howard from the couch, "bring some coffee. Hey, Mel, do you give Arlene the attention she deserves. She's a real improvement on Heather Figaro."

As Jim Hook emerged from the dean's private bathroom, Arlene McDonald-Ishimura entered the office with a tray bearing four cups, a pot of coffee, sugar, cream, and spoons. "Anything else, Dr. Druse?" she asked.

Jim, who had resumed his place in the chair, said, "Arlene, do you miss Amore, old lover boy? Mel sure doesn't have the oomph of Amore."

Arlene, wisely, scurried from the office, leaving the four academics to their deliberations.

"My God," said Mel, "you guys act like the Three Stooges."

"Right-o," said Howard Mathis, and, addressing Freddy Gaylord, "Hey, Moe, who wrote 'Hamlet'?"

"You trying to trap me, Curly?" said Freddy. "Same guy as wrote *Moby Dick*." Freddy again flipped the switch on the dean's intercom. "Hey, Arlene, the dean wants a couple of custard pies. Got any on hand?"

Mel exploded. Jumping up from his chair, he shouted, "Enough! Enough! The three of you are a disgrace. A disgrace. Sleep learning. My God!"

Freddy Gaylord removed himself from the dean's desk and stood at parade rest before it. Howard Mathis sat up attentively on the couch. Jim Hook leaned forward to catch the dean's every word."

"Let's get serious, you guys," said Howard. "The dean means business."

Relieved, the dean again took his seat behind the desk.

"Yes, he means business," said Freddy Gaylord. "So, Dean Druse, how much of cut do you want in our business, Moe, Curly, and Larry Learning Consultants, Incorporated? Let me confer with my colleagues."

Hook, Mathis, and Gaylord retired to the far corner of the office and muttered. Hook slapped Gaylord on the head, and Mathis kissed Hook on the cheek. Hook farted mightily. "That's very crude, Larry," said Howard. "Larry's got no manners," said Gaylord. Then the three huddled, arms around one another. After a couple of minutes, they shook hands and took their places, with military correctness at ease, before the dean's desk. "I have consulted with Moe and Larry, and we're ready to offer you one-fourth of the action in our enterprise, Moe, Curly, and Larry Learning Consultants, Incorporated, on the condition that you won't insist on including a Vanbrugh unit in our course."

"Ah, come on, you guys, let's knock off the clowning," said Mel with great forbearance. "We need to talk about this sleep learning business."

Howard Mathis once again stretched out on the couch, Jim Hook resumed his seat in the chair, and Freddy Gaylord sat in the yoga position on the floor.

"What about the sleep learning business?" asked Mathis.

"You guys know it's just a bunch of hooey," said Mel.

"It's no more hooey than Waldo's course in nineteenth-century American lit or Phyllis's Chicano lit course," responded Freddy. "Phyllis claims that her course creates tolerance and understanding. From the feedback I get, I think all she accomplishes is to bore students and piss them off. And do you really believe that Potty brings tolerance, understanding, and humanity to his students? No, Mel, in the context of the English Department, Hook,

Mathis, and Gaylord Learning Consultants, Incorporated is pure as driven snow."

Jim now took up the discourse. "You don't really think we're serious, do you, old buddy? After all, the joke's on you and the rest of our colleagues. I thought a literary gent like you would immediately sniff out the irony of what we're doing."

Mel was irked. "And what irony is that?"

"There's no such entity as Hook, Mathis, and Gaylord Learning Consultants."

"But what about the advertising on the radio?"

"Have you heard any ads?" asked Howard.

"No. But. . . ."

"But," Howard continued, "that's part of our gag. You might think we advertised on the radio. We didn't."

Freddy arose from his lotus position on the floor and took a seat on the couch by Howard's feet. "Let me explain. "The English Department is as phony as our learning consultants scam. It's a term-paper culture. All we do is make unexamined claims about how much good we're doing for society and then write papers that no one reads to be published in journals that don't matter a whit to the course of history. Our work doesn't really relate to the human condition. Look, Mel, as an undergraduate, you learned to write short term papers. As a graduate student, you learned to write longer term papers. And that's all you know how to do, so that's what you do. Of course, the stuff you crank out now isn't called term papers, but that's essentially what it is. We're a term-paper society, even more phony than Hook, Mathis, and Gaylord Learning Consultants because we—we literary people—take ourselves so seriously. The English Department as a genre is as much bullshit as HMGLC."

Mel rose from his chair and left his office, closing the door behind him and leaving Hook, Mathis, and Gaylord victors in the epic battle.

"I'm going home," he informed Arlene Mcdonald-Ishimura.

attitudes

* * *

Mel sat in the family room at 1415 Dimple Dell Drive. A bottle of Beefeater was on the end table beside him, and the TV remote was in his hand. As he sipped the gin, he channel surfed. Suddenly a familiar face appeared. The Reverend Gerald Bunker.

He stands beside a smoldering altar that looks as if it were constructed of cement blocks. The backdrop for the scene is a huge microwave dish pointed heavenward. Two others are with Bunker: Pastor Johua, a black man in a clerical collar, and a white man in a sport blazer and open collar. The white man has a bumper crop of wavy hair.

"Let us all bless the Lord, bless the Lord with all our hearts and souls. His blessings will live everlastingly in our hearts. Welcome to all the faithful!" says a perky Jerry Bunker to the audience viewing this telecast. A man of perhaps sixty, he is paunchy and jowly, with a head of silver hair. The occasion is a joyous debt burning. "Thousands of you," he says, "have already planted your seed in the good soil of The Universal Family Church Mission, and many of you have written to us and told us you are already out of debt or are coming out of debt."

The ceremony being televised is a debt burning, the promissory notes, mortgages, bills, and liens of the faithful being consigned to the fire in the cement-block altar. "God gave me a message today, a sweet message for you," intones Bunker, "and that is that as the smoke from this altar rises heavenward, it will smell mighty sweet unto Him because it says that *thousands* have put their trust in Him and are stepping out in faith. This is a faith fire, and faith smoke always pleases God." Pastor Joshua interjects, "It gives old Satan a headache, but it blesses the Lord." Bunker continues: "And that faith smoke goes right up through the devil's kingdom. It doesn't smell sweet to Satan. He gnashes his teeth and tries to fan it away."

As the ceremony proceeds, Bunker ridicules those who put a George Washington in the collection plate; the Lord wants more, wants not a spoonful, but basketsful or pickuptrucksful. Bunker's monologue goes on while his acolytes burn stacks of paper, presumably the debts of the faithful. And Bunker reads scripture. "Give, and it will be given to you. A good measure, pressed down, shaken together, running over, will be put into your lap; for the measure you give will be the measure you get back."

The two thousand dollar sums for which Bunker appeals are not, of course, really donations to The Universal Family Church Mission, but love gifts to the Lord, Who will, in spite of the promise of measure for measure in Luke 6.38, repay them many fold. After one has accepted Christ's salvation, which is a gift, completely free of charge, the Lord begins to return offerings with interest. Give, and ye shall receive in overabundance.

Pastor Josiah offers a prayer, and then, as Bunker and his cohorts burn debts, the scene alternates between the cinder-block altar and a very stout man singing "Fire, Fire, Fire" and dancing around an unidentified site with ancient buildings and ruins.

Mel pours himself a finger or two of gin, gulps it down, and falls asleep with the TV blaring.

* * *

"Do you all know one another?" asked President Amore. "Father McDenough, university Catholic chaplain; Ted Sturm, professor of biology, and, I might add, member of the National Academy of Sciences; and Dean Mel Druse.

"So, what are we here for? You know that we're being asked—even pressured—by various constituencies to sponsor a conference on intelligent design. One member of our board is particularly interested in such a conference, and Reverend Gerald Bunker has enlisted his followers in the cause. Reverend Bunker wants the conference held at the university to give it at least tacitly the academic stamp of approval."

attitudes

"In 1996, the big names in ID held a conference at Biola University. Why don't they just go back there?" said Professor Ted Sturm.

"As I understand it," said President Amore, "Reverend Bunker and his group want to secularize ID. As of now, it's viewed by many as a fundamentalist attempt to get God back into the schools and into government. In one of his blogs, Bunker says that Dawinism is godless naturalism and must be debunked, or, if you will, deBunkered. Father, McDenough, your thinking?"

"Certainly I want to get God back into the schools and into this university. I'm simply giving my own version of John Henry Newman's argument. It's a pity that the general public—including the faithful who follow the lead of Reverend Bunker—don't know anything about religion. My goodness, the general education requirements in this university include history and sociology, but not religion. That's a shame. On the other hand, there should be a firewall between religion and the rest of the university's subject matters. Throughout history, religion has suffered when it tampered with, for instance, science. Galileo is just the best known instance.

"It's interesting," continued Father McDenough, "that the first real debate about evolution was between Anglican Bishop William Wilberforce and Thomas Henry Huxley, who was called 'Darwin's Bulldog.' Amazingly and rationally, Wilberforce based his argument on a critique of Darwin's science, not on Biblical truth. Of course, Wilberforce's science was shaky, but the spirit of his argument was enlightened. Compare the intelligence and civility of the Wilberforce-Huxley debate with that low point of creationism, the Scopes trial. Clarence Darrow really did make a monkey out of poor William Jennings Bryan."

"Is there anything to ID, Ted?" asked Mel.

"Well, the gist of the argument is that some elements in nature are irreducibly complex and can't be explained through evolutionary theory; ergo, there must be an intelligent designer. Gee, I don't want to give you a lecture on the flagellums of bacteria or the beaks of finches on the Galapagos. The ID people argue that they couldn't have developed by chance, but they're dead wrong. These are just two of the technical pitfalls that the ID folks dig for themselves. There's one that should embarrass them, the old mousetrap analogy. Mike Behe, one of the big ID names, uses the argument. If you omit one part of a mousetrap, it won't catch mice. Say you omit the catch that the mouse must press to be caught, you could still use the faulty mousetrap as a paper clip. Three hundred years ago, David Hume demonstrated the faultiness of the mousetrap analogy, but the ID people keep using it.

"A much better analogy is a stranger wandering about in a city he wants to explore. The visitor to Vienna wanders about, turning this corner and then that one. Suddenly, he comes upon Demel's coffee house. He has coffee with whipped cream and a slab of Sacher Torte and thanks whatever power there be for this miracle. Of course, if he had turned other corners, he might have encountered even more miraculous sights—and tastes.

"Golly, if you think about it, the designer couldn't have been all that intelligent. He gave us knees that wear out after forty years and an appendix that has no use whatsoever but that gets infected and can kill you. If the designer had been a decent engineer, he'd have given us much more durable spines, and he certainly would have made it easier for women to bear children. I'm afraid Reverend Bunker's intelligent designer didn't do a very intelligent job."

Father McDenough added his blessing to Professor Sturm's verdict. "I've been interested in ID ever since it started popping up in theological discussions. I really think it's junk science and junk religion."

"So we agree," said President Amore, "sponsoring an ID conference would be an embarrassment to the university."

"Definitely," said Professor Sturm.

"Undoubtedly," said Father McDenough.

"By all means," said Dean Druse.

attitudes

"Gentleman, thank you very much for your time and your wisdom. I won't keep you any longer. Uh, Mel, could you stay for just a moment?"

When Father McDenough and Professor Sturm had departed, President Amore said to Dean Druse, "Mel, we have a problem. Actually two problems, Ben Hadley and Gerald Bunker. I'll take care of Hadley. You handle Bunker."

"How?" asked Mel.

"Oh," that's your problem.

* * *

"What an honor," said Kate. "This is the first time you've ever visited me in my office. I'm afraid I don't have the amenities that you keep in your desk drawer."

"God, Kate," said Mel, "I didn't know what I was getting into with this dean business. It's just one hassle after another."

Kate was in her executive mode, glasses low on her nose, prim white blouse buttoned with frills around her neck.

Mel briefed Kate on the Reverend Bunker dilemma. Informing Bunker that there would be no ID conference at the university would bring the wrath of the whole Universal Family Church Mission down on Mel. "Damn it, Kate, Les has put me on this spot. He's president of the university. He could tell Bunker that the ID conference is impossible, but Les leaves that little task up to me. You and I both know that Les enjoys making people squirm, just for the hell of it. So tomorrow when Bunker calls, I'll tell him that the university has decided an ID conference would be unwise, and Bunker will translate 'university' as 'Dean Mel Druse.'"

"Mel dear, you and I have solved greater problems than this one. Suppose I were to invite Emma Zucker to have lunch with me tomorrow, and suppose I were to mention, in strict confidence, that Dean Druse, with his typical open-mindedness, would support the idea of the conference, but that President Amore is dead set against it. I think that bit of news would get back to Reverend Bunker post haste. And I'll bet the Reverend would consult Ben Hadley. You know that Ben Hadley is one of Bunker's enthusiasts, don't you?"

"You know everything."

"I like to keep myself informed. Wouldn't it be interesting if President Amore got himself so entangled in religion and academia that his position became. . . ."

"Les Amore is too smart to get himself trapped like that. He might be a ruthless son-of-a-gun, but he's smart."

"Oh, Mel, there are wheels within wheels that you don't know about. Someday the light will dawn."

"Have dinner with me tonight. Come to the house. I'll order Thai or Chinese. We can be alone. We can talk. I need to talk with you."

"I really don't think I should come to your home with Bobby in Nevada, but we can do Chinese at the Ding Ho together."

"But I want something more than. . . ."

"All of us want something more than. I do. I've never known anyone who doesn't. But there's always a something more that we can't have and shouldn't want. So. Chinese at the Ding Ho? I'll meet you there at six thirty."

* * *

"The Reverend Bunker is here," announced Arlene McDonald-Ishimura via the intercom.

"Send him in," responded Dean Druse.

Reverend Bunker and his smile entered the office. Not taking the chair to which Mel had motioned him, the Reverend went behind Mel's desk and embraced him in a brotherly hug. "Dr. Druse, a little bird told me that you're on our side, and I appreciate that. I've talked with Mr. Hadley. He had a conference with President Amore, and Amore explained the difficulty of bringing the ID conference to the university. Some day. Some day. But not yet. We can wait. God is not impatient."

"I appreciate your understanding, Reverend. Why don't you have a seat?"

Bunker took a chair in front of Mel's desk. "I'd like very much to have you as a guest speaker at the Mission. How about next Sunday. In layperson's terms, you could outline the conflict between Intentional Design and godless Darwinism."

"Thank you. Thank you. But I must decline. I don't think it would be proper for me to inject myself into the controversy." Mel felt that itch, that irresistible twitch, of malicious humor and said, "Why don't you invite Professor Theodore Sturm? He's a real expert on the subject."

19. Fortune Cookies; or, Transitions

Mel removed the plastic wrapper and broke open his fortune cookie. "A change awaits you," he read aloud.

"You see, you have something to look forward to. Fortune cookies are never wrong. So what does mine say?" Kate broke her cookie open and read, "A change awaits you." She laughed. "There's a good deal of perversity here. Fate gives us both the same fortune, but doesn't tell us what or when."

"Boy, do I ever need a change," said Mel. "I was living a peaceful life, and then Warren's death came along, and then Bobby decided to take off for Nevada, and then I became chair and had to put up with all the departmental crap, and, as if that wasn't enough, now I'm dean and have to put up with all the crap in the university. God, Kate, I owe you an unrepayable debt for getting me out of the fix with Reverend Bunker, may God rest his flabby, bombastic soul."

"Know what I'd do if I were you? Next weekend I'd go to Nevada and spend some time with Bobby. I know one thing about you. Bobby is your fate, your destiny. You've had other thoughts, but you should forget them. You'd never be happy with anyone but Bobby."

"You're right, I'm sure. But I want. . . . Look, Kate, you don't really know me. No one does."

"Bobby knows you much better than you think she does."

"If Bobby knew what goes on in my deepest soul, she wouldn't have anything to do with me. Neither would you."

"Mel, you're not at all unique. Don't you think that, late at night, I have thoughts about myself that I would never reveal? I believe that in our secret hearts we're all monsters of one sort or another."

"God, I wonder why I ever got into the racket I'm in. I'll be honest with you, Kate. You're the only person in the world that I can be completely honest with."

"What about Bobby?"

"Not even Bobby. I've never liked the literature that I teach. The Restoration bores me silly. How can I be honest about that? I look at the faces in front of me in my undergrad classes, and I see boredom or animosity. Nothing else. If I keeled over dead in a class, the students would yawn and take off for the Union Building to drink Coke and play grab ass. Know what I read for pleasure, actually for reasons even deeper than pleasure? D. H. Lawrence. Walt Whitman. I'm a phony, Kate. And my own real desires. . . ."

"We should stop our confessions at this point. We'll embarrass ourselves if we go any further."

"Kate, remember your thought experiment? Now I'd like to posit one. Could you imagine a life with me?"

Kate was blunt. "No." But she quickly mellowed: "Spend a couple of days with Bobby. She'll get you back on track."

* * *

Just north of Barstow, the billboards advertising casinos started. "Xanadu, the ultimate. Luxury rooms as low as $39.50." "The

Palace. Nevada's loosest slots." "The Athens. 12 ounce prime rib dinner. $2.99. 24 hours."

The driver, being absorbed in his own meditations, noticed the ads only subconsciously, and the Chevy guided itself up I-15 toward Las Vegas.

Bursting through the California-Nevada line, the Chevy faltered, chugged lamely on, and then stopped. Out of gas. Mel shook himself out of his trance, muttered an "Oh shit!" and looked to his right and then to his left. To the left, Whiskey Pete's Hotel and Casino. To the right, Buffalo Bill's and Primm Valley Casino and Resort. To the left, gigantic neon signs. To the right, gigantic neon signs. To the left, neon announcing the presence at Whiskey Pete's of the Bonnie and Clyde auto. To the right, a whoop-dee-do roller coaster. Directly ahead, I-15, with mirage puddles glistening in the hundred-and-fifteen-degree heat.

Mel extracted himself from the Chevy, now, with the air conditioning off, starting to become uncomfortably warm, and stood in the searing heat from the sun reflected and magnified by the paving of the highway.

"Oh shit!" said Mel. Resolutely and sweating, however, he walked down the offramp to the service area at Buffalo Bill's Hotel and Casino. In the service station convenience store, the slot machines were tooting tunes and belching coins. A group of road warriors, their hogs parked just outside the door, were sipping Bud from cans and feeding the slots. Their black leather jackets and leather caps seemed incongruous, even though the convenience store was air conditioned.

Mel took his place in line to wait for the cashier. Three bikers ahead of him, cans of Bud in hand, were discussing the next leg of their run.

"A couple of hours and we'll be in Mesquite," said one of the bikers.

"And then all hell breaks loose," replied another.

"I've got to cool it this weekend. I'm scheduled to start the audit of Yorba Linda Savings and Loan Monday."

"You have it easy. Hell, I'll drill 'em, fill 'em, and bill 'em from eight in the morning until five. Can't be shaky when I use that jack hammer on bicuspids and molars."

"I'd hate to be one of Jake's patients Monday morning. You know, after he hones that scalpel and starts carving, just one slip and its bye-bye for the guy on the table."

It was Mel's turn with the cashier. "I'm out of gas, just by the offramp. Could I borrow a can so I can get some gas for my car?"

"We don't loan cans," said the clerk. "We sell them. Five bucks."

"But I just. . . ."

"We don't loan cans," said the clerk emphatically, pointing her index finger at Mel.

He noticed that she had a silver ring with topaz on each finger and her thumb and that she was toothless, her lower jaw almost touching her nose when she closed her mouth in a scowl.

Mel paid the five bucks, got the can, filled it with a gallon of gas at the pump, and trudged through the heat back to his car.

He drove to the service island, filled the car, and was on his way to the Xanadu, where, for old time's sake, he had made reservations for the night.

* * *

Kate paused in the doorway and then slowly pirouetted. Norbert, lounging in a chair across the room, gazed at her brilliantly red lips, parted slightly in an enigmatic smile; at her breasts hazily visible through the diaphanous, ankle-length gown; at her thighs and legs; and at her derriere as she turned.

Norbert had chosen the music. The liquid flow of the Hovhaness harp concerto was the perfect accompaniment for Kate's pavane.

She turned a second time, and then, in keeping with the music, she flowed across the room to where Norbert was sitting and curled up on the floor, her thighs resting on his bare feet.

attitudes

Norbert lit a cigarette and placed it between Kate's lips. She inhaled deeply, holding the smoke in her lungs for several seconds, and then let it curl out of her nose and mouth. Norbert lit a cigarette for himself and inhaled.

"So it's goodbye," said Norbert flatly.

"Why should it be?"

"Well, when you're Mrs. Schwann. . . ."

"Bertie, I'll never be Mrs. Schwann. I'll always be Kate Reese."

"You're going to marry the guy."

"So?"

"So this is the end for us."

"Bertie dear, why should my marriage to Donald change our relationship. You know that we've always gone our separate ways—except when. . . . Except at times like this."

***

Having filled his tray at the Xanadu all-you-can-eat buffet, Mel surveyed the provender he had gleaned from the steam tables. Corned beef and cabbage with boiled new potatoes, three-bean salad, and corn bread. He hacked off a slice of corned beef, contemplated its pinkness momentarily, and shoved it into his mouth. He chewed unenthusiastically and choked the wad down. He sampled the soggy cabbage. He took a forkful of bean salad but put it back on the plate. He got up from the table and wandered from the buffet into the main casino.

With the astuteness of a literary scholar trained in the hermeneutic skills of structuralism and post-structuralism, Mel "read" the casino as he would interpret, for instance, "The Relapse," by Vanbrugh.

"God," he muttered to himself, "slot machines. How many? Maybe a thousand. Video poker. Gaming they call it. Not gambling. Gaming masturbation. Jesus, look at that woman with the blue hair. She's pumping the slot like she'd pump a dildo. May the great god Chance give her a jackpot orgasm."

Mel knew that there was no use in seeking variety by going to another casino. All of the joints up and down the strip had the same clients, the same "games," the same sounds, the same smells. He had read somewhere that the casino bosses scent the slots. The right smell keeps the players playing.

He laughed aloud at the thought, the insight, that occurred to him. The casinos are a perfect analogy for the professional meetings he had attended. You could go from one to another year after year, and you saw the same faces, heard the same drone of presenters reading their papers. The same obsessive playing of the game.

Or maybe the analogy wasn't so perfect. After all, in a casino you might hit a jackpot, but what payoff could you gain at a professional meeting? Well, if you attended enough of them, you might get promoted from associate professor to full professor.

Mel bought a stack of chips and played five of them. Numbers 14 and 15, for his address on Dimple Dell Drive. Numbers 5 and 1, for his age. And double zero. The ivory ball whizzed around the wheel. It fell and clicked into number 2, jumped out and clicked into number 33, jumped out again and landed securely in 00. Mel was thirty-two dollars ahead.

At the cashier's window, he changed his thirty-six chips for money and went to his room. He stripped down to his jockey shorts, took a Budweiser from the mini-bar, pulled back the covers, flopped on the bed, and clicked through the channels on the TV. The menu of movies included "Comedy," "Drama," "Adventure," and "Adult." He chose "Adult" and read through the possibilities: "Bottoms Up," "Young Studs," "Teenie Titties," "Sex Slaves," "Hell Bent for Leather," "Experienced and Hot," and "Naughty Nurses." He opted for "Naughty Nurses" and settled back for an evening of libidinous pleasure.

However, before the nurses got very naughty, Mel was asleep, his bottle of Budweiser half full on the bedstand next to him.

He awoke just as dawn was breaking, the crimson rim of sunlight on the horizon visible from his room on the fourteenth floor

attitudes

of the Xanadu. Invigorated, eager to be on his way, Mel showered, repacked his bag, and was off. Bacon, eggs, and pancakes, with plenty of coffee, at the Xanadu coffee shop. Then pointing the Chevy northward once more on I-15.

As the Chevy carried Mel beyond Las Vegas and then past Nellis Air Force Base, Mel thought of his Chinese dinner with Kate. "A change awaits you" had been the message in the fortune cookie. "A change awaits you."

He began to hum a melody, "Jeanie with the light brown hair." And then he added the words: "A change awaits you, yes it does, old Mel. A change, but what's to come I just cannot tell. A change awaits you. . . ."

A highway sign brought the crooning to an end. "US 93, Next Exit. Great Basin National Park. Ely."

The Chevy effortlessly made the transition from I-15 to US 93, and Mel stared at a stretch of highway that ran on for miles—no curves, just straightaway through heat mirages, and then an upward grade before the asphalt made a curve and disappeared.

On each side of the road, creosote bush, dark green, wiry, clinging to the alkaline soil. The mountains, rising abruptly from the flat aridity of the valley, were deep purple, almost black, with, here and there, bits of mica gleaming like sequins under the desert sun.

Mel turned off his air conditioner and opened the Chevy's windows. The desert air was clean, blowing over Mel like a hot shower scented with the almost medicinal aroma of the creosote bush. The Chevy slowed from seventy MPH to forty, and Mel gazed at the mountains, the patches of bush, the intensely blue sky, the mirage puddles on the highway ahead.

Now, as the highway climbed upward, leaving the creosote bush behind, Mel pulled the Chevy off the tarmac and onto the shoulder. He got out of the car, stretched, and walked into the desert, touching the green-silver leaves of the sagebrush, crushing them between his fingers and sniffing at the clean, herbal fragrance. A horned toad scurried away from Mel's step, and a jackrabbit sat poised to run. Mel took a step toward the rabbit, and it bounded away, zigzagging through the sagebrush.

Mel relieved himself, watching the urine disappear into the dry, sandy soil.

As he got back into the Chevy and continued the drive northward on US 93, he felt strange, elated yet disembodied.

The Chevy chugged onward at forty MPH. Mel read a sign: "Pahranagat NWR, 1 mile."

He saw poplar trees ahead, and as he topped a slight rise, a lake appeared. He pulled off US 93 into the grove of poplars and climbed from the Chevy. Blackbirds by the dozens were clamorous, and the grove was cool and, above, all, peaceful and deserted. Mel strolled to the shore of the small lake and gazed at flocks of ducks and coots swimming about and diving for—for what?

As Mel gazed at the lake, a breeze came up and ruffled the water. Mel idly went through his mental Rolodex. Les Amore. Waldo Clemens. Harvey Newburn. Potty Tinker. He was indifferent, detached. He muttered to himself, "Who the hell cares?"

And then Kate Reese. Kate Reese. He paused. Kate Reese. The paradox. She should have roused him from his cool indifference. He knew that. But Kate Reese. Kate Reese.

He began to count the coots and ducks on the lake. One, two, three, four, five. . . . At twenty he stopped counting and returned to the Chevy, once again heading it north on US 93.

A sharp eastward turn, a downward wind through a narrow canyon, and he pulled into Caliente.

The demands of his body were now ascendant, and Mel looked for an eatery. He saw a large sign that looked as if it had been painted by a not-very-skillful artist: Hank's Café. He pulled the Chevy to the high curb and dismounted.

He sat at the counter in Hank's Café, feeling out of place. Three old-timers at a table eyed him, not suspiciously, no, but with curiosity.

"Where you from?" asked a bearded gent in a cowboy hat.

"Los Angeles," answered Mel.

attitudes

The three locals chuckled.

A clean-shaven questioner with silver hair flowing down his back asked, "You a movie star?" The intent was patently ironic.

"I'm a professor," said Mel.

Now the chuckles were laughter.

"So what do you profess, Professor?" asked an aged and skeletal man who looked amazingly like the old actor John Carradine.

"Literature," said Mel flatly.

"No shit! We're impressed." The cowboy hat shook hands with his companions.

Wearing a white apron and an Anaheim Angels cap, Hank appeared from the kitchen. "Don't pay any attention to these geezers. They sit around all day solving the world's problems, and I'm lucky if they order a bowl of chili or a cup of coffee. So what'll it be for you?"

"A sandwich, I guess."

"Do you have hemorrhoids?" asked Hank.

Mel was stunned. "Hemorrhoids? No. Yes. So what—"

"Buddy, if you have hemorrhoids, you need a bowl of Hank's chili, guaranteed to cauterize hemorrhoids." And Hank pointed to a hand-lettered sign on the wall: "Hank's Chili. Garanteed to coterize hemroids."

"Bring on the chili," said Mel. "And some crackers or something to go with it."

The chili was, indeed fiery. Mel tempered the heat with soda crackers from the box that Hank had placed on the counter and with a frosty bottle of Coors. As he took a long swig of beer, he noticed another placard on one wall: *How can you soar like an eagle when you're surrounded by a bunch of turkeys?*

Mel read the wisdom aloud: "How can you soar like an eagle when you're surrounded by a bunch of turkeys?" He laughed, took another pull at the Coors bottle, and scraped up the last spoonful of chili.

Revitalized, cleansed by the fire of the chili, Mel was ready for the final leg of his journey, the hundred and fifty or so miles to

Ely. "How can you soar like an eagle when you're surrounded by a bunch of turkeys?" Mel shouted to Hank. "I'll be back through in four days. See you then."

"Hey, hold on Perfesser," called the silver-haired old timer. "Come and set a while. You're not in any hurry. Hank, bring the Perfesser a cup of coffee."

Mel took a seat at the table with the three, and silver-hair introduced himself. "I'm Lyman. And this here's Clyde." Lyman indicated his gaunt companion. "And Charlie behind them whiskers."

Mel shook hands with each and took s wary sip of the coffee that Hank had placed before him.

"Where you headed?" asked Lyman.

"To Ely."

Clyde leaned toward Mel. "Why Ely? What's in Ely?"

"My wife. I mean I'm going to visit my wife."

"What's your wife doing in Ely?" asked Charlie.

"She's planning to start a resort. Casino, hotel."

"Shee-it!" said Lyman. "Your wife's crazy. Who the hell's going to go to Ely when there's Reno and Vegas and Tahoe? There aint any airline service to Ely. Ely's on the road to nowhere. Vegas is on the main north-south route between LA and Salt Lake City. Elko and Reno are on the way to San Francisco. Ely is on US 50, known as the loneliest road in America."

Charlie raked his fingers through his whiskers. "Lemme tell ya about Nevada. Reno and Vegas, they're not Nevada. Matter of fact, I don't think they belong on this planet. Last time I was in Vegas ten years ago, the place scared me to death, and I'm fearless. Now in the real Nevada, you can find peace and quiet and do what you want without havin' somebody tellin' ya what ya oughta be doin.' See, Caliente's almost Nevada—not quite, but almost. Don't no tourists come to spend the weekend in Caliente. Now Ely, it's not as much Nevada as Caliente, but it's still Nevada. Got a Ramada Inn. Two whorehouses. Real Nevada don't have no Ramada Inns or whorehouses."

attitudes

Lyman leaned back in his chair and gazed at the ceiling. "Drive west on US 50 for seventy-five miles or so to Eureka. That's Nevada. No Ramada. No Holiday Inn. No whorehouses. No McDonald's. Hell, Ely has a McDonald's."

Charlie interrupted. "Hell, Eureka's got a Best Western now. It's getting' to be a damn tourist trap. But Austin, now that town's still real Nevada. About seventy-five miles west of Eureka. No damn motels. No damn McDonald's. And no goddamn traffic. Just the wind blowing down the canyon and the sweet smell of sagebrush. That's Nevada."

Mel had finished his coffee. He rose and shook hands all around.

The Chevy climbed gradually along US 93 into the junipers and piñon pines. Mel knew about this flora and felt quite at home. After all, juniper berries flavored his Beefeaters, and since grade school he had known that pine nuts, from the cones of piñons, were a staple of Native American diet in the areas where the trees grew.

Dreamily steering the Chevy along the highway, he was thinking of the real Nevada, of Austin. It was in a valley, austere mountains rising sharply on each side—he knew that much. The details he supplied from his memory of the Westerns he had seen and loved: "Shane," "Stagecoach," "Rio Bravo." The Austin of Mel's imagination had board sidewalks. He could envision making a new start there, he and Bobby away from everything they had known previously. The wind gusting down the canyon would sweep the air forever clean of the smells of civilization. The locals, the Austin natives, would know nothing of . . . of . . . nothing of Vanbrugh, not even anything of Shakespeare. They would be clean, uncorrupted.

He braked sharply. A Badger was waddling across the highway. He watched it disappear into the undergrowth. And now, over a rise, before him lay a panoramic view of Ely. For Mel it was less a town than the gateway to a mythic land where there was no pretense. In the real Nevada, he could truly be himself.

Mel pulled the Chevy onto the shoulder and got out. He gazed at the town before him. And then he repeated this mantra: "It's hard to soar like an eagle when you're surrounded by a bunch of turkeys."

Finis

On the morning of September 11, 2001, Mel was sashaying down the main drag in Ely. He was wearing black cowboy boots with burgundy inset designs; crisp new levis; a large silver belt buckle with a piece of turquoise in the middle; a tan, tailored shirt with fringe around the pockets on each side; and a glorious, magnificent hat, black with a stiff brim and topped by an uncreased dome, the sort of chapeau favored by the great Native American chiefs.

> From: BDruse@eec.com
> To: KReese@dsl.com
>
> Sept. 11, 2001. The world just ended. That is, the world that I've known. George W. Bush just got the best break any Texas cowboy could hope for. The Trade Center catastrophe will be the president's reason for going to war. Anyone who has ever watched a John Wayne movie knows how Bush will react to the tragedy. A couple of weeks ago, Bush said, "My administration has been calling upon all the leaders in the—in the Middle East to do everything they can to stop the violence, to tell the different parties involved that peace will never happen." That was a real Freudian slip.
>
> Well, here's how our lives have shaped up. Mel is resigning from the university and has resolved to move to Austin, Nevada. He's in total revolt against his old life. You should see him in his new cowboy duds.

attitudes

Really quite a sight. The way I feel now, I'm ready to get as far away from civilization as possible, so I'm willing to give Austin a try, and if Austin doesn't work out, we'll find some place in the Mohave.

I've given up on the idea of making Ely into a world famous resort. It was a half-baked notion anyway. I talked to Steve Wynn about the idea, and he convinced me that Ely is a lost cause.

Cora seems to have found a home here. It turns out she's a red hot bridge player, and she's making good dough playing all comers for ten cents a point. She'll keep the house. As far as I'm concerned, she can live there as long as she wants to.

How does life as Mrs. Schwann suit you? My old pal, I bet Donald has met his match. Once Mel called him a raging bull elephant, but I think that with you, his roar probably comes out as "Baa." Keep in touch. I suppose Austin has internet service, and anyway, you can always call me on my cell phone.

So, for now, adios.

about the author

W. Ross Winterowd is the Bruce R. McElderry Professor Emeritus, University of Southern California, where he founded its PhD program in Rhetoric, Linguistics, and Literature. He has authored, coauthored, or edited many essays, reviews, poems, and books, including *Searching For Faith: A Skeptic's Journey* (2004, Parlor Press), *Senior Citizens Writing* (2007, Parlor Press), *The Culture and Politics of Literacy* (1989, Oxford), and *The English Department: An Institutional and Personal History* (1998, Southern Illinois). He has been leading writing workshops for seniors in Huntington Beach, California, since 1997.

www.ingramcontent.com/pod-product-compliance
Lightning Source LLC
Chambersburg PA
CBHW031559170426
43196CB00031B/201